Julian Fisher was born in what has been called the poorest post-code in Britain: B16 in inner-city Birmingham. His youth was marred by tragedy, severe emotional challenges and self-inflicted injury. But, while in hospital, conversations with a brave and extraordinary Iranian refugee altered forever his outlook on life. Her story sparked in Julian an ardent determination to strive for academic, personal and professional fulfilment.

He overcame long odds to win a place at Oxford University, where he read PPE. Subsequently, he embarked on a varied career, quickly spurning the financial sector to work for the government in the field of international relations. Moving back into the private sector, he worked for a global private security company in various challenging locations, before founding his own private intelligence boutique, specialising in Africa. In 2017, he was lead trainer on the Channel 4 series *Spies*.

Julian divides his time between the Welsh Borders, south London and Cape Town. But, for him, home is where the hound is.

Praise for *Think Like a Spy*

'If I were a young graduate looking to gain an advantage in the workplace, this is the first book I would turn to. Part memoir, part tutorial, *Think Like A Spy* is as close as readers are likely to get to the secrets of intelligence recruitment. A fascinating and instructive guide'
Charles Cumming, bestselling author of *BOX 88*

T0385293

'*Think Like a Spy* is an indispensable guide to influencing and persuading others. Fisher has walked the talk. In it, he shows you how to apply the secret techniques used by spies the world over to achieve your goals in both your personal and professional life'
Scott Walker, kidnap-for-ransom negotiator and *Sunday Times* bestselling author of *Order Out of Chaos*

'A veritable treasure trove of intelligence gems . . . an espionage tradecraft handbook from an authentic insider'
Nigel West, intelligence historian

'Fisher deftly guides us into a secret world, then demythologises it, illuminating how the ordinary can achieve the extraordinary. The world's second-oldest profession, he reveals in this thrilling account of human behaviour, was not built on betrayal and blackmail, as Hollywood fantasists would have it, but the not-so-dark art of influence and alliance building. Fisher gives us the tools we need to achieve our goals and live a life of adventure and intrigue. Spies, he teaches, are made not Bourne'
Tyler Maroney, author of *The Modern Detective: How Corporate Intelligence Is Reshaping the World*

'For anyone looking to grasp the art of persuasion, interpersonal skills and alliances, Fisher's book belongs in your back pocket. Peppered with case studies and personal anecdotes, *Think Like a Spy* is at once instructive, insightful and entertaining'
I. S. Berry, author of *The Peacock and the Sparrow*

THINK
LIKE
A
SPY

JULIAN FISHER

PIATKUS

PIATKUS

First published in Great Britain in 2024 by Piatkus

Copyright © Julian Fisher, 2024

1 3 5 7 9 8 6 4 2

The moral right of the author has been asserted.

A CIP catalogue record for this book is available from the British Library

ISBN: 978-0-34944-060-6

Typeset by Hewer Text UK Ltd, Edinburgh
Printed and bound in Great Britain by Clays Ltd, Elcograf S.p.A

Quotes on pages 144 and 145 are from *Schindler's List* (1993),
directed by Steven Spielberg and written by Steven Zaillian, based
on the novel *Schindler's Ark* (1982) by Thomas Keneally

Papers used by Piatkus are from well-managed
forests and other responsible sources.

Piatkus
An imprint of
Little, Brown Book Group
Carmelite House
50 Victoria Embankment
London EC4Y 0DZ

An Hachette UK Company
www.hachette.co.uk

www.littlebrown.co.uk

Author's note

The professional and personal anecdotes in this book are all based on actual events. However, in order to protect those involved and to respect confidentiality, certain key details have been changed, including amalgamating events and characters where appropriate. Any similarity between composite characters and real people is accidental. Dialogue exchanges are not verbatim, nor should they be treated as such.

To Amanda and Tim, loving allies still,
even in the chasm of their absence.

Contents

Stop! An invitation to think about what spies do   xi

Introduction   xiii

A Note on Terminology   xxv

Part 1: Getting Ready (Operational Groundwork)
1 The Focused Power of Targeting   3
2 The Transformative Power of Cover   30
3 The Bonding Power of Cultivation   68

Part 2: Getting Together (Recruitment)
4 The Paradoxical Power of Elicitation   103
5 The Enabling Power of Identifying Motivations   137
6 The Pulling Power of the Perfect Pitch   175

Part 3: Staying Together (Agent Handling)
7 The Keeping Power of Influence   213
8 The Revealing Power of Effective Debriefing   244
9 The Protective Power of Controlling the Environment   270

Final Thoughts about Thinking Like a Spy   297

Acknowledgements   301

Index   303

Stop!

And think.

I know you have just picked up this book. But I'd like you to put it down again. Just for a minute or two. And please spend that time thinking about the following question.

What do spies do?

Ignore the obvious answers: spies work in the shadows; they deal in secrets; they conduct covert operations. All true. But not very helpful.

I want you to think about the gritty details. *Who* are these spies? *What* do they do in the shadows? *Why* do they deal in secrets? *Where* and *when* do they conduct operations?

And, crucially, *how* do they set about their work?

Discard the Hollywood stereotypes. The superheroes of the screen bear few resemblances to their off-screen counterparts. Spies are made, not Bourne. As we shall see. And you can make yourself in their image.

But, before we set off on that journey together, I invite you once again to set down this book for a few moments and ask yourself:

What do spies *really* do?

Then, when you are ready, turn the page. There I'll explain why I think the answer to that question is more remarkable than any novel or movie can hope to portray.

Introduction

A spy does something extraordinary.

She travels abroad, often under cover, to hostile territories. Once in-country, she engages with senior political, military and legal personnel. Some of them, she peels off from their professional settings and draws them into close, personal friendships. Over time, she focuses on the most promising of these relationships and deepens them, strengthening the bonds of mutual trust and understanding. Then, after careful assessment and with exquisite timing, she strikes.

When the right day comes, she sits down with one of her new friends, somewhere quiet, unobtrusive and relaxing. A plush hotel restaurant, perhaps, or a park bench on a balmy summer's evening. She pours him a glass of wine, soothes any nerves he may have and settles him into an easy rhythm of attentive conversation. She reads his body language and listens intently to his words, her emotional antennae attuned only to him. Her sense of time, place and occasion heightened but her posture relaxed and her facial features open. And, as the evening mellows and the edges of the day begin to soften, she asks him to do something for her.

She asks him to betray his country.

* * *

She asks him to work for her, to become her willing partner in the world's second oldest profession: espionage.

He hesitates, of course. But it is only hesitation, not refusal. She has opened the narrow window of agent-recruitment and all that remains is for him to climb through it and join her on the other side. Her side.

Eyes on him throughout, she explains what it will mean. That he will be expected to get hold of secret information about his country's political, military and economic plans and to share it with her. That he will help her to undermine his country's national security in support of her country's interests. He will be breaking the law, of course. And, if caught, he may be subject to frightening sanctions: public shame; imprisonment; torture, maybe. Execution, in some countries.

And she is honest with him about the risks. If it all goes wrong, he will need to rely on his wits to survive. She will do what she can to help. But she is a visitor in his country and there will be limits to what she can do. At the worst and most threatening of times, when his heart is pounding, his mouth is dry and his innards have turned to icy liquid, he will have to manage on his own. Because that is the life of the traitor.

All this she asks of him as the buzz of unconcerned conversation around them fades to a hiss in his ears.

And he says, 'Yes'.

*   *   *

Yes, despite knowing the consequences of failure. Despite knowing Oleg Penkovsky's fate, for example.

Visitors to the Spyscape centre in Manhattan[1] learn about Penkovsky, a CIA asset in the 1960s and 'the most important spy of

1 https://spyscape.com/

the Cold War'.[1] An officer in the GRU (the Soviet military intelligence organisation), he provided intelligence concerning Russian military capabilities that proved crucial during the Cuban missile crisis. This intelligence gave President Kennedy 'the confidence to pursue a diplomatic solution to the crisis, backed up by a naval blockade'.[2] His actions led the CIA to give him the codename HERO. But his heroism was seen as treachery by the Soviets, who may have discovered his actions through a tip-off from a Soviet source from the West. Whatever the reason for his uncovering, he was to die an ignominious death. Most reports note that he was given a show-trial in Russia and shot to death on 16 May 1963. Other, more gory accounts suggest he may have been tied to a stretcher and fed, while conscious, into a crematorium furnace. Either way, the whereabouts of his remains are unknown.

Yes, despite knowing the story of Robert Hanssen, an FBI agent who turned to work for the Russians, selling them countless classified US documents. He is described by Spyscape as the Soviets' 'superspy'.[3] No doubt his KGB handlers considered him a hero. But the US authorities disagreed: on his discovery in 2001, they sentenced him to fifteen life terms in prison, with no possibility of early release. At least his guilty pleas spared Hanssen the death penalty. But they robbed him of the remainder of his life, nonetheless. He was to die in prison in June 2023. Retribution is not the preserve of any one side in the game of espionage.

Yes, despite knowing what happened to Joe Fenton, shot in the head by the Provisional IRA's so-called 'nutting squad' in 1989, on suspicion of acting as an agent for the British Army during the 'Troubles' in Northern Ireland.[4] And to others such

1 *Spyscape Museum Booklet*, p. 140.
2 Ibid.
3 Ibid. p. 32.
4 Jennifer O'Leary, 'Army's IRA spy Freddie Scappaticci admitted killing suspected informer', BBC News, 30 May 2023. https://www.bbc.co.uk/news/uk-northern-ireland-65748734

as Alexander Litvinenko and Sergei Skripal, apparently hunted
down by ruthless Russian hit-squads on suspicion of being
enemies of the state. Death by poisoning or a life forever on the
run: hardly an appealing choice.[1]

Despite knowing all of this, and more, he says 'yes'.

*   *   *

Unthinkable, isn't it? That an ordinary person – for spies are ordinary people too – could persuade someone to risk everything in
such a way. To jeopardise their reputation, their freedom, their
life, in the service of another country's national interests.

That's what I thought in 1989, during my first year at university, when I first started to ponder the world of espionage.

I was moved to do so by footage of thousands of East Germans
storming the Berlin Wall on 9 November that year. The Berlin
Wall! That symbol of the Cold War, of communist oppression,
that had stood since well before I was born, for twenty-eight
years; 10,316 days. The Berlin Wall! That barrier to humanity,
that had seemed impenetrable for the first eighteen years of my
life. I watched in awe that cold November evening as East
Berliners, freed after decades of Soviet tyranny, took pick
hammers and chisels to the concrete and chipped away at the
standing horror of it.

Just days before, the wall had been protected by the *Deutsche
Volkspolizei* (German People's Police, commonly known as
VoPos), an organisation that numbered up to a quarter of a
million officers. They had used deadly force to prevent the citizens of East Germany escaping across or under the Wall. More
than six hundred would-be escapees were shot or killed in other

1 https://www.nytimes.com/2018/03/06/world/europe/alexander-
litvinenko-sergei-skripal.htm

ways between 1961 and 1988.[1] Behind the VoPos stood the Stasi, the sprawling Ministry of State Security, dedicated to identifying, arresting or killing 'enemies of the state', including those brave souls who reported to western intelligence services. By 1989, the Stasi was a fearsome force, with some 274,000 employees.[2] This was a truly intimidating environment, in which the west's spies were expected to make just the sorts of recruitments described above. And in which recruited agents were always only a whisper away from betrayal by the Stasi's network of neighbourhood informers.

To me, back then, the idea of such recruitments was unimaginable. But they were happening. There, in East Berlin, and elsewhere, in other hostile operating environments. And they were being made by people like me. And like you.

What I couldn't know, at that time, was that ordinary people can be trained in a suite of skills and techniques which – when deployed in a structured, conscious way – enables them to achieve the unimaginable. It would certainly never have occurred to me that, already and unknowingly, I had absorbed some of the lessons learned by new intelligence officers. And I would have laughed at anyone who suggested that I had already applied those lessons, to take me further in life than I had ever expected to travel. This was something I came to realise much later. That realisation led me to recognise something else: that everyone can be taught to think like a spy, thereby transforming their lives.

And that epiphany led me to write the book that you are holding now.

* * *

1 https://www.berlin.de/mauer/en/history/victims-of-the-wall/
2 Helena Merriman, *Tunnel 29*, Hodder & Stoughton, 2021.

I was born in the poorest postcode in the UK: B16, in inner-city Birmingham.

There was no shortage of privilege. I had amazing, intelligent, musical, loving parents. I was surrounded by books and music. And, as my late mother used to say, I had won the lottery of life, being born a white male in England. I won't deny that. But perhaps I didn't get all six numbers and the bonus ball.

My early years were tough. It was the 1970s, money was tight for everyone and I was the fifth of seven children. I still have vivid flashbacks to the smell of my older brother Tim's holey socks, worn against the cold, as we lay head to toe in our shared bed. All seven of us were educated at home until the age of eleven. In practice, this meant lessons in the morning with Mum, before sloping off to trespass on the playing fields that belonged to the nearby Mitchells & Butlers Brewery. There, we were joined by local truants, to play raggedy games of football or forage for unripe apples that made our stomachs ache.

My first day at 'big school' – a sink comprehensive in a nearby suburb – thrilled me. I looked forward to learning and to making friends. But I returned home to hear that, while I had been sitting my streaming tests, my beautiful, talented, clever sister Amanda had jumped to her death from the window of her psychiatric hospital. She was twenty. I stood in the lino-ed kitchen, a half-dried coffee mug in one hand and a tea towel in the other, stupefied by the words I had heard from my mother but could barely comprehend. I saw the room before me become two, each version tilting through the other, before coming back to a single whole. I looked again and the room was the same. But nothing would ever be the same again. Including me.

After that, school didn't work for me. I was stumbling through the days in a daze of grief, as though observing the world from the outside. I would hear my fellow pupils and my teachers speak but their words came to me from a distance, as if

I was hearing them in that moment of dropping off to sleep in a room full of people. I withdrew from my classmates, which led them to think me aloof. In return they bullied me endlessly, teasing my skinny build and my sporting ineptitude. I didn't much care at first. Little could hurt me compared to the aching hollowness and desperate helplessness that followed Amanda's suicide.

Later, though, as the bullying continued, there didn't seem much point in going to school. There, I would only be taunted by classmates and face stonewalling from teachers who had no clue how to handle a grief-stricken child. So I didn't go. Not often. I was probably absent as much as I was present, sometimes with my parents' knowledge, just as often without. Fourteen months after Amanda's death, while walking myself to school after a two-week absence, dread curdling in my lower stomach, I contrived a way to get out of school altogether.

I stepped into the road, in front of a fast-moving car.

*   *   *

I find it difficult to write those words. My parents had suffered enough tragedy and, even now, I won't allow myself to contemplate how they would have felt if I had not survived the impact. But I do not regret the months I spent in hospital, my leg held together by a titanium plate, much of the time encased in plaster of Paris from my chest to my toes. It was a transformative time for me. First, because it taught me that there were many in the world who were much worse off than me. Gavin, an eight-year-old in the bed next to mine, had an incurable condition which meant that his skeleton was not growing fast enough to accommodate his maturing organs. He had been abandoned by his parents and was in the care of his loving grandma, who devoted herself to bringing him to hospital for repeated surgical procedures. His body was a mass of scars and he could move around only with the aid of a miniature Zimmer frame. But the smile never left his face and his optimistic company was a delight.

Second, my extended stay in hospital taught me that I could survive. That I was not the physically weedy, broken reed that I had previously thought myself to be. I had time to read and think about what I wanted from life. I would trawl through old copies of *Reader's Digest*, looking for the IQ tests they would periodically publish. Discovering that I had a knack for such quizzes, I concluded that I must be cleverer than I had previously supposed. All this combined to imbue me with renewed strength to face the world and to make my way in it, on my terms.

But the most important lesson I learned was from one of the student nurses who cared for me. Mehr was little more than a child herself, maybe seventeen or eighteen when I met her. I remember the small pools of tears that formed in her eyes as she told me the story of her family's flight from Iran's revolution, in 1979. She described hiding in a linen closet, listening to bodies slam against walls and hands slap against faces as Mehr's father, a medical doctor, was arrested as a counter-revolutionary. All for some unguarded comments he had made earlier that day in a coffee shop. He was not to be heard of again. Her mother and she were helped to leave the country by a distant relative who had managed to keep his job as a border official. The two made their way to Pakistan and, from there, to the UK, with only one small bag of belongings each. They ended up in Birmingham, living in a one-bedroom flat close to my own family home, from where Mehr's mother eked out a living as a cleaner.

Mehr was determined to help her mother financially, as soon as she was old enough. And she resolved to honour her father by following him into the medical profession. But there was one major obstacle. On arriving in the UK, Mehr spoke very little

English. The local authority found her a place at a state school, but there were no Farsi-speaking teachers there and she struggled to make progress. Until she awoke one June morning with an idea already formed in her mind. She asked a teacher to find out which universities offered courses in Farsi and to write letters to their language departments offering free conversation classes for students. A few weeks later, a letter arrived from Daniel, a student who was studying Farsi at the School of Oriental and African Studies in London. He was staying with his parents in Edgbaston, an affluent Birmingham suburb, for the long summer break. Daniel and Mehr met under her mother's watchful eye and the two became immediate friends. Over the summer of 1980, they got together every day for two hours of conversation, the first in Farsi, the second in English. These encounters gave her the confidence to engage strangers – bus conductors, passersby, the postman, neighbours – in conversation. By the end of that summer, Mehr was almost fluent in English.

But Daniel's help did not end there. His father was a well-to-do entrepreneur who worked in Birmingham's Jewellery Quarter and was involved with the City Council. He had connections in most professional fields and agreed to help Mehr secure a place on a training course to become a State Enrolled Nurse. But, first, she had to pass her school exams, all set in her second language, of course. She failed them first time round and despaired that she would have to abandon her dream of nursing, leave school and find menial work to help her mother. Daniel's father intervened again. He paid for Mehr to continue conversation classes with his son, while she studied to re-sit her exams, this time successfully.

Mehr called me 'Ko', an abbreviation of *kocholo*, or 'little one' in Farsi.

She told me her story sitting on the end of my bed. Afterwards, seeing my astonishment, she wriggled my big toe, where it stuck out beyond the plaster cast, and said, 'You see, Ko, Daniel and his father were kind people but I could help them too. My father always taught me never to take without giving. So, I gave something to Daniel and, in return, they became my allies.' She paused. Then, suddenly serious, she spoke again.

'Allies are the most important things you will need in life,' she said. 'Never forget that.'

I never have.

*   *   *

I emerged from hospital determined to listen and to learn from people around me. To take the lessons I needed and to find the allies required to propel me into a different life. That stay in hospital was a reset for me and Mehr had been the one to press the button. I was not going to let her down.

I learned the skills to forge extraordinary alliances from ordinary people in ordinary jobs, as I will explain in this book. I discovered that, just by listening – even to the most unlikely seeming mentors – we can learn vital lessons in how to navigate the world with more assurance and more success.

In time, the skills I acquired took me to places I had never dared contemplate as a comprehensive schoolboy from inner-city Birmingham: I moved schools, twice, seeking out the one most likely to get me to a good university; I landed a place at an Oxford college, where I was surrounded by the polished products of the best fee-paying schools; I wangled a job with a blue-blooded stockbrokers in the City of London, where I was surrounded by sophisticated aristocratic socialites; I represented the UK abroad, in the Chanceries of two High Commissions; I worked with British military men and mercenaries, advising presidents and prime ministers in fascinating and challenging countries; I fronted a Channel 4 TV series; and

I founded my own specialist intelligence company, providing esoteric services to blue-chip clients.

*   *   *

I am extremely fortunate to have lived – and to continue to live – a life full of adventure, intrigue and interest, despite an unpromising start. I credit this to the skills I absorbed from people around me, from all backgrounds and sometimes in the most unlikely settings.

It wasn't until much later that I realised I had been, without knowing it, absorbing and applying some of the skills taught to spies all around the world. Skills that enable them to achieve the unthinkable, as described above. And here's the thing. If I could do that, you can too. So, I invite you to join me on a journey, in which you too will learn to Think Like a Spy.

This will involve examining nine separate skills, grouped under three headings:

- Getting Ready, covering target-profiling, cover and cultivation;
- Getting Together, covering elicitation, motivations and pitching; and
- Staying Together, covering influence, debriefing and detection of deception, and tradecraft.

For each of the nine skills, we shall begin by reviewing how and why they are taught to spies the world over. It is important to note that these skills are used universally: they are not proprietary to any specific national intelligence service; they are employed widely by private intelligence consultancies, such as my own; and the techniques are taught to security and intelligence specialists working for global corporates. You will read stories about the use of the skill in real-world examples, in both intelligence-gathering and personal settings. Perhaps most important, I shall make suggestions about how you, too, can develop and use these skills to improve your chances of personal and professional fulfilment.

But before we get going, it is important that we have a shared understanding of the words and phrases that you will come across repeatedly, as you learn to master the art of influence and build life-changing alliances.

A Note on Terminology

'Spy' is an imprecise term.

It is often used to refer to employees of state intelligence agencies, such as the CIA, Mossad or France's DGSE. Another term for these individuals is 'intelligence officer'. Equally often, the word 'spy' is used for the people recruited by intelligence officers to supply them with secrets. Other terms for this category are 'agent', 'source' and 'asset'. Confusingly, though, the word 'agent' is used in America interchangeably with 'intelligence officer'.

To make matters – appropriately – even more murky, intelligence officers have a variety of functions. Some are engaged in intercepting messages sent by electronic means: Signals Intelligence or 'SIGINT'. Others might spend their time analysing publicly available information, to spot patterns or provide leads for other types of operations: Open-Source Intelligence or 'OSINT'. Yet others pore over photographs taken from military aircraft or drones: Image Intelligence or 'IMINT'.

But the category of interest for present purposes is Human Intelligence or 'HUMINT'. This involves, at the operational sharp end, the type of operation that I outlined in the introduction – identification, cultivation and recruitment of human sources of intelligence. Once such sources have been recruited and have begun supplying a stream of intelligence, other categories of officers get involved: to process, analyse and present the intelligence to interested parties. Everyone involved in this chain of intelligence generation and management may be referred to as a spy.

However, I use the term throughout this book in a very specific manner. I use it solely to refer to the human source intelligence officer who is directly recruiting and running assets on the ground. To make this crystal clear, an alternative title for this book could be 'Think Like an Intelligence Officer'. Their recruits, I refer to as 'agents', never intending that phrase in the American sense (officers of intelligence and law-enforcement agencies). Their colleagues in analysis and distribution of intelligence I refer to as support officers. And we shall not be concerning ourselves here with those agencies or departments involved in SIGINT, OSINT or IMINT, so I shall not trouble you with establishing terminology for them.

PART 1

Getting Ready (Operational Groundwork)

'When we succeed, we succeed because of our individual initiative, but also because we do things together [. . .] You're not on your own, we're in this together.'

President Barack Obama, 13 July 2012

CHAPTER ONE

The Focused Power of Targeting

Where do we start when learning to think like a spy?

At the beginning, of course. The beginning of the cycle.

Cycles govern our lives: as youngsters, the academic cycle gives us structure; later, in our workplaces, project cycles occupy us, as do taxation cycles; beyond our windows, the cycle of the seasons dictates the cycle of sowing and harvesting; above us, some people believe that the lunar and planetary cycles determine our fates. So, I urge you to start thinking about cycles. One in particular: the intelligence cycle.

This is what a typical intelligence cycle looks like:▶

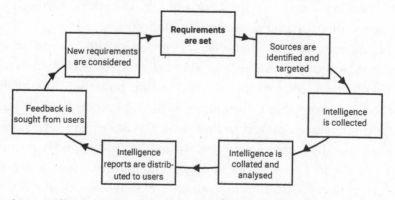

You will see from this that intelligence management is an iterative process. Intelligence gathered in the first turn of the cycle is used to reset the requirements for the second turn. And so on, as policymakers hone their responses to the information delivered to them.

Each stage of the cycle shapes action to be taken at the next. The information required determines where sources might be found. When relevant sources have been identified, operations can be planned to engage with them and collect intelligence. The intelligence collected determines policy conclusions. These conclusions guide who should see intelligence reports (the 'customers'). Customers respond to the reports and their feedback is used to adjust requirements. Revised requirements are then put back to the spies for further action.

There are parallels with a business project life cycle, in which there are five phases: project initiation phase (requirements setting); project planning phase (source identification and targeting); project executing phase (collection, analysis, and distribution of intelligence); project monitoring phase (seeking of feedback); and project closing phase (the re-setting of requirements to re-start the cycle).

In the case of the intelligence cycle, the first stage of *operational* action is targeting. This is, put simply, a case of identifying the best person (or people) for the job. It is done through a process of narrowing down or elimination.

Requirements are usually for specific information that cannot be found through open sources: more or less the definition of secret intelligence. So, the starting point is to establish who is privy to that information. Who is likely to know what the spy has been tasked to find out? The answer to this question is usually to be found in institutions. The most likely group of people to know about military capabilities? Senior army officers and civilian staff in ministries of defence. About a president's plans to invade neighbouring territories? Apparatchiks in the office of the president. About the availability of foreign exchange reserves in developing countries? Central bank officials. And so on.

But these are large groups of people and not all of them will be able to get to the intelligence needed. Therefore, it helps to know more details about a target institution. How is it organised? What departments are there and what are their responsibilities? Organograms are very helpful to map out an institution's structure. And, here, the internet is the spy's friend. Government departments and other organisations often divulge large amounts of information about themselves on their websites. After all, that is the primary purpose of a website: to showcase what the outfit behind it is all about. And there is a natural temptation on the part of website designers to load a great deal of content. Content that is there to be mined by the determined spy.

However, some organisations have more savvy than this, with greater organisational awareness of information security. They may have staff dedicated to ensuring that sensitive organisational data is not published online. In this case, the spy's targeting job is more difficult and requires more imagination. They might turn to existing agents who know about arrangements within more secure departments. Academic works can also be useful, as can discussions with filmmakers, journalists and businesspeople who have been active in the country of interest to the spy.

Diving deeper, the challenge is to find out who works in the departments of interest. Again, this information is sometimes made available online, alongside contact details for each member of staff. That's the dream. The nightmare is when organisations keep details of their employees under impenetrable wraps. Again, short of hacking into Human Resources databases, the spy may be reliant on other contacts to provide details about the identities of specific job holders. Alongside this, intensive online research can yield fruits. While there may be no formal organogram to turn to, it is often possible to piece together a reliable personnel-map of an organisation from other online resources: social media profiles; media reports of events attended by relevant staff; and speaker lists at conferences pertinent to the intelligence required.

I conduct similar exercises at the outset of every project I work on for clients. Over time, this approach has built up a significant database of knowledge about government departments and other agencies across Africa, the focus of my consulting business. And one soon gets a feel for where information is to be found about different types of organisations in particular jurisdictions. As a result, targeting has become easier for me each time I have conducted it.[1] But there is another stage of profiling to complete before the organisational data is actionable.

PERSONALITY PROFILING

Once equipped with a list of names of people likely to have access to intelligence of interest, it is necessary to develop individual personality profiles. This stage of assessment benefits from some psychological insights. In their informative book *The Psychology of Spies and Spying*, John Taylor and Adrian Furnham[2] outline 'six dimensions of personality profiling'. Of these, I want to look in some detail at three.

First to be considered is the impact of culture: that is, how societal norms and expectations are likely to have exerted their influence on targets of interest. For example, a sense of cultural

1 A note of caution here. There are legal constraints on what personal information businesses and other entities are allowed to hold. If you plan to build a database that identifies people, you should first familiarise yourself with legal obligations in this area.
2 John Taylor and Adrian Furnham, *The Psychology of Spies and Spying*, Troubador Publishing, 2022.

alienation will often incline someone to seek meaningful relationships and alliances elsewhere.

Silas, a long-standing contact of mine from Senegal, is a case in point. He has influential friends in government, and often provides me with analysis about political developments that goes well beyond anything available from open sources. Silas is in his forties and is childless, in a culture that prizes children, particularly boys. He once told me that some of his older friends and family members do not consider him to be 'a man' because he has no sons. Consequently, Silas leans heavily on his non-Senegalese friends, including me, because he is not made by any of them to feel somehow inferior due to his family circumstances. I take this sensitivity into account in all my dealings with Silas. In return, he is willing to share with me information and insights that he would be unlikely to make available to someone less attuned to him. Such is the power of cultural awareness in the intelligence world.

Upbringing is the second dimension to consider. The events of our early years have great bearing on our personalities and attitudes in later life. For example, it is useful to consider the circumstances of a potential target's education, which may have the effect of developing a personality receptive to ideas and people from outside their immediate communities.

Janet, a Zimbabwean friend of mine, was educated at the International School in Harare, where she was surrounded by the sons and daughters of diplomats and NGOs from all over the world. This outward-looking experience fundamentally altered her relationship with the insular government of Zimbabwe, which she regards with some distaste, despite being one of its senior officials. I am sure you will be able to assess the significance of that fact for yourself.

Third is intellect. It is not straightforward to assess an individual's intellect without meeting them. But it is possible to gather some evidence. They may have published papers online, for instance, or they may be active on social media, commenting on current affairs or cultural matters. Spies study such clues about their targets because intelligence is good for intelligence. Potential agents with developed intellects are attractive because they will have penetrating insights into and understanding of the subjects on which they will be asked to provide information. They are also likely to be more creative in developing access to intelligence of interest. And, in my experience, highly intelligent people have a more pronounced tendency to boredom, a trait which may lead them to seek stimulation by entering new alliances with interesting interlocutors.

This was the case with Susan, a police officer in Africa, who worked with me to spirit an opposition-supporting journalist out of the country, when we found out his life was in imminent danger. I return to this tale elsewhere. For now, the important point to note is that Susan was the right person to help me partly because she was frustrated by her day-to-day duties as a traffic cop. Flagging down speeding motorists and issuing parking fines was not drawing fully on the intellectual capacity of a linguistics graduate and holder of a private pilot's licence. But fulfilling job opportunities were thin on the ground and Susan was thrilled to turn her mind to an interesting and worthy operation.

Furnham and Taylor go on to examine personality dark-side traits (such as personality disorders) and motivation, in their review of profiling. But these elements don't belong in the targeting phase since they are very difficult to assess from afar. We shall return to them in later sections.

Spies develop these target profiles because they are after something: secret intelligence. The purpose of the profiles is to make an early assessment of who has access to information of interest, who is likely to be open to an approach and how that approach might best be framed.

Later in this chapter, we will examine how you can adapt and adopt the targeting model, to help you get what you are after. This might be a helping hand into your dream job, an invitation to speak at an important conference, the opportunity to appear on a television programme, or myriad other ambitions. But first, I'll tell you a story about how I unconsciously used profiling and targeting to land my first serious job, in a firm that was not accustomed to recruiting state-schoolers from the inner cities.

* * *

Winston Churchill MP won me my first graduate job.

It all started as I stood next to the then-prime minister, Margaret Thatcher, in a ceramics factory in the Black Country. I was surprised at how much shorter she was in real life than she appeared on-screen. And the smell of rose-water on her reminded me of my grandmother, who was about the same age. But she exuded charisma and greeted me with some charm. I felt privileged to be part of the group showing her around, as she picked up floral-patterned cups and plates, examining them with a convincing impression of interest. And, as I thought about how unlikely it all felt, an idea occurred to me.

It was 1989 and the Conservative Party was about to get caned in the European parliamentary elections of that year, the first vote in which the Labour Party polled higher than the Tories since 1974. That election was, arguably, the beginning of the end for Thatcher's premiership.

But this story is not about that.

I'd had high hopes for my gap year, having applied to volunteer in Africa for an organisation called The Project Trust. This Scotland-based charity was one of the first organisations to offer meaningful experiences to students taking a year out before university – an unusual phenomenon back then. It arranged for its lucky applicants to spend their year in a developing country, working with local communities and getting under the skin of its cultures. I had passed the initial selection phase and could not have been more excited about packing my bags and heading off.

But then the fundraising pack arrived. I had not properly appreciated that the experiences were financed through funds raised by the applicants themselves. The target was hefty and I had no idea how to set about meeting it, despite helpful suggestions in the literature, such as organising a fun run or a tombola. All reasonable enough, but such capers would barely make a dent. It was obvious that I would need one or two serious financial mentors and I didn't have any. I was yet to reach the stage of my life when I could set about consciously recruiting valuable allies to my cause.

The Project Trust set me up with Chloe, a volunteer who had recently completed her year abroad and was charged with offering me advice. She lived in one of Birmingham's wealthier suburbs and I had a shiver of apprehension as I approached the large, detached Victorian red-brick house where I was to meet her. This was not the kind of property I was accustomed to visiting. I perched on a leather sofa, trying to control a fit of the shakes that was rattling my teacup in its saucer. I didn't trust myself to put them down without spilling the tea, nor to lift the cup and drink from it, so I sat immobile, clutching the saucer in one hand and the cup in the other as the tea went cold. Finally, after thirty minutes or so of Chloe telling me about the terrific time she had enjoyed abroad and the magical places that she had managed to visit after her volunteering stint, her imperious mother took pity on me and removed the cup and saucer from my hands.

She ushered me towards the door and Chloe followed me out, for final goodbyes and to wish me luck on my own adventure. I looked at the ground as I asked her the only question that I had wanted all along to pose: how had she managed to raise the money for her travels?

'Oh, I didn't have to worry too much about that,' she said, airily. 'Mummy and Daddy paid for it.'

In that moment, the dream of volunteering in Africa during my gap year evaporated.

This meant that I had a year on my hands, with nothing to fill it. That is, until I met Mike (now Lord) Whitby. Mike is a salt-of-the-earth Brummie, with a successful track record in manufacturing business, and I liked him immediately. Not the sort of person to judge me, or anyone else, on their background and social standing. He had been selected as the Conservative Party candidate for the European parliamentary constituency of Midlands West and was looking for someone to help him run his campaign. Someone who was not going to cost him or the constituency association a great deal of money. I fitted that bill and was keen to get my teeth into something challenging and interesting. So every day I would travel by bus to offices in a vacant car lot that had been loaned to Mike's campaign by the Richardson brothers, twins who had dedicated their business lives to bringing wealth and opportunities to deprived areas of the Midlands following deindustrialisation. There I would help Mike plot his campaign events and conduct research to support his candidacy.

It soon became clear that the national campaign was going badly for the Tories. Opinion polls made for dismal reading and the party in Westminster became increasingly desperate to identify potential bright spots to celebrate on what was shaping up to be a terrible election night. Midlands West was held by the Labour Party with a very narrow majority, following a by-election in 1987 that had unexpectedly seen their vote share fall. Conservative Central Office lit on this fact and decided to prioritise the campaign there, believing that it was a potential gain for them from Labour. So, as the race got under way in earnest, the party sent some of its biggest names – including Thatcher – to campaign alongside Mike. I got to meet them all. At the time, to my younger and more impressionable self, that felt like a big deal.

It was also a golden opportunity for me to create life-changing alliances. I resolved not to waste the chances that came my way. At each event, I would make sure that I had some face time with whichever bigwig had been sent to us that day. And I would ask each of them if they needed a parliamentary researcher, who would have some time on his hands after the campaign and was prepared to spend that time working for expenses only. I figured that this was the most likely way of getting my foot in the metaphorical door with them.

Most gave me a polite brush-off. But the then-Leader of the House of Lords, Lord Belstead, invited me to write to him and promised to find out if any of his colleagues would be able to make use of my time. He wrote back. One of his MP friends needed someone to help with the task of sorting and filing several suitcases of papers that he had accumulated over his years in the House of Commons. The work was uninspiring but that did not matter to me, given my wider intentions. The key thing was that, a few weeks later, I was in possession of a House of Commons pass and enough funding to make the trip to London once a week.

That was when my targeting work started for real. So far I had simply been opportunistic. Now I intended to be artistic. Or, maybe, artful.

I found a spare hour and settled into the House of Commons library with all the information I could find about the cohort of Conservative MPs. I was clear about my objectives: I had, in a manner of speaking, set my requirements. I wanted to identify

MPs whose names would look most impressive as referees on my CV, for when it came to finding a career after university. From that shortlist, I would work out who already employed their full quota of staff and who might have some capacity to take me on, as someone already holding a parliamentary pass.

It didn't take long to narrow down my search to one person. That was Winston Churchill MP, grandson of the wartime leader. Churchill Junior had been elected to Parliament almost as of familial right but had not distinguished himself especially once elected. I guess he had a hard act to follow but that didn't matter to me. His name was what I wanted. And, having scoured Hansard for his contributions in the chamber, I reckoned he could do with someone to help write his speeches. So, I set about making sure I was the person who would do that.

I hung around central lobby when I knew he would be likely to head through on hearing the division bell. I found out the whereabouts of his office and made sure I had regular occasion to be in its vicinity. I drifted into the Strangers' Bar if I saw him heading that way. I all-but stalked him, in fact (not something I recommend). In time, we were on nodding terms and then, one day, I found him outside the library, hunched over a Reuters printer that spooled out global news headlines on that old fashioned green and white paper with holes running down each side. We got chatting about some developments in Middle East politics, as the machine whirred and chattered between us. After a while, I plunged in and asked if he would be interested in taking me on as a speechwriter. He jumped at the idea.

It probably wasn't my most impressive period of endeavour. I recall Winston forwarded to me a copy of Hansard which contained a speech I had written for him, on the subject of nationalisation. The opening words of his respondent, a Labour frontbencher, made me cringe. They were something along the lines of

'I don't know who writes the Honourable gentleman's speeches but I suggest he finds a replacement.' Again, though, performance wasn't the point. I got on well with Winston and he happily agreed to provide me with a positive reference when the time came for me to venture properly into the world of employment.

That time came a few years later. I hauled open the heavy oak door to the Cazenove & Co. offices on Tokenhouse Yard, behind the Bank of England, to be greeted by a concierge in tails. He ushered me to a Chesterfield porter chair, where I waited to be carried to my interview by means of small rickety lift, accessed through a folding metal door. The narrow corridors, with their Victorian-era wallpaper and deep-pile carpets, smelled of industrious opulence: leather, wood polish and paper.

Cazenove is celebrating its two-hundredth year in the stock-broking business as I write, though it was bought by the US investment bank JP Morgan in 2009. Prior to the acquisition, it was a venerable City institution, respected universally for its values of integrity and discretion. It was an anachronism even at the time of my interview, in the early 1990s. Staff members were predominantly white men from wealthy backgrounds. Many were aristocrats. Almost all had been educated at expensive private schools. When in town, they lived in Chelsea, Kensington and Mayfair.

They moved in shoals: to upmarket ski resorts in January and February; country estates over Easter; the Royal Enclosure at Ascot, Wimbledon, Lord's, Henley, Goodwood and debutantes' balls during the social season; Cornwall and Tuscany for summer holidays in July; the grouse moors for the Glorious Twelfth.[1] Their accents and jargon were refined, unmistakeably upper-class drawls. They dressed in bespoke clothing cut to a set of accepted norms: braces, not belts; single-breasted suits made of

1 12 August, the first day of the grouse-shooting season.

conservative cloths with colourful silk jacket-linings; double-cuff shirts without breast pockets; polished black Oxfords or brogues. Little sayings helped establish the code: 'when in town, never wear brown'; 'only butlers and chauffeurs wear black socks'.

In short, I was not one of them.

A sense of *noblesse oblige* meant that my colleagues-to-be were impeccably polite and friendly towards me, if a little condescending at times. But I was never to be one of them. There would always be a glass partition between me and them, no matter how far I rose in the firm's ranks. Because I literally could not speak their language.

This was driven home to me one day when I took a phone call for a colleague who was away from his desk. The caller asked me to leave a note to say that they should meet at Val d'Isère. I had never been skiing, had no idea how to spell the name of the resort and was too embarrassed to ask. This was before the dawn of the internet and I had no easy way of checking. So, I wrote it phonetically: 'Valdisair'. Later, returning from lunch myself, I was unnoticed by a small group that had gathered at the desk where my colleague was passing around the note I had written, for their amusement and derision. I retreated for five minutes, to spare them (and me) the embarrassment of discovery.

I was surprised and delighted when I was offered a job at Cazenove, given the chasm between my experiences and those of its natural recruits. It felt like I was storming a social bastion. My delight was not misplaced. My years at 'Caz', the odd episode apart, were instructive, enlightening and great fun. One of the salesmen there, sadly now no longer with us, was fond of quoting *Liar's Poker*: that a job at Cazenove was not so much like working as turning up each day 'to collect lottery winnings'. I remain friends with a handful of people I worked with there and they are intelligent, thoughtful, generous, warm souls. Most were. But it was something of a puzzle how I had managed to be accepted into this elite club, with its arcane rules and its impenetrable social cliques.

At least a part of the answer lay in my earlier use of the targeting technique. This was revealed to me a few months into my time at Cazenove, when I was chatting idly with my boss. John was everything that I could have hoped for in a mentor at that stage of my life. Kind-hearted, down to earth, wise, generous with praise, acute in his criticisms. And he had a sense of humour. He had a twinkle in his eye when he said to me, 'Of course, I had to offer you a job.' I asked him why.

'Because,' he said with a smile, 'I really liked the idea of phoning Parliament and asking to speak to Winston Churchill.'

I'm sure there was more to his decision than that. But I sometimes wonder.

*   *   *

You've now been introduced to the first important technique in the operational cycle of intelligence gathering and seen how I applied it in my civilian life, even without being able to name it. Next, I will outline an adaptation of the targeting technique to help you meet your professional and personal goals. This chapter will then conclude with a story about the use of targeting in my professional life. But first, let's review what we have learned so far.

RECAP

- Spies define exactly what they want before setting out to get it. Requirements-setting – the first stage of the intelligence cycle – is vital preparation for an operation.
- Requirements shape the targeting process. Who are the people able to get the intelligence required? Who amongst them may be open to an approach?

- Some targeting data is available from open sources, primarily the internet and social media. But some can only be acquired through friendly intermediaries.
- Targeting data is used to develop personality profiles, with a focus on cultural context, social background and personal intellect.

* * *

Let's pull all this together to develop a practical system that you can use towards achieving your ambitions.

There is one thing I must make clear at the outset. The targeting technique is not the same as networking or building a social media following, though both these things may play into it.

The crucial difference is that networking is about building a bank of contacts from all walks of life who, one day, *might* be useful. Targeting is about setting out to identify the people or person best placed to help you achieve something specific.

It will help to start thinking about your personal cycle of achievement. At this stage, I'll introduce some alternative terminology, to adapt the intelligence process:

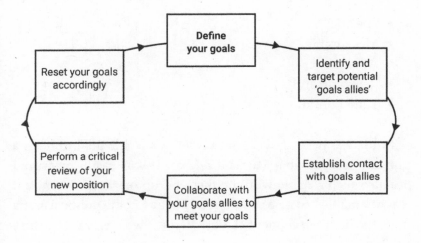

It should be obvious from this that each cycle is but one part of the process of developing the life you want to lead. For example, you might set a goal to land a job in a specific sector or country and collaborate with goals allies to do so. Once in that job, you will wish to refine your goal: to be promoted, for example, or to be published in a trade journal as an expert in your field. Refined goals will require new targeting exercises and collaborations with new goals allies. And this process will continue throughout your career.

Of course, it is important to know broadly where you want to end up in five or ten years, or even on a longer time-horizon. But it is also important to be flexible and to recognise that we are not in full control of our destinies. It may be necessary to adjust your overall ambitions in the light of achieving specific, time-limited goals that build towards them. We shall come back to the place of longer-term goals in Chapter Two (p. 30), when we look at how to adapt the principles of cover in the service of our ambitions.

For now, you may find it helpful, when considering short- and medium-term goals, to adopt the SMART model, which is frequently applied to objectives-setting in business. Your goals should be:

- Specific;
- Measurable;
- Attainable;
- Relevant; and
- Time-bound.

In the example above, I set myself a specific goal to have a publicly recognisable MP as a referee. It was easily measured because such a name would either end up on my CV or not. It was attainable because I was already active in the political arena (note the iterative element at work here). It was relevant because

I originally wished to work in government affairs or lobbying (it got me into stockbroking, so there's the flexibility bit at work). And it was time-bound because I knew when I would need to start distributing my CV for graduate jobs. I recognise, of course, that few of these elements will apply to most readers of this book. But that is the point of your personal cycle of achievement: it will be unique to you.

Once you have described your personal goals, the next stage is to draw up a profile of the types of people who might help you achieve them. I call these people 'goals allies'. Note that there are two necessary conditions for someone to be a potential goals ally.

First, they must be *able* to help you. This is equivalent to the spy looking for potential agents who have access to the intelligence required. A fantastic agent who is motivated, creative and energetic is of no use to a spy if the information they are able to share is not relevant.

Second, they must be *willing* to help you. As far as the spy is concerned, access to intelligence is of no value by itself. So, their targeting exercise will examine those factors that might incline the agent to take risks in support of another country's national interests. Your bar is likely to be set much lower than this, but willingness to help is still of vital importance.

With your goals ally profile completed, it is time to start the targeting exercise for real. This means mining information to draw up a short-list of people who match that profile. You can think of it like a dating profile if that helps. You are on the hunt for matches.

There are various sources that you can turn to in this process. Your social media connections are an obvious starting point. But do be prepared to go beyond first-order connections. Examine also contacts of contacts and suggestions under headings such as 'You May Also Know'. It is worth reviewing all your social media accounts at the outset of a targeting exercise but some are more useful than others for particular purposes.

The obvious one is LinkedIn as a resource for contacts in the business world. But you will also have a sense of the likely user base for others.

Beyond social media, the internet offers a wealth of resources, some paid but many free. Depending on your available budget, you may find it useful to subscribe to a handful of sites that focus exclusively on your area of interest but there is no compelling need to do so, given how much information is freely available.

Don't forget your local library. There, you may be able to access subscription-only websites. And it will hold up-to-date copies of useful reference works, such as the *Writers' and Artists' Yearbook* (thinking close to home), journals published by the Law Society, *The Academic's Handbook*, specialist business sector publications and countless others. Libraries may also have access to newspaper and magazine articles that are not easily located online.

Finally, the best information source of all: other people. Family, friends, colleagues, social media contacts, maybe even careers counsellors or other such mentors. All these people have knowledge in their heads that may be valuable to you. It is always worth asking if they have ideas about who might become a goals ally to you. Algorithms and search engines are great but people are creative, imaginative and connected. Remember Karinthy's concept of six degrees of separation?[1] It's not so far-fetched. The idea was stress-tested by the more famous psychologist Stanley Milgram in the 1960s and found to be reasonably sound.[2] In 2008,

1 Frigyes Karinthy, 'Chain-Links', 1929. http://vadeker.net/articles/Karinthy-Chain-Links_1929.pdf
2 Jeffrey Travers and Stanley Milgram, 'An Experimental Study of the Small World Problem', *Sociometry*, Vol. 32, No. 4 (Dec., 1969), pp. 425–43. https://snap.stanford.edu/class/cs224w-readings/travers69smallworld.pdf

a study by Microsoft of 30 billion conversations on the Messenger platform concluded that there were 6.6 degrees of separation between any two individuals in the world.[1] On average, of course, there being no such thing as 60 per cent of a person.

Contacts in common can also be very useful when calculating the trickier side of the targeting equation: willingness. We all know the power of referral. Better the email or letter that opens with 'Simon suggested that I get in touch with you' than with 'You don't know me but . . .'. Best is the email from Simon that starts with 'I'd like to introduce you to my brother Jules.' It is a characteristic of human nature that we are more willing to help someone with whom we have something in common.

Don't panic if, having identified a handful of potential goals allies, you are unable to find a way to them through shared contacts. There are many other points of commonality to explore. Does your target live in the same area as you? Were they born in the same town? Did they go to the same school as you? Did their children? Have they worked at the same organisations as you in the past? Are they of the same religion? Do they play cricket at the same club? And so on. The possibilities are endless and research can turn up the most useful things, as this case study illustrates.

CASE STUDY

Tom is a talented fashion designer with a long-term ambition to work for one of the leading fashion houses in Paris. However, despite having a first-class degree in design from a good university and an impressive portfolio, his work applications have so far been unsuccessful.

---

1 https://www.microsoft.com/en-us/research/publication/ instant-messagers-really-six-degrees-kevin-bacon-big-microsoft-study-supports-small-world-theory/

He decides to break down his ambition into a series of attainable goals and discusses with friends in the fashion industry how he can improve his chances of landing his dream job. His friend Sophie suggests that he should try to get a celebrity endorsement of his work, perhaps by their posting an image of them wearing one of his pieces on social media.

At first, Tom feels daunted by this prospect, thinking only of Hollywood A-listers. Why would someone like that be willing to give up even a small amount of their time to help him? Then, one day, he goes to a musical at his local repertory theatre and realises several of the cast are from his hometown. But one of them has a national profile and this gives him an idea.

A simple Google search quickly finds several celebrities who were born in Tom's town. He selects five that he thinks would be well placed to help him. He bases his selection on clear criteria: a profile in Europe, because he wishes to work in Paris; at least 250,000 social media followers, because this base would make them a mid-tier influencer; and a reputation for dressing well and fashionably, because this will place him alongside some of the labels previously worn by his goals ally.

Having selected a manageable number of targets, Tom starts to research them in more detail, to identify those that might be motivated to help him. During his research, Tom finds an interview with one of his shortlisted targets in the local evening newspaper. The celebrity – an actor, first name Moussa – tells the interviewer that he is passionate about his hometown and frequently visits to give motivational talks at local schools. It seems he has a desire to help talent from the town of his birth.

That's the targeting exercise completed. We'll follow Tom's subsequent progress later in the book.

It won't be wasted on you that what Tom set out to do first was establish a commonality with his target. But this was not his only consideration when it came to establishing Moussa's willingness to help.

In general, people are surprisingly happy to lend assistance if asked in the right way (we'll come back to this later). But, as with everything, there are degrees to this truth. You will need to be imaginative in how you assess whether a target is likely to give up their time and energy for you. Look for evidence such as reports of your target mentoring younger people. They might be known as donors to charities that seek to develop opportunities for the disadvantaged. They could be politically active in a progressive cause. They might have established a foundation to help others. A fine example of this is the Sutton Trust, established by financier-turned-philanthropist Sir Peter Lampl, which aims to improve social mobility.[1] I'm not recommending him specifically; there will be many other such examples. It is for you to go looking for them, in the fields that are relevant to your personal cycle of achievement.

It is also important to think about what interacting with you can offer a potential goals ally. Which brings us to the important question of ethics. You may think the approach I have outlined above is self-seeking or manipulative. And there is no denying it can be turned to these ends. But it is your responsibility to ensure that it isn't. It is vital that your research into another person does not become stalking. That is to say, it should not be intrusive, threatening or alarming to them in any way. Stick to gathering information

1 https://www.suttontrust.com/

that you can be confident your target would be happy for you to know about them. Respect their boundaries. When you do make contact, be honest and straightforward about your intentions. Be ready to accept rejection: there are always others who will be more accepting. Honouring these principles in yourself will yield better dividends in the long term, I promise you.

All that said, human beings are social animals and collaboration comes naturally to most of us. Collaboration, of course, suggests some degree of reciprocity. This does not mean that your first contact with a target should be purely transactional: 'If you do X for me, I'll do Y for you.' In fact, many people find such approaches distasteful and off-putting.

What it does mean is that you should be conscious that you are seeking alliances, not favours. There needs to be something in it for your collaborator, even if it is simply an alignment of values.

In the end, all the above is academic, until you take the plunge and ask to meet your target. The old saying that 'if you don't ask, you don't get' is usually true. In the next two chapters, we'll examine both how to set about demonstrating an alignment of values and how to optimise your chances of getting a first meeting.

But I'll close this chapter with another story, about a time when I was forced to employ the targeting technique in real time.

* * *

The year 2008 was a bad time for Zimbabwe.

It might have been better to avoid going there in a year when former President Mugabe's thugs had intimidated and beaten his way to re-election, following his shock defeat in the first round of voting. Things had gotten so bad that the opposition leader Morgan Tsvangirai had withdrawn from the second round, declaring that to run would risk the lives of his supporters (not to mention his own). Mugabe 'won' the second round with over 80 per cent of the vote but nobody serious could recognise the result as anything other than stolen. Eventually, international pressure led to the formation of a coalition government, with Tsvangirai as prime minister to Mugabe's president. But this was largely a papering over of the cracks and bad feeling rankled on all sides.

Including towards the British, whom Mugabe had spent the past decade demonising. Many members of his party – Zanu-PF – had drunk the Kool-Aid on this and blamed British-led sanctions (that were, in truth, very mild in their effect) for the economic devastation wrought by Mugabe's own policies.

But I was not too concerned as I walked into the party's headquarters on the appropriately named Rotten Row in Harare, some months after the election. In my experience, most Zimbabweans were unfailingly friendly and polite in person, even if they were capable of being whipped into anti-British hysteria when part of a mob. It wasn't part of my plan that day to tangle with any mobs. Instead, I was on my way for a very civilised and friendly discussion with a senior ally of Mugabe, who occupied party offices in a high-rise building in downtown Harare.

I had met the politician in question – whom I shall call Tafadzwa – some years earlier, when working at the British Embassy. It turned out that he had been educated in the Midlands and had fond memories of the area. Thus was our commonality established. Our friendship flourished, despite the heightening diplomatic stand-off between London and Harare. He had a habit of laughing at the situation and telling me that 'it is all just politics'. He claimed that Mugabe continued to harbour warm feelings towards Britain. While I doubt that was true, it was certain that Tafadzwa did.

My call was social. A chance to catch up and renew our friendship after some years apart. But I had donned a jacket and

tie because Tafadzwa was always immaculately turned out and
I knew he appreciated a reciprocal effort. I guess this could have
made me look like an official caller, which became a problem
soon after I left his office.

I've never much liked elevators as I am slightly claustropho-
bic. But the lights were out in the stairwell, so I took a deep
breath and walked in. I was the only person in the lift as it
descended a couple of storeys. I was quite relieved for the
company when the lift pinged, the doors opened and a couple
of young men joined me. But my relief was extinguished as a
gang of others hurried in behind them. The compartment was
full as the doors slid closed, a group of muscular men pressing
me against the back wall. They were, unmistakeably, members
of the Zanu-PF Youth League, a rag-tag bunch of party faithful
who were often sent to knock heads at opposition rallies. And it
seemed like they were on their way to cause trouble again,
fuelled by copious amounts of Chibuku, an evil local beer
brewed from sorghum. A mix of rancid beer fumes and stale
sweat had me holding my breath. One or two of the gang were
carrying pangas, sharp scythes with diverse uses, from hedge-
trimming to bodily assault. Pangas had been the weapon of
choice during the 1994 genocide in Rwanda.

The youngsters ignored me, much to my relief. They were
chatting excitedly amongst themselves in chiShona and I was
unable to follow their conversation. It sounded bellicose but
perhaps that was just my imagination. I pinned myself against
the wall and took shallow breaths through my mouth, willing
the ride to be over.

But the elevator was overloaded and the strain was audible,
metallic creaks protesting against the weight. Somewhere between
the third and second floor – agonisingly close to my escape – it
gave up the struggle and jolted to a stop, with a final lurch of
resignation. The only thing that continued sinking was my heart,

as I realised it was likely to be several hours before an engineer could be roused to release us: the work ethic was not thriving in Mugabe's Zimbabwe. Having sunk as far as it was going to, my heart began to pound. I could feel sweat coating my palms and soaking my shirt. At least I wasn't going to stand out because of that. I felt dizzy and feared that I might have a panic attack.

Then the lights went out.

It was pitch dark. Not even an illuminated alarm button. The group of Youth Leaguers fell silent but I could feel them pushing harder up against me in the confusion. So, I reached into my jacket pocket and found the torch on my mobile phone. The sudden flood of light brought some relief but it also directed attention to its bearer. I was conscious of eyes on me and mutters of discontent beginning to swell.

Then one of them came right out with it. 'Are you British?' he asked, rolling the 'r' in a characteristically Zimbabwean way.

'I'm not with the Embassy,' I said. 'British' and 'British diplomats' were almost synonymous in Zimbabwe at the peak of the bilateral dispute.

'That is not what I asked.' There was more than a hint of menace in the speaker's voice now. 'I asked if you are British.'

I wasn't going to get away with pretending not to be, so I admitted my Britishness.

Another voice from somewhere in the group spoke up. 'You are in the wrong place, my friend.' Rarely have I heard the phrase 'my friend' spoken with such insincerity.

'I have just been visiting my friend Tafadzwa,' I said, with a vague idea that an appeal to seniority would help my position. I was wrong.

'Ahh, that one,' spat another voice. 'He is a traitor.' Again, the rolled 'r'. 'Always hanging with the British.'

The situation was escalating, several of the group now staring at me with open hostility. I swallowed my panic – both at the claustrophobia and at the growing threat – and looked around for someone I could appeal to.

Looked around for an ally.

One of the two men who had first got into the lift was standing close to me. Unlike the others, who were clad in jeans and t-shirts, he was wearing an ill-fitting suit, so I figured he might be in a position of some authority. A good start. My eyes were drawn to an enamel badge on his lapel. It had one word on it, in bronze on a red background: 'United'. I knew from experience that many Zimbabweans followed Manchester United FC avidly and was pretty sure that it was an antiquated club badge. I pointed to his chest and the wearer looked down at his badge.

'Good game the other day,' I said.

He stared at me for a few seconds, as the others turned to watch for his reaction. Then a smile broke through and he twisted himself in the limited space to lay a hand on my shoulder.

'Yes. A great game,' he said. 'Two fantastic goals by Ronaldo. The greatest player ever.'

Somewhere on the other side of the lift, someone snorted.

'That one is not the greatest,' came a voice. 'Wayne Rooney is the greatest.'

And they were off. In an instant, thanks to my newly recruited ally, my sin of Britishness was forgotten. Instead, my would-be tormentors entered into a strenuous but good-hearted debate about the greatest player in British football.

Ironic.

But the greater irony is that I have never seen Manchester United play. In fact, other than World Cup fixtures, I've never seen a game of football. Commonalities can be invented, as well as real, it seems.

And that's where cover comes in.

*   *   *

RECAP

- In our adapted model, your personal achievements cycle replaces the intelligence cycle. Iterative goals-setting is the key. Define exactly what you want.
- Then start a targeting exercise to find goals allies. There are two parts to this. Who can help you meet your goals? And who is likely to be willing to help you?
- Much targeting data is available from the internet and social media. But some may only be available through family, friends, colleagues and mentors.
- Referrals significantly increase the likelihood of targets being willing to give up their time and expertise for you. But other points of commonality can be powerful too.
- Look for evidence that your targets are inclined to help or mentor others. And be ready for collaboration. You are seeking to build alliances, not to exploit others.
- Set yourself high ethical standards. Respect others' boundaries and don't be intrusive. Be ready to accept rejection. This will pay dividends in the long term.

CHAPTER TWO

The Transformative Power of Cover

Cover is arguably the most important of a spy's repertoire of skills. It is also probably the most remarked upon.

As I write, news is breaking of six people arrested in the UK on suspicion of spying for Russia. Almost all the reporting I have read on this matter is fixated on the lives led by the suspects. Fixated, in other words, on their covers. From the BBC, I learn that 'former neighbours' describe two of them as 'a couple' and that 'the pair, who moved to the UK around a decade ago, ran a community organisation providing services to Bulgarian people, including familiarising them with the "culture and norms of British society"'.[1]

The *Daily Mail* informs me that three of the arrestees 'had allegedly posed as journalists to carry out surveillance on targets in London and Europe' and were found to be in possession of 'forged press cards and branded clothing from the Discovery and National Geographic channels'.[2] I have also

1 Daniel De Simone and Jeremy Britton, 'Suspected spies for Russia held in major UK security investigation', BBC News, 15 August 2023. https://www.bbc.co.uk/news/uk-66504350
2 George Odling et al., 'Bulgarians arrested for being "Russian spies" had "posed as journalists" to carry out surveillance on targets as forged press cards and clothing for the Discovery and National Geographic channels found', Mail Online, 16 August 2023. https://www.dailymail.co.uk/news/article-12411019/Russian-spies-journalists-surveillance-UK.html

learned from the same newspaper that the Bulgarian 'couple' frequented a local café, where they would 'usually order the "Super Breakfast" – a £7 dish of egg, bacon, beans and tomato, accompanied by four slices of bread'. One of them 'who frequently went in alone, also ordered hash browns'. They at least understood the principles of cover, it would seem, as 'the couple did not stand out in Harrow'. with a journalistic source adding that 'no one would give them a second glance'.[1]

At the more cultivated end of the newspaper market, the *Guardian* reveals that one of the suspects is 'described as a driver for hospitals' and, while 'his Facebook page lists no friends', it 'features several videos of nightclubs and parties'. These details are rounded out with the shocking news that 'a live stream from 2018 appears to show [the suspect] teaching English to a group of mature Bulgarian students. In one class held in Wembley another teacher sings the song Jamaica Farewell by Harry Belafonte as pupils join in.'[2]

So, we know quite a bit about the covers deployed by the suspected spies. But very little about what they got up to under them. It is likely that the journalistic emphasis placed on cover is useful for the authorities, who would probably rather not see laid out in public details of the operations they ran or intelligence they retrieved. In this case, stories about cover may be

1 Tom Pyman, ' "Russian spy couple" rowed with neighbours over satellite dish they fitted the wrong way round – while another "intelligence agent" used seaside guest house as his "HQ"', Mail Online, 16 August 2023. https://www.dailymail.co.uk/news/article-12412195/The-Russian-spy-used-rundown-three-star-seaside-guest-house-English-coast-HQ-007-email-address.html
2 Luke Harding and Matthew Weaver, 'Three Bulgarians suspected of spying for Russia charged in UK', *Guardian*, 15 August 2023. https://www.theguardian.com/uk-news/2023/aug/15/three-bulgarians-suspected-of-spying-for-russia-reportedly-charged-in-uk#:~:text=The%20three%20alleged%20spies%20are,suburban%20properties%2C%20the%20BBC%20reported

acting as cover for the really interesting stories. Welcome to the hall of mirrors that is the spying game.

The mundanity of some of the details about the six suspected spies' quotidian lives is pertinent to a key distinction in the use of cover. This is that it can be both a shield and a sword; 'defensive' and 'offensive'.

TYPES OF COVER

In the spy's world, defensive cover is part of the everyday and is vital. It helps to prevent them being identified as intelligence officers by hostile agencies. As Christopher Felix puts it in *A Short Course in the Secret War*,[1] 'cover shields the secret agent from his opposition. It puts him in a position to accomplish his mission.' Note again the comments above that the suspected spies 'did not stand out' and 'no one would give them a second glance'. For defensive purposes, grey is good. It is important that such cover can withstand more than a cursory interrogation. But the starting principle is that it should not cause its bearer to invite scrutiny in the first place.

Now, there is some tension between this type of cover and offensive cover. The term 'offensive' sounds militaristic but I do not mean it this way. Offensive cover is not designed to cause harm or to defeat an adversary. Rather, it is created to draw a target to a spy and to hold their interest. In that sense, offensive cover is designed precisely to *make* the spy stand out. Otherwise, why would an intended target be drawn to the spy? This tension is resolved because the attractive element of cover is tailored to specific targets: it may be thought of as a 'dog-whistle'. Felix,

1 Christopher Felix, *A Short Course in the Secret War*, Madison Books, 2001, p. 65.

again: 'All good cover [. . .] reaches into the mind of the opponent, thinks as he would think, and then creates a combination
of fact and fancy, of actual arrangements and contrived impressions, which the opposing mind is prepared to believe.' He goes
on to note that 'good cover is an intimate relationship between
deceiver and the deceived'.

And there is the key point. Properly conceived, cover provides
a sound basis for a relationship between the spy and their target
to be established and to flourish. That is why the targeting technique is so vital. Offensive cover is designed according to the
dictates of the target's position, personality and circumstances.
Naturally, the defensive and offensive elements of cover must
be in accord for a successful operation. They must work together.
Contradictions between the two would likely condemn a cover
to fail on both counts.

There is another distinction in the formal world of espionage. As detailed in *The Psychology of Spies and Spying* by
Adrian Furnham and John Taylor, there are two main categories of cover: 'official cover' and 'natural cover'. Official cover
'entails the handler using other government departments as
the officer's parent department'. This use of cover usually
falls into the 'defensive' category and will not detain us here.
Natural cover 'is when the handler adopts a business,
academic or other non-government cover'. Evidently, natural
cover offers more options and greater flexibility to create a
persona that is attractive to a spy's target: to create effective
offensive cover. And – in a later section of this chapter – we
shall adapt this type of cover to help you meet personal and
professional objectives (p. 45).

Therefore, it is worth examining in some detail the common-
sense principles that underpin design of natural cover for offensive purposes. I should make clear here that this is not a rehearsal
of a training module offered by any one intelligence service.

There is nothing proprietary about use of cover. It is part of every intelligence officer's *modus operandi*, wherever they are from. And the principles taught by spy schools all over the world are the same. What follows is my summation of those teachings, based on an extensive review of material that is available in the public domain.

THE PRINCIPLES OF COVER

It seems to me that there are nine principles of effective cover. They each fall under one of the following three headings:

- Practicalities: the ease with which a spy can adopt a particular cover;
- Presentation: how the cover appears to a spy's target; and
- Proposition: how the cover invites a target to engage.

Under 'practicalities', perhaps the most important principle is one that applies to so many walks of life: 'keep it simple'. However, it is not always simple to keep things simple. After all, creation of cover is an art and the untrained artist is often tempted to add rather than subtract detail. There really is no need. Consider for a moment how people tend to respond to the classic cocktail-party question of 'What do you do?' Usually, the response is a single word, preceded by 'I am a': stockbroker; doctor; consultant; writer; carpenter; topiarist; mechanic; butcher; baker; candlestick maker. Okay, that last one is a composite of two words. But the basic point stands. This is not to say that the story won't need backing up with some detail as conversation proceeds. Only, rather, that more convoluted answers tend to raise rather than dampen suspicion. As in this following exchange, between me and a newly introduced fellow guest at a birthday party:

She: 'So, what do you do?'

Me: 'It's a bit complicated I'm afraid. I'm not sure there's an easy way to explain it.'

She: 'Well, have a go.'

Me: 'Okay, then. I run a consultancy that advises investors in Africa on how to identify and manage political and reputational risks there.'

She: 'Oh, so you're a spy!'

The irony is that, on this occasion, I wasn't trying to use any sort of cover. I was just bored with explaining my job for the umpteenth time that evening. Had I been deploying cover, my first response would have been 'I am a consultant.' When pressed, I might have added that I consult on investments in Africa. Usually, the response to something like this is 'That must be interesting,' which can be met with a shrug and 'It earns me a living.' Unless in the presence of a target, in which case the follow-ups would be more nuanced and designed to entice.

Simplicity notwithstanding, any decent spy must be able to defend their cover beyond the most basic questions. Which brings us to the second practicalities principle: 'keep it as close to the truth as possible'.

Of course, there are limits to this. There is no point in a spy adopting cover so close to reality that it invites suspicion in its own right: 'information broker' might raise eyebrows, as might 'private intelligence practitioner'. But equally, there is no point in pretending to be something that you obviously aren't: it would be brave for a Brit to try and pass themselves off as a New York bagel vendor, for one ridiculous example. It is usually a safe bet to adapt cover from another part of life. Academia for someone with several higher degrees, maybe. Or financial adviser for someone who has moved from the City into the intelligence world.

The second practicalities principle is closely related to the third: 'make it something you know about'.

This stipulation is so obvious that it would be insulting for me to offer up examples. You will be able to think of a great many yourself. But some spies succumb to the temptation of cover roles that confer a degree of glamour. This can lead them into a trap of ignorance. The would-be luxury yacht dealer would be well advised to do a good deal of homework about manufacturers, models and markets before handing out business cards, just in case they meet someone who is thinking about trading in their Benetti for a Royal Huisman and would appreciate some advice. And that example probably caught your attention: another good reason to avoid that cover, which is not consistent with the idea of fading into the foreground.

Which brings us onto 'presentation', concerning how the spy under cover comes across to their targets and others. Getting this right requires a degree of self-awareness. There is no point in a wallflower claiming to be an after-dinner speaker. Hence, the first principle to be aware of under this heading is: 'ensure plausibility'.

It is important to look and sound the part. This is not about adopting disguises, which have only a limited place in real-world spying. Rather, it is about choosing attire and accessories that are consistent with the chosen cover. And, conversely, limiting oneself to choosing covers that are consistent with immutable personal characteristics, such as physical build and appearance.

Spies also need to remember that every front has a back end, leading us to the second presentation principle: 'develop a believable backstory'.

Sometimes called a 'legend' in the intelligence world, this may include adopting an alias identity and buttressing it with biographical details: date and place of birth; parentage;

education; and career path. For operations with a high degree of security risk, it is also necessary to ensure that a spy has a residential address and, if appropriate, a business address capable of being checked and vouched for. There are departments in professional agencies that specialise in constructing such artifices.

As there are for production of documents to fulfil the third presentation principle: 'carry credentials'.

These may range from government-issued passports or identity documents, through work passes and work phones, all the way to what is sometimes termed 'wallet litter'. Wallet litter is the detritus that all of us accumulate in our day-to-day lives, that says so much about us: boarding pass stubs, receipts, loyalty cards, stray memory cards with one PowerPoint document on them, passport photos, redundant keys, scribbled shopping lists and so on. The point about all of this is that we are so much more than what we say we are. We are also the sum of what we carry with us, mentally as well as physically.

The mental and emotional aspects of identity permit development of the *proposition*. This is the offering to a target that will entice them to engage with the spy and persuade them to remain connected. A proposition is the crucial nexus of any relationship between spy and target. It is what brings them together. Looked at another way, it forms the 'offensive' element of cover, with practicalities forming the defensive element and presentation straddling the two.

The proposition element is the most relevant to use of cover in the adapted personal achievements cycle. It is, therefore, worth taking especial note of the three principles that underpin it.

The first principle should be obvious: 'establish an interest in common with the target'. The point of a spy's offensive cover is to attract a target and the best way to do that is engage with the latter's interests. In an effective operation, the targeting phase will have identified such interests and the spy's cover will have been designed around them. If the target is known to be a committed Christian, for example, the spy may familiarise themselves with the scriptural basics and discover an enthusiasm for churchgoing. If they are classical music fans, a subscription to *Gramophone* may be in order. If hard rock, *Revolver* would be the more apt choice. Should the target go hiking every weekend, our spy may be found selecting a pair of walking boots in their nearest outdoors shop.

It is important to note that this alignment of interests is not necessarily related to *specific intelligence* sought by the spy. In fact, apparent focus on this element at too early a stage is likely to repel many targets. Rather, shared interests are the soil in which a relationship will grow. The real purpose of that relationship is unlikely to be revealed until it has taken strong root and flowered: at a much later stage and only then after extensive further assessment of the target. Cultivation and assessment techniques are dealt with elsewhere. Our interest at this stage is how spies initiate relationships.

Mutual trust is integral to the beginning of any relationship. And trust is based partly on authentic behaviour. Humans are instinctive mammals and we can often spot when someone is behaving disingenuously. Hence the second proposition principle: 'engage the part of your personality that identifies with the shared interest'.

It quickly becomes obvious when someone is feigning enthusiasm for a subject, especially a specialist subject. Returning to our examples above: a committed atheist should probably not attempt to come across as devout; tone-deafness is not a great start when seeking to demonstrate an interest in classical music, though it may work for heavy metal; a spy who suffers from chronic plantar fasciitis may wish to avoid taking up hiking. When seeking to create commonality with a target, some degree of knowledge in the subject matter or competence in the practice is desirable. Failing this, avid curiosity is the minimum required. Genuine enthusiasts for a pastime may be willing to take novices under their wings but only if the novice demonstrates an authentic desire to learn. If the spy is unable to find even curiosity about one area of a target's interests, they will move onto another without wasting too much time.

This is important because development of an effective proposition requires diligent observance of a third and final principle: 'engage actively with the interest'. Please don't confuse this with method acting. The idea behind this principle is not that spies have to live in character day to day. But they do have to perform enough activities in line with their cover to maintain authenticity when in contact with targets. Of course, some spies do live cover day to day – such as the six suspected spies that we looked at in the opening section of this chapter and spies living under official cover. But such a requirement usually applies to the defensive element of cover rather than the offensive. When it comes to the *offensive* element, the principle is that the spy should train his or her mentality to bring the interest in question to the forefront of their mind. This way, they will remain familiar with relevant subject matter and connected with it in a meaningful way. Done properly, this means that the spy will not be dredging their mind for conversational gambits of relevance when interacting with their target. Put simply, a spy passing themselves off as a Rugby Union enthusiast should know how a line-out works and keep an eye on recent scores, for example.

In other words, some mental adjustment is required to create effective cover. It is remarkable how quickly a conscious mental adjustment of this nature becomes unconscious. You can probably think of times in your educational or professional life when forced engagement with a subject led to a genuine ongoing interest in it. This is a very useful trick that our minds work on us. It keeps us focused on study, occupations and personal interactions of which we might otherwise tire.

Furthermore, this mental trick can work just as effectively when it comes to engagement with our latent personality traits, turning them into naturally forward-facing characteristics. This can be turned to advantage as part of our personal achievements cycle.

It took a broken heart for me to learn that lesson.

*   *   *

I was not a very pleasant young man. But cover changed me.

Someone once said that 'damaged people are dangerous. They know they can survive.'[1] I had certainly learned to do that: survive hunger and the cold, grief, being physically broken. Survive bullying. And survival had hardened me. Hard-boiled me, even.

I was a Thatcher's Child, as you might have guessed.

Margaret Thatcher – a woman who certainly invoked strong reactions, positive and negative – was elected shortly after my ninth birthday. Close to the time when I began to witness my sister's descent into illness. In a way, Thatcher was a constant during my formative years of loss, confusion and anger. And I admired her take-no-prisoners approach. So, I adopted it. This meant an arrogance of manner, certainty in the rightness of my views, intolerance of weakness and impatience with those whom I didn't see as useful to my life. At school, I would openly mock those I thought less clever than me. I would stage public takedowns of teachers I thought were not up to the job. I moved from school to school, determined to find the one that offered

1 Josephine Hart, *Damage*, Virago Press, 2011

me the best chance of getting to a top-tier university. In the process, I abandoned friends and learned to embrace loneliness. That was my take on Thatcherism. It seemed, to my insecure younger self, like a good way to survive.

Problem was, it won me few friends. And no girlfriends.

My first casual job was at an Examinations Board. I was eighteen and had recently completed my A levels. While waiting for my results, I joined a gang of other youngsters who were employed by the Board to tot up marks on examination papers. For written papers, it was a case of adding up the numbers scrawled by examiners in the margins and loading the resulting tallies into a spreadsheet. For multiple choice, it involved holding a template with holes for the correct answers over those marked by the exam-taker and counting where they matched. It was not a difficult job but I worked alongside a group of young men and women of my age, all of whom liked a drink. And that suited me. Alcohol melted the edges of my awkwardness and blunted my hurt.

I wasn't the centre of the gang. My abrasive attitudes and unfashionable political views saw to that. But I managed to strike up friendships with one or two of my colleagues. And I was tolerated on the outskirts of evenings spent in the pub. For the first time in my adolescence, I started to feel like I might belong.

And there was a girl in that gang who I liked. *Really* liked.

As I got to know Emma, I realised that she was the opposite of me. Generous, kind-hearted, open-minded and inclined to believe the best of everybody. Even of me, up to a point. Often, we would sit together on the outskirts of our gang, she sipping white wine spritzers, me quaffing hoppy pints of real ale, the August sun warming our faces. And she would ask me about my childhood, my views, my feelings, my day. I soon noticed that our conversations were always about me. She seemed very interested in *me*. So, one day, after a second pint, I screwed my courage to the sticking point and asked her out.

She said 'No'.

Kindly, but emphatically, she rejected my advances. I was confused, so I pushed her for an explanation. Why, after several months of intense one-to-one discussions, during which she had shown an unusual level of interest in me, was she not prepared to go on a date with me? Her reply ran something like this: 'I am interested in you as a person. You are hurt and that distorts the way you see the world but I like to hear what you think about current affairs. I'm afraid, though, that I don't want to take our friendship beyond a friendship. This is because, a lot of the time, *you come across as not very nice.*' She added, 'You should try it one day, being nice.'

Talk about a sucker punch. And, with that, she left. Not right then, but a few days later, to go back to university in Manchester, for her second year. And I was left behind because I had my gap year to fill. Over the next few weeks, my temporary colleagues drifted away to different universities, polytechnics or full-time jobs. So, I moved on. I didn't take away very much from my stint at the Board. Workplace friendships petered out, as they tend to, and the experience faded into intermittent and unimportant memory. Save for Emma's final words to me.

'You come across as not very nice. You should try it one day, being nice.'

They rankled. And rankled. Reverberated in my mind every time I interacted with someone in my accustomed manner: abrupt, dismissive, uninterested. I began noticing how others were reacting to me. The distance they would create and the coldness of their responses. Before Emma spoke to me so bluntly, I would have been impervious to the effect I was having. Now, Emma had forced me into some self-awareness. It was a painful process. I realised with a shock that many people didn't like me.

And I soon discovered that I didn't like me very much, either.

After some weeks of reflection, it dawned on me that the critical words in Emma's summation were *come across*. Perhaps she was not commenting on my core character but on the arrogant cover I had adopted to disguise my insecurities and inner pain. Perhaps people could 'come across' as nice if they worked at it. She had advised me to 'try it sometime', so, one day, I decided to give it a go.

I remembered an English teacher who had been dismissive of the word 'nice', which he characterised as anaemic and clichéd. But it seemed to me that he was mistaken. There is a quality – niceness – that people value and which can change social experiences for the better. I set about observing friends and family who seemed effortlessly nice and compiled a mental list of properties and behaviours that they displayed. I took note of what they said and how they said it. And then I began to mimic them. Self-consciously, at first. Perhaps without conviction. But I worked at it, developing habits of niceness until they became automatic.

And a magical thing happened. Almost without noticing it, my character changed – genuinely and at its core – for the better. I became instinctively more engaging. I found myself empathising with the experiences of my friends and family members. My default mode became to listen, rather than to pontificate. My curiosity about people blossomed. I opened myself to, and welcomed, views opposed to my own. Humility replaced arrogance. This is not to say it was an easy process. Far from it. But, over time, I became the person I thought I was only pretending to be.

I had adopted niceness as a cover but, in time, niceness had adopted me.

This was my first introduction to the principles of Cognitive Behavioural Therapy (CBT) but we'll come back to that. It was also my first introduction to the principles of good cover.

We've looked at how intelligence agencies everywhere train their recruits to think about cover. Next, I'll offer some thoughts on how to adapt that training for use in your everyday life. We'll learn that there are interesting overlaps with my early experience of adopting a form of personality 'cover'. A cover which, in fact, came from within me. A cover that – unexpectedly – turned out to be a better reflection of the person I am than the shell I had developed in response to adversity.

I was to meet Emma one last time, by coincidence, at a party thrown by one of our former colleagues from the Examinations Board. It was a year or so after she had told me the truth about myself and she was on her summer vacation. She was with a boyfriend from university. Jonathan was a bright and sociable guy, with whom I struck up an immediate rapport. The three of us chatted for much of the evening, laughing at one another's jokes and learning from each other. There was a real warmth in our small group. But Jonathan had to leave early, as he had a dawn flight for a family holiday the following day. After he had gone, Emma and I drifted apart, to mingle with others. But as the evening drew to a close, she made her way back to me. And she had more words for me that I have never forgotten. She said, 'I can't believe how much you have changed. You are not the Jules I knew. It's like you are a completely different person.'

She said she regretted having turned me down when I asked her out. She asked, 'Can I take you out one evening soon?'

I said 'No'.

Nice Jules wasn't going to do that to Jonathan.

*   *   *

RECAP

- Cover can be 'defensive' or 'offensive'. We are more interested in the latter: that element of cover designed to attract a target to a spy and to hold their interest.
- Offensive cover is tailored to a target's position, personality and circumstances. 'Natural' rather than 'official' cover offers optimum flexibility to achieve this.
- There are nine principles of effective cover, which divide under the three headings of practicalities, presentation and proposition.
- 'Practicalities' govern ease of use. 'Presentation' relates to how cover comes across to its audience. 'Proposition' is that which makes the cover attractive to a target.
- The proposition is an interest in common with the target, with which the spy can mentally identify and is prepared to engage actively.
- A strong offensive cover requires some mental adjustment, which can lead to a genuine and unforced engagement with a new area of interest.
- Similarly, orientation towards specific personality traits can turn them into forward-facing characteristics. Anyone can put this to use in their personal and professional life.

*   *   *

It is exciting that you can turn some of the principles of cover described above to advantage in your personal achievements cycle. This section lays out in detail how to set about doing that.

But first, an iron rule. When using cover in your personal life, never pretend to be somebody or something you are not.

This may sound like a contradiction in terms. I'll come back to why it is not, after a brief review of the reasons behind this rule.

First, and most important, it is unethical to misrepresent yourself to potential allies. In certain cases, it may also be illegal. In the business intelligence and private investigator worlds, use of cover to retrieve information is sometimes referred to as 'pretexting'. It is frowned on by most ethical practitioners. And it is illegal under the Fraud Act 2006 (which uses the term 'false representation'), if used dishonestly and intended to secure a financial gain or cause financial loss to another. It is easy to see how these stipulations might be interpreted to cover pretexting by commercial investigators. And it is not much of a stretch to see how it might apply to individuals using pretexting for their own gain.

Second, you are very likely to be caught out. Professional spies are backed by well-funded governments and have resources and legal protections that are not available to ordinary citizens. For the rest of us, maintenance of alias identities and false occupations quickly becomes unmanageable. A few well-placed online searches can easily uncover misrepresentation (we shall return to this when we look at techniques for detecting deception in Chapter Eight (p. 248)). In this case, any advantage gained through use of deception will be lost and there may well be a price to pay. Related to this is the point that, if you are pretending to be someone you are not, it is unlikely that any gains accrued through new alliances can be credited to the real you. So, the start point is flawed.

Finally, and most happily, there is no need to use deceit. The principles of cover of most use in the personal achievements cycle relate to those that fall under the 'proposition' heading. Your aim should be to frame your authentic self in such a way that your goals allies:

- will be able to identify with you;
- will be happy to engage with you;
- and, in time, will be willing to help you achieve the goals you have set for the relevant turn of your personal achievements cycle.

Moving away from the language of cover but remaining true to its more positive intentions, you will do this by working on your 'personal brand'. Let's think a while about what we mean by 'brand'. The word might naturally draw our minds to visual matters: a popular fizzy drink with a ubiquitous logo and distinctive glass bottle design, for example. Or to verbal statements: the bank that promises to be 'by your side', maybe, or a chocolate bar manufacturer that once claimed to help us 'work, rest and play'. Already some parallels with cover are emerging. How does a company present itself or its products to us? What is its proposition? How comfortably do the presentation and the proposition sit with reality?

However, this is just the beginning. A brand, like a cover, is much more than an image, a front, or a façade. Properly constructed, a brand should tell a story about the organisation to which it belongs, providing a reason for a consumer, client or other target to engage with the organisation *and to remain engaged with it*. Indeed, a brand can be thought of as part of an organisation's DNA. It is the collective impact of a company's qualities, values and reputation. It is what forms potential and existing customers' perceptions of the company: is it seen as reliable, trustworthy, ethical and able to deliver consistently high-quality products and services?

Take, for example, the case of my first post-graduate employer. Cazenove's logo was a simple rendition of the firm's name in bold capitals. But its brand was so much more than that. The phrase most commonly applied to the firm was 'blue-blooded'.

It was frequently – perhaps erroneously – referred to as the 'Queen's stockbroker'. It was renowned for the quality of its staff, its positioning as adviser to many of the FTSE 100 companies and for its adherence to discretion. I think I am right in saying that the firm issued only two press releases in its distinguished two-hundred-year history. In the City of London, when I joined the firm in the early 1990s, Cazenove had a rock-solid brand that had little to do with the font chosen for its logo.

Likewise, as the most successful social media influencers know well, a personal brand is about more than how you look. Appearance will certainly come into it; Cazenove employees all dressed in a similar way, according to old-fashioned notions of business attire. But looking the part is only a small element of the package. Building a rich and compelling personal brand takes much more than that. As Richard Branson once said: 'Branding demands commitment; commitment to continual re-invention; striking chords with people to stir their emotions; and commitment to imagination. It is easy to be cynical about such things, much harder to be successful.'[1]

'Where do I start?' I hear you ask.

DEFINING YOUR PERSONAL BRAND

Start at the beginning, of course. First, it requires working out what you want to achieve, longer term. Each revolution of the personal achievements cycle will be in the service of your long-term goals: where you want to be in five years' or ten years' time. Of course, as we have noted previously, such goals will be subject to amendment and revision, as your life turns through

1 Jenna Lorge, 'Words of wisdom from the world's greatest branding experts,' CEO Magazine.com, 15 June 2022. https://www.theceomagazine.com/business/marketing/best-branding-quotes/

its cycles. But they are an unavoidable start point. And, despite revisions, excisions and additions, they will remain your lodestar, unless and until you abandon them altogether.

So, you need first to be clear about your over-arching life goals. Then, decide what part your personal brand will play in meeting them. For example, let's imagine you have a burning desire to work in international development in tough parts of the world. A personal brand that exudes empathy, emotional robustness and strong planning skills may persuade potential employers to take a second look at you. Or, if you are determined to break into investigative journalism, you might want to come across as inquisitive, determined, able to work with people and a strong communicator.

For successful engagement with potential goals allies, your personal brand *must* align with your personal and professional goals. It seems obvious but it is worth repeating. Far too often, otherwise capable interviewees let themselves down by mismatching their personal brands and their goals. Such dissonance can have destructive consequences. If you doubt this, ask yourself how often you have walked away from a conversation thinking something like 'she didn't look like an estate agent' or 'he didn't sound like a lawyer'. Mismatches between perceptions and realities are not always a bad thing. But, as a rule of thumb, you are more likely to reach your goals if you come across as the sort of person who is apt to do so.

Having established your over-arching goals, I want you to start a fresh list. This list should include *all* the attributes and qualities that, in an ideal scenario, goals allies would associate with you. This is *your* list, created to meet your requirements. So, you should not be trammelled by the following suggestions. But your list *might* include some of the following:

- Likeable;
- Trustworthy;
- Dependable;
- Ethical;
- Academic;
- Knowledgeable;
- Well-read;
- Informed;
- Assured;
- Calm;
- Reflective;
- Proactive;
- Curious;
- Supportive;
- Approachable;
- Open;
- Robust; and
- Adaptable.

Keep going for as long as you continue to think of qualities that you would like potential goals allies to associate with you.

It is tempting at this point to say to yourself, 'But I can't be something I am not.' Very well. If there are items on your list of desirable attributes that are outlandishly unlike you, strike them out. Look again at the section above, in which we examined how to apply the principles of cover. We noted there that authenticity is vital.

Don't rush this exercise. I suggest you put this book down now and spend some time thinking about it, adding to your list as ideas occur to you and deleting those that strike you as implausible. But it is critical to remember, as you produce your list, that anything which seems unlikely to you will certainly seem unlikely to others. Even public health philanthropist Bill Gates does not present himself as a trained doctor.

*   *   *

Are you done? Have you created a list which covers all the qualities that:

1. Are aligned with your long-term goals;
2. You would like goals allies to associate with you; and
3. Are not *totally* unrealistic? (We can cope with a little unrealistic. Always have something to aim for.)

It need not be a long list, once you have reviewed and considered a range of possibilities. Indeed, it will most likely be quite short: the key qualities and attributes that you associate with your goals. If it is too long, I recommend that you go over your list again, paring it back to those elements that cannot and should not be cut out.

BUILDING YOUR PERSONAL BRAND

With your revised list finally at hand, let's turn to how you can set about 'creating your cover'. Or, rather, building your personal brand.

There are three steps to this process: observe; adopt; and internalise.

It is frequently said that imitation is the sincerest form of flattery. Well, get ready to do some serious flattering. Think about people you know, in person or through their public personae. Who among them displays the characteristics you have identified as the core of your personal brand? Make a list. Then, narrow it down. Who *epitomises* the qualities you want to make your own? Who shall be your role models? Try to get the list down to no more than two or three people. People who you will be able to observe, one way or another, without intruding on them.

And do just that. Observe. This is an active process. It is not simply a case of spectating. We all do that, every day. The idea is, rather, to make a conscious effort to understand and appreciate the way your role models behave in a variety of situations.

Watch their appearance and their body language. How do they dress? Do they adopt an open posture? Do they lean in when speaking with others? Cup their chin when concentrating? Are they at ease or poised for action? Which of their actions seem to display the qualities you seek to emphasise in yourself?

Listen carefully to them. What tone of voice do they use in different situations? Do they speak fast or slow? Question more than pronounce? Are there specific words and catchphrases that they use? Which of their speaking habits announce the qualities you seek to emphasise in yourself?

Note your emotional reactions to them in different contexts. This is important because your reactions are likely to be similar to other people's responses. Seek to understand the interaction between your role models' actions and words and your own feelings. This way, you will develop a keener self-awareness: a better sense of the impact of your own actions and words on others. And it is feelings that matter. A popular saying often attributed to Maya Angelou[1] is 'people will forget what you said, people will forget what you did, but people will never forget how you made them feel'. So, register how *you* feel in response to specific stimuli from your role models.

1 Not un-contentiously. See Rebecca Seales, 'Let's save Maya Angelou from fake quotes', BBC News, 13 November 2017. https://www.bbc.co.uk/news/41913640

Build a mental reference library of outfits, expressions, actions, mannerisms, styles, phrases and words that project the qualities in your role models that you seek to emulate. Let's call these individual building blocks 'traits'.

The next step is to adopt some of or all these traits. Again, this must be a conscious process. It is of little use to tell yourself 'I will behave more like my role model.' If this is the extent of your self-coaching, you won't. Instead, try telling yourself that, faced with a particular situation, you will respond in the manner of your role model. The key word here is 'respond,' which is very different from 'react'. Take time to assess situations as they arise and choose the appropriate response, making use of the reference library of traits that you compiled in the observation phase.

Soon enough, you will notice that people around you change their behaviours in response to the changes in your own. This can be a prize in itself but your true goal should be to internalise the qualities you seek to project. The most effective way to achieve this is to adopt routinely the desirable traits of your role model. Each time, remind yourself that you do so because you have the internal qualities with which they are associated. The chances are that you really do.

Imagine, for example, that your ambition is to become a dog trainer, specialising in problem animals: a 'dog whisperer'. You have identified a role model and seek to emulate the sense of calm energy she exudes, even when faced with a pack of howling hounds. But you find yourself battling panic or freezing in stressful situations. Well, remember an occasion on which you were the one who kept your head when all around were losing theirs. It might be the time a football teammate was injured and you swung into action as a first aider, calmly reassuring them while staunching the flow of blood or improvising a splint. Or the night out when a bar brawl threatened and you were the one with the presence of mind to get your mates out of there before it turned ugly. Then, take some time to recall how you felt in that situation. What was your breathing like? How did you hold your body? What was the pitch of your voice? The next time you encounter a stressful situation, channel *that* feeling and *those* behaviours. You won't get it right every time but don't fret about that. You will be surprised how quickly a calm energy becomes part of your physical and psychological muscle-memory.

Most personalities are like Rubik's Cubes: multifaceted and capable of manipulation to present your preferred combination to an observer. Sirius Black was talking about the same point when he told Harry Potter that 'we've all got both light and dark inside us. What matters is the part we choose to act on. That's who we really are.'[1]

ADOPTING TRAITS AND COGNITIVE BEHAVIOURAL THERAPY

Talking of wizardry, there is an almost magical iterative loop between acting and becoming: between adopting and internalising. Think again about the story I told above about my early life, when conscious adoption of a set of personality traits had the unexpected effect of altering my personality for real, and for the better. I mentioned that this was my first introduction to the principles of Cognitive Behavioural Therapy (CBT). What did I mean by that?

CBT is a form of therapy that was developed in the 1960s by Dr Aaron T. Beck (though Beck was working with ideas and techniques that had been around for decades before he formalised them into a structured practice). CBT is widely used by

1 *Harry Potter and the Order of the Phoenix.* Warner Bros., 2007.

therapists and counsellors working with patients who face a range of emotional problems, from alcoholism and anger issues, through obsessive compulsive behaviours, to complex personality disorders. At its core lies an examination of the relationships between context, thoughts, feelings and behaviours.

Patients are encouraged to recognise that the actions of others or developments in their local environment do not have a direct effect on their emotions. As one excellent therapist put it to me, 'People don't make you feel anything, they just do things.' Rather, emotional responses are determined by a combination of external events and the *thoughts* one has about those events. Furthermore, emotions do not inherently cause specific *behaviour* in response to an external event. Hence, to put it simplistically, it is sometimes possible to modify emotional responses and behavioural responses to external events by working towards altering harmful beliefs we have about ourselves.

In my own, younger, case, I had internalised a set of beliefs that included the idea that I was an eternal victim. The loss of a close family member, bullying at school, the daily privations of economic under-privilege, physical harms from my road accident. All these combined to make me defensive and put me in permanent 'fight or flight' mode, waiting for the next blow to land. So, I tended to interpret the slightest setback or rejection as an attack, leading me to feel angry, resentful and retributive: I would often choose 'fight', at least in the verbal sense, when flight did not seem to be an option.

But Emma's way of framing her rejection of me – with kindness and clarity – enabled me to rework assumptions about myself. It was this, I believe, that subconsciously led me to change my behaviours – to adopt the personality cover of 'niceness'. In other words, I began to interpose a more positive set of beliefs between events around me and my feelings about those events. And, crucially, between my feelings and my behaviours

in response to events. While it felt like I was adopting an external cover, I was in fact working with my inner self in a construc-
tive way, to project a different exterior than I had done hitherto.
I believe this is the key to effective use of cover: because the
process started to change the way people behaved around me,
with a positive feedback loop emerging.

I have no idea if a clinical psychologist would agree with me.
But I am sure that I am right because I experienced for myself
the truly transformative effects of adopting a 'cover'.

And you can too.

In the next chapter (p. 68), you will learn how to bring
together targeting and cover to lay the foundations of life-
changing alliances. But, first, let me tell you a story about how I
once used impromptu cover both defensively and offensively,
with impressive results.

* * *

The South African Airways flight from Johannesburg hit stom-
ach-churning turbulence. Like driving over the potholed highways of our destination, Kinshasa, at foolhardy speed. An overhead luggage-bin sprang open and spilled its contents onto
screaming passengers. Behind me, a Congolese man with the
booming voice of a TV evangelist prayed aloud for our surely
doomed souls.

The chaos matched my mood.

Back then, in the mid-noughties, the Democratic Republic of
Congo (DRC) was emerging from a long and complex conflict.
A conflict that had drawn in powers from across Central, East
and Southern Africa, so bloody and drawn-out that it had been
dubbed Africa's Third World War. Millions had died and the
country's dictatorial leader, Joseph Kabila – a man reputed to
have orchestrated his father's assassination – barely controlled

most of its territory. His father, Laurent, had been able to hang onto power only with military assistance from nearby Zimbabwe, under the equally despotic rule of Robert Mugabe. Zimbabwe's then-minister of justice has been accused of orchestrating deals that saw the country awarded a chunk of DRC's mineral wealth in return for military assistance. That man, Emmerson Mnangagwa, is now president of Zimbabwe, having deposed his one-time ally Mugabe in November 2017. He is, not-so-affectionately, known as 'the Crocodile'.

The war had officially ended in 2003 but this guaranteed little on the ground. Militias, bandits and foreign armed personnel continued to stalk areas of the country, especially in mineral-rich regions. So, I was flying into a storm, figuratively, as well as literally. Alone, unarmed and without back-up. There was no cavalry on which I could call, should I find myself staring down the barrel of a gun. Or, I should say, *when* I found myself staring down the barrel of a gun.

Guns, in fact. Plural.

My mission was to assess the security environment for a company with dormant mining interests in the DRC. The company had operated for many years in the east of the country, which had got hairy very fast in the late 1990s, when the war broke out. Many of my client's local staff had simply defected to safer areas of the country or fled across the border into Rwanda. The client had pulled out its expatriate staff soon after, declared *force majeure* and mothballed its operations. Now, with peace papers signed in South Africa's Sun City, they wanted to know if they could start digging again without risking the lives of too many employees.

And I was the man who was going to tell them. At first, I had tried to persuade members of the board that they could learn what they needed to know from a desk-based exercise: I didn't fancy stepping into crocodile-infested waters. But it turned out my senior contacts in the company had an appetite for risk. At least they did when it came to my safety. So, I agreed to go in, to gauge the temperature in their former theatre of operations. To gather 'ground truth'; the best intelligence there is.

We finally broke through the thunderous cloud cover over Kinshasa and started a more rapid descent, the pilot slipping the aircraft to get us down faster. Not a wise manoeuvre on a commercial plane but South African pilots live by their own rules. With the plane tilted, I had a view along the runway and was surprised to see it lined with crouched soldiers on either side. A welcoming committee of sorts. A jab of pain across the back of my head reminded me of my hangover. I rather wished that I was back in the bar of my five-star Sandton City hotel. There, the previous night, I had met Paul Grosvenor.

Nice guy, Paul, and someone who had been sensible enough to avoid the perils of the self-employment path that I had trodden after my government service. Instead, he had worked his way up through the pay scales of an international consulting firm; one with a name familiar to pretty much anyone with access to a radio, a TV or a newspaper. A top-dollar outfit, respected all over. As we touched down, I pulled Paul's business card from the breast pocket of my linen jacket and made a mental note to follow up our unplanned drinking session with a more formal meeting on my way back through Johannesburg. It would be handy to be in contact with the Head of Government Consulting – Africa for a firm of his employer's stature. Maybe I could turn him into a client.

But that was for the future. Right now, I had to navigate my way through N'djili Airport, without resorting to bribery. This involved watching as a taciturn customs officer turned out the contents of my suitcase with one hand while caressing the butt of her sidearm with the other, then patiently repacking under her resentful gaze while waiting for her to turn her attention to a more willing victim. She lit on a slight, Belgian businessman. He had his wallet open before she had his luggage open and I took the opportunity to lug my case away without having eaten into my small wad of dollars. I was going to need them, with credit cards by and large unusable in the Congo and inflation running rife: some days later, hungry for goodness after a diet of burned meat and under-cooked French fries, I would find myself paying twenty dollars for three oranges in a Lebanese-run supermarket. They tasted good.

A taxi was not difficult to find. The challenge was to select one from the throng of would-be drivers that pressed against me and marketed their services with linguistic gymnastics, hopping from English to French and from French to Swahili with ease. One guy seemed quieter than the others, so I chose him. Florian drove me to the old Hilton in a station wagon which had one of its doors tied to the body of the vehicle with several threads of faded blue wool. He became my chauffeur and guide during my stay.

I say 'old' Hilton because the chain had, many years previously, abandoned the hotel which continued to bear its name. It nonetheless remained the most salubrious of Kinshasa's residential offerings, as attested by the large number of European businessmen huddled in corners of the hotel atrium with uniformed military men. Brown envelopes changed hands without shame, cigars were cut, and half-litre bottles of beer were downed to toast the bartering of the Congo's extensive reserves of minerals – effectively its only source of wealth. The only women in the lobby, so far as I could tell, were harassed reception staff and harassing prostitutes, who wasted little time in laying out to me their own wares for barter.

There was some relief to be had in my room, when I made it that far, pushing the door closed with a sigh and positioning a tilted chair under the handle as an additional form of security.

But some of my would-be amours were not deterred. I took the first knock to be room service, only to discover one of the women from the lobby, crouched panther-like outside my door, positioned so that I would not be able to see her through the spyhole. She was delightfully good-natured, even as I declined her services and refused to 'tip' her instead. Later supplicants, who came to my door in ones, twos and small groups throughout the night, would not all be so gracious. But I had learned by then not to open up, so their insults and imprecations were at least muffled by an inch and a half of wood.

Not the best night's rest and not fabulous preparation for the following day's attempts to get my research under way. But a few cups of indescribably awful black coffee kickstarted my brain over breakfast, as I pondered my plan.

What was I going to do? Well, my intention was to fly east, to see the situation on the ground for myself. But I knew better than to do this without local support. So, the previous week, I had called a contact in Kinshasa, a minor politician who was a former soldier and had his own commercial interests in the mining sector. Bellowing into a crackling and patchy mobile phone connection, I had arranged to meet him that morning at the Palais du Peuple, home of the Transitional National Assembly of the Democratic Republic of the Congo, of which he was a member. The transitional assembly was an appointed body, formed in August 2003, following the conclusion of the peace treaty which formally ended the war. It sat intermittently and I was surprised that my friend – let's call him Patrice – would be in his office on a Saturday. But he had promised me he would be there, so I set off with Florian in his battered station wagon, spirits aloft, if not high. My idea was to persuade Patrice to sponsor me for a place on a UN, commercial or NGO flight into Goma International Airport, near the Rwandan border. Better still, I might be able to coax him into travelling there with me. I had first considered getting in from Rwanda but figured I would be better off with top-cover from someone with clout in Kinshasa, in case things turned ugly. And Patrice was my man. He had sounded keen to assist, as far as it was possible to tell on a broken call.

The Palais du Peuple is not an attractive building. Its 1970s-style ensemble of clean lines and concrete uniformity reminded me of my crappy comprehensive school in inner-city Birmingham, albeit with a grander sweep of stairs to the entrance. But I am sure that had nothing to do with Florian's refusal to park anywhere near it. More likely, he had an instinctive caution around governmental authority that I have encountered in Africans across the continent: an inevitable result of the abuses of colonialism and some less-than-ideal regimes following that unfortunate period. After all, the Palais du Peuple was the seat of the country's legislative body.

I was surprised, therefore, to find that getting into the building was simple. There was no apparent security. So, I walked up the steps and into an imposing entrance hall unchallenged. Not that that got me very far in any meaningful sense. For I had no idea how to find Patrice's office. I had naively assumed there would be a reception desk manned by helpful staff who would point me in the right direction. Instead of which, there was . . . nothing. And nobody. Just a vast empty space, that felt unnaturally chilly in the clammy, tropical heat of Kinshasa. I loosened my tie as I ventured up an internal staircase, imagining I might find corridors with labelled offices. Encountering no such luck, I called Patrice's mobile and was relieved when he picked up after two or three rings.

'Jules, my good friend,' he said. 'How nice to hear from you. Where are you?'

'I'm here,' I said.

'Where?'

'At the Palais du Peuple.'

A pause. 'The Palais. What are you doing there?'

There? Not here?

'I'm here to see you, Patrice, as we arranged.'

Another pause, longer this time, during which I heard over the crackles the sound of pages being turned.

'I am sorry, but I think we have our wires mixed,' Patrice said. 'When you said *la semaine prochaine*, I thought you meant *next* week, not this week.'

'I said that last week. Next week then is this week now.'

'Oh. *Désolé*. I thought you meant the one after. Not this coming week.'

I started making my way back down the stairs, to the entrance. 'Never mind. No problem. I will come to find you. Where are you right now?'

'That would be good, thank you,' Patrice sounded relieved. 'I am at the Bronté Hotel.'

'The Bronté? In Harare?'

'Yes.'

Harare. In Zimbabwe.

Oh, shit.

Time for Plan B. Or Plan A? Maybe shoot back to Jo'burg and work my way to Kigali in Rwanda and from there to Eastern DRC? Or work the phones and find someone else who could help me from the Kinshasa side? I quickened my pace, planning to sprint the couple of blocks back to Florian. If I was quick, I could make that day's flight back to South Africa and regroup. But I wasn't sure that was the best plan. At least I was in the DRC, and I had a visa for my visit. Would that work for multiple entries? I couldn't remember. I needed to get back to the hotel, retrieve my passport from the room safe, check the visa conditions and make a plan from there. Maybe Patrice could pass me to another contact. I shouldn't have hung up on him so abruptly. I dialled him again, planning to claim the line had dropped out, pressing phone to ear as I pushed open the heavy-grille door and stepped into the oppressive heat.

In my confusion, I had lost situational awareness.

The slap to my cheek humiliated more than hurt. And it sent my phone spinning across the concrete flooring. I raised my head sharply, to find myself looking beyond the barrel of an AK47, into bloodshot eyes hooded by the green beret of the Congolese army. To my right, the crunch and thud of a heavy military boot landing on my mobile. Turning towards the sound by instinct, I saw another weapon pointed at my head. A metallic tang of motor oil masked the smell of sweat from five, maybe six, soldiers that now pressed in to surround me.

I raised my hands well above my head.

'What are you doing here?' I couldn't tell who spoke, only that the question was barked at me with menace. I was confused that the questioner spoke in English rather than French. And there was something about his accent. It took me a moment to place it as Zimbabwean. Obviously, a Zim soldier who had been accorded a rank in the DRC's army, for whatever reason. I didn't much care why. I was just grateful that it would be so much easier to explain myself.

That posed a problem of its own, however. A truthful explanation of my presence would make me sound like a spy.

Ahem.

It was, I figured, too much to expect a rank-and-file soldier to understand the difference between business intelligence and espionage. And I wasn't in a hurry to try. So, I played for time.

'I'm here to meet Patrice Mtoto.'

'Who is he?' That bark again.

'One of the members of the National Assembly.'

'Take me to him. He can confirm you.' The AK47 to my front inched a little closer to my forehead. I realised my interrogator was its bearer. I dropped my eyes respectfully, avoiding direct eye contact.

'I'm afraid, sir, that Monsieur Mtoto could not make today's meeting after all.' I glanced towards the remains of my mobile phone. 'But I could call him if you can lend me a phone.'

'No phone,' my tormenter barked.

'Okay. Perhaps we could go to my hotel and we can call from there.'

'No. You are trespassing and you are in a protected zone. This is a criminal offence.' The thought of a Congolese prison weakened me. Ice water flooded my belly. 'You will explain who you are and what you are doing here to me. Now.'

I had no options. I would have to invent a cover story. Unusually, though, I hadn't prepared one in advance. It was a rookie error, but I had relied on Patrice's patronage to get me through any difficulties. And, in my planning, I had failed to consider the 'left of arc' possibility that he might not be in the country or might otherwise be unavailable. I cursed myself silently, for getting sloppy and complacent. Never a good idea in a Third World country riven by conflict and distrust.

But a glimmer of an idea occurred to me.

'Well, okay. Let me explain.' AK-man lowered his weapon, a little, and met my gaze full on; defiant, challenging me to persuade him of my innocence, of my right to be on government property at a time of heightened insecurity. 'I work for an international consulting group. You have probably heard of us.' No further downward movement of the rifle, so I pressed on. 'We have been awarded a project by the office of the president here.' At the mention of the president, the rifle slipped a little, its holder a fraction less confident than he had been. 'And I am here to meet Monsieur Mtoto because he holds the military rank of brigadier general.' This was not true but it rarely harms to claim association with senior ranks when faced with a military thug. 'He promised to introduce me to some of the ranks because our project is to report to the president about how to improve pay and conditions for the army, now that the war is over.'

Now, my interrogator lowered his gun. 'So, you want to talk to us about what we need?'

'Yes. Exactly. That, and to discuss your experiences of the war.' I took silence as encouragement. 'You, for instance. Where did you serve during the conflict?'

'I have just got back from the east,' said the soldier, now lowering his weapon fully, to rest it across his chest. His eyes were a mix of curiosity and suspicion. I just had to hope that the first could conquer the second. But he wasn't going to give in too easily.

'Could we sit down and you tell me about your experiences?' Maybe this man could solve my dilemma. If I couldn't make it to eastern DRC on this trip, at least I could get a first-hand account of security conditions there, from a security-professional who spoke fluent English. Something like hope stirred in me.

And I had anticipated his next demand.

'I don't believe you,' the soldier said. 'Prove it.' With those two words, he had got to the nub of cover: plausibility and credentials. I was sure I had the former but I now needed the latter, if this situation was not to go wrong. More wrong.

'Of course,' I said. 'But can I lower my arms, please?' Always ask first.

The soldier nodded and I lowered my arms inch by inch, gesturing with my right hand to the breast pocket of my jacket: too small to conceal a weapon. He nodded again.

I fished inside the pocket with two fingers and produced a business card, which I handed to him.

'Pleased to meet you,' I said. 'My name is Paul Grosvenor'.

With a dose of good luck, I had been able to improvise a cover story that achieved both defensive and offensive ends, to my great relief. I was protecting myself by inventing a reason to be somewhere that, at least in the minds of my captors, I should not be. And the story I made up also made an attractive proposition to my interlocutor. It seemed like I had something to offer him: a way to amplify his voice; air his grievances; perhaps to improve his lot through better pay and conditions. I transformed myself – with a few words – from enemy to potential ally.

And I got the pay-out. The soldiers and I spent the next three hours together, smoking, drinking tea and discussing two things: how the government could and should improve the miserable lives of its soldiery; and the state of the conflict in eastern DRC. A lot of what my new friends told me ended up in the report to my client and helped them reach a decision to resume limited operations.

I owe a lot to Paul Grosvenor.

*   *   *

Of course, the circumstances I faced in the Congo were extraordinary. With my life in danger, I felt it was acceptable to lie, thereby creating the impression the soldiers had something to gain by cooperating with me. This is not something I recommend in ordinary circumstances. But the underlying principle remains: effective cover is about making yourself attractive to interlocutors.

RECAP

- Use of cover techniques in a personal capacity is not about pretending to be something or someone you are not. It is counterproductive and unnecessary to do so.
- Instead, aim to build a personal brand so that goals allies will be able to identify with you, will be happy to engage with you and be willing to help you achieve your aims.
- To do this, identify role models who display the characteristics you wish to define you. Then observe, adopt and internalise their traits.
- Tap into the relevant parts of your character. Your personality is multifaceted and capable of orientation to present your preferred combination to an observer.
- There is a positive feedback loop between behaving, external reactions and becoming. Counsellors use this iterative process in applying Cognitive Behavioural Therapy.
- Effective cover, therefore, comes from within. And it can be truly transformative of us without exploiting others in any way.

CHAPTER THREE

The Bonding Power of Cultivation

Cultivar: a plant that has been created or selected intentionally and maintained through cultivation.[1]

Cultivation: the act of making a special effort to establish and develop a friendship.[2]

In *The Constant Gardener*, the hero is a diplomat rather than a spy. But I suspect that le Carré's choice of title was a nod to something spies and gardeners have in common. Both talk a great deal about cultivation.

In the spy's case, this refers to a specific stage of agent recruitment: that which follows conclusion of a targeting exercise and development of appropriate cover. It is the stage at which the spy engages with her target and starts to build up a relationship with them. At this point, it is not an espionage relationship but a series of interactions between two people that may lead to one.

Harry Ferguson breaks down the cultivation process into four stages in his book *Spy*.[3] These are: approach; acquaintance; friendship; trust.

---

1 American Heritage Science Dictionary: https://www.ahdictionary.com/word/search.html?q=cultivar
2 Cambridge Dictionary: https://dictionary.cambridge.org/dictionary/english/cultivation
3 Harry Ferguson, *Spy: A Handbook*, Bloomsbury, 2004.

Ferguson's 'approach' is the first encounter with a target. Encounters can be engineered and they often are. It may be that a spy attends a conference at which the target is a speaker. Or is a guest at a party thrown by a willing intermediary, to which the target is also invited. Occasionally, it is possible to contrive an apparently coincidental and natural-seeming encounter at a bar, restaurant or even on the street. Imagination is key to this. Persistence and patience may also be necessary, as the best-laid plans 'gang aft agley' (Robert Burns). In this case, the apt response is that described by another Robert (the Bruce): to 'try, try and try again'. Up to a point. It is important not to try so hard and so repeatedly that the spy becomes conspicuous or a nuisance. Sometimes, it is advisable to cut losses and move on to other targets.

Bullseye will be struck eventually.

When it is, and the spy is finally in front of their target, she has one apparently simple aim. That aim is to secure a second meeting.

As with many apparently simple things, the reality is compli-cated. People are busy and, increasingly, curate their schedules with care. Asking a target to commit to a follow-up is to ask them to give you some of that most precious of resources, time. Why should they?

This is where the offensive element of cover comes into play. The spy needs to be able to present their target with a 'proposi-tion' that is attractive enough to persuade the latter to promise them more facetime. It is important that the proposition is snappy. There may only be limited time for the spy to secure the next encounter. Of course, it is preferable that the target should like and identify with the spy. First impressions do indeed count. But, at this stage, there is little room for nuanced aspects of relationship building. Those come later, once the initial aim of securing a second meeting has been met.

Ferguson separates the 'acquaintance' and 'friendship' stages of cultivation, with acquaintanceship revolving around a planned series of semi-formal meetings, before the armoury of personal interactions is factored in. There is no hard and fast rule about this. Approaches will vary according to the precise circumstances of the cultivation. But a good spy will set about creating bonds of friendship as soon as possible, preferably during the second meeting. It could be, for example, that the second encounter between spy and target takes place at the latter's workplace, especially if the proposition element of cover is work-related. But, by the end of that meeting, it is desirable for the spy to have established enough rapport to make the offer of casual drinks, or an invitation to a conveniently scheduled party, a natural segue.

COMMENCING CULTIVATION

This is the beginning of the friendship phase, which is crucial to any successful recruitment.

It represents the move from 'something casual' to 'relationship', in dating parlance. At its heart – appropriately – is an effort by the spy to get their target to like them. To be attracted to them. There are various stratagems that can be employed to achieve this end, none of them exclusive to the espionage world. They are used by salespeople, suitors, seducers and shysters everywhere. And by good people who want to be good friends to others. Many of them have been proven as effective through psychological experiments. Most are intuitive. You may find it interesting to reflect on how many of the following ploys you have subconsciously (or consciously) used to strengthen your personal and professional relationships.

Perhaps the most important aspect of attraction – and one that is frequently overlooked, as we allow our friendships to drift – is familiarity. Scientists call this the 'mere exposure effect' and it doesn't apply only to attraction between people. It is one of the principles that underpin effective advertising and it helps to explain why we turn again and again to the same music when we want to lift our moods. In the case of interpersonal attraction, familiarity is one of the reasons why friendships and romances so often bloom in shared environments, such as universities and offices. Hence, spies make special efforts to see their targets repeatedly, rarely letting one encounter pass without at least laying the groundwork for the next.

Exposure is not enough by itself, of course. It is also important to be outward facing, when in the company of those whom we hope to attract. One way to do this is to use warm and positive language about contacts in common. A phenomenon called 'spontaneous trait transference' leads us to attach to a speaker the words they use when describing others. Comments like, 'Do you know Elaine? She is such a lovely person' will nudge the listener towards seeing the speaker as lovely, in a verbal sleight of hand. And you get to double-dip with this one, because positivity will itself enhance your attractiveness, thanks to 'emotional contagion'. Happy people tend to make us feel happier and we are naturally attracted to those who bring us happiness. Spies tend to smile like they mean it. And to use humour, which has been shown to make people more likeable.

In short, don't be an emotional vampire.

But do show some vulnerability. Spies recognise that 'emotional openness' helps friendships along. Admission of some fragility is often seen as a sign of strength. So long as it is not overdone, of course. Similarly, it is a good idea to own up to some mistakes and imperfections. We are able to relate more easily to those who, like us, are not perfect. This is why we root for the public speaker who admits their nervousness and cheer the likes of Eddie the Eagle. (For younger readers, Michael Edwards was the first athlete to represent Great Britain as a ski-jumper in the 1988 Olympics. He came last. In 2016, a movie was made about him.)

Truly skilful spies might combine this stratagem with another powerful device: confiding in their target. Coming back to public speaking, imagine someone giving a rousing speech while apparently oozing self-confidence. Now imagine that you compliment them on their performance. And they reply, 'Let me tell you a secret. I was terrified up there. When I was twelve, I broke down in tears when I was told to read an essay in front of my class. I've worked hard to manage my nerves since then. Now, I really need a drink.' You are going to like that person more for confiding in you than you are for their rhetorical skills, right?

Imagine how much more you would like them if, having said they need a drink, they added, 'Let me get you one, too. Then let's find a quiet corner somewhere. I want to hear all about your day.'

Which brings us to a surefire technique for winning friends: *make it all about them.*

There are various strands to this technique. First up is 'reciprocity of liking', which is just a fancy way of saying that we like people who like us. We know this instinctively and use it to our advantage, even as kids. 'Tell your friend Sally that Jamie really likes her' is a pretty good opening gambit for a would-be childhood sweetheart. When Sally hears from her friend that Jamie likes her, there will be a flicker of interest in Jamie from her. At the very least, she will conclude that Jamie has good taste. And we continue to fall for this trick well into adulthood. I was at a New Year's Eve party in 2020 when I met Dan. He was on his way to work at the local pub but stopped to have a quick chat with me, at the end of which he said, 'I think we are going to be friends.' I felt a frisson of pleasure and thought to myself, 'Yes, I think we are.'

A second strand is 'mirroring'. We all know the significance of body language but not everyone knows how to use it to advantage. The spy does. They will make a conscious effort to mimic a target's physical behaviours. For reasons that are not obvious, but maybe because imitation is a form of flattery, mimicking someone tends to increase the chances of their liking you. So, tell someone you like them and show that you like them by imitating them. A handy reminder to carry with you in social settings is 'show and tell'.

Third is establishing values and interests in common. The 'similarity-attraction effect' is rarely far from a spy's mind. Finding out what interests someone is part of the point of a spy's targeting exercise. And laying the basis for shared interests is one aspect of tailoring cover for that target.

The final strand is recognising that the subject most people find most interesting is themselves.

This lies behind Dale Carnegie's famous saying, 'If you want to be interesting, be interested.'[1] The comedian and broadcaster Bill Maher was groping towards the same point when he said, 'Curious people are interesting people. I wonder why that is.'[2] I can tell him. It's because curious people are likely to be interested in *him*.

The best way to show someone that you are interested in them? Let them talk about themselves. MRI imaging has shown that parts of the brain associated with reward are active when people do this. One study has shown that 'self-disclosure was strongly associated with increased activation in brain regions that form the mesolimbic dopamine system, including the nucleus accumbens and ventral tegmental area. Moreover, individuals were willing to forgo money to disclose about the self.'[3]

1 Dale Carnegie, *How to Win Friends and Influence People*, Vermilion, 2006.
2 https://twitter.com/NtlComedyCenter/status/1616557252084748310.
3 Diana I. Tamir and Jason P. Mitchell, 'Disclosing information about the self is intrinsically rewarding', *Proc Natl Acad Sci USA*. 2012 May 22; 109(21): 8038–8043. https://www.ncbi.nlm.nih.gov/pmc/articles/PMC3361411/

In less scientific terms, talking about ourselves gives us an emotional high. So, a spy will listen intently as their target speaks and then ask follow-up questions. About the target, their interests, their views. Better still, spies will often ask questions designed to establish how a target sees themselves. Then, they will be at pains to let the target know – subtly, of course – that they see them in the same way that the target sees themselves. 'Self-verification theory' suggests that reinforcement of some-one's self-image may be a quicker way to their heart even than through their stomachs, though it is also a good idea to buy them lunch.

The KGB realised this. And they were pretty darn good at recruiting people. Just look at their successes with the Cambridge Five, as brilliantly reconstructed by the writer-historian Ben Macintyre.[1]

It is worth quoting at length from a translation of a KGB training document that bears the clumsy title 'Some Aspects of Training the Operative for Psychological Influence of Foreigners During Cultivation'.[2] This manual says, 'In understanding the target as a person, the operative's ability to put himself in his place, using the possibilities of his own imagination, is very important. It is necessary to mentally penetrate the target's internal world, so to speak, to imagine his desires and problems and "see" their solution. Such an ability is one of the most powerful instruments for psychological influence.'

It goes on to say, 'The law of psychological reciprocity is manifested in the sphere of interpersonal relations. Consequently, most people experience affinity and positive emotions toward

1 Ben Macintyre, *A Spy Among Friends,* Bloomsbury, 2014.
2 KGB, 'Some Aspects of Training the Operative for Psychological Influence of Foreigners During Cultivation'. https://www.4freerussia.org/wp-content/uploads/sites/3/2019/11/Some-Aspects-of-Training-the-Operative.pdf

those who express empathy and understanding and agree with them, approve their actions and so on [. . .] Therefore, each time a person says something with which you can agree, you should let him know that. For his part, he will feel the need to agree with your statements or, to put it another way, to show reciprocity.'

The manual notes that 'the best method of forcing a person to talk about himself is to ask questions showing authentic interest in him. A skilfully posed question can help a target open up and explain clearly what in fact he wants.'

And the lunch? 'Influence on a person's mind may [also] be material,' notes the KGB, 'achieved largely by a change in the material conditions of the life of the target.' It recommends, for example, 'bringing him presents; paying monetary rewards; organising trips, visits, etc'.

All of this is designed to work towards the fourth of the cultivation stages outlined by Ferguson: trust. The KGB, again: 'People accept an idea offered to them far easier when they sense that the person making the offer understands their problems and their difficulties. It is important to achieve trust in relations. If we want to attract a person to our side, first we must convince him that we are his sincere friends.'

It is the establishment of trust that, eventually, allows the spy to move to the recruitment stage of a HUMINT operation. But that is for later.

For now, the main point to note is that there are three things, above all others, that enrich the soil of cultivation. The first is a positive, outward-facing attitude. The second is a cautious degree of emotional openness. The third is an authentic interest in the cultivar.

As I learned from an unexpected source.

* * *

Mr George was a small man, but he had a big impact on me.

He was short and wiry, with a diffident manner that made him seem to shrink further into himself. He wore bottle-bottom glasses that refracted his irises to the diameter of a pencil and his pupils to pin pricks. He combed strands of thinning grey hair over his scalp, wore the same fading green mackintosh every day and carried newspapers and magazines around in a Sainsbury's plastic bag. I liked him a great deal.

Not least because he seemed to like me and to be interested in me, at a time when I felt inconsequential and frustrated.

It was summer 1992 and I had recently graduated. Not that a degree from Oxford University was doing me much good in the jobs market. I was living with my parents in Birmingham, while I accumulated a pile of rejection letters. Mum was supportive, reassuring me that everyone would be struggling in the face of a recession. She had no answer to the point that most of my course-mates had already landed jobs with leading law firms, management consultants, stockbrokers and broadsheet news-papers. I was sure I was doing something wrong. But I wasn't sure what.

Dad was also supportive, finding me casual employment at a cultural institute in Birmingham. He had started there as a part-time receptionist in his forties and worked his way up to run the place. He put me to work painting walls in the various theatres and meeting rooms. It was lonely, repetitive work, during which I had plenty of time to brood on my apparent unemployability.

It was there that I met Mr George. The institute operated as a sort of social club for the less well-off but culturally minded. Mr George (I don't believe he ever told me his first name) was one such person. He was either unemployed himself, or retired, because he had plenty of time to spend in the members' reading room or the library, when he wasn't attending the programme of regular talks and other events.

So, I could always find him for a chat if I fancied a break from slapping paint onto walls. A frequent occurrence.

I would wander into the reading room and, if he was there, Mr George would place his newspaper to one side, stand and peer up at me, shading his eyes as though looking up at the sun. He would always ask the same question: 'How's the weather up there?' My mood would determine the answer, tracking the state of my job search at that time. 'Raining' would suggest that I had received a job rejection that day. 'Some sunshine with scattered clouds' might follow an invitation for a second interview.

One morning in late August was particularly bad. I had been out the previous evening, celebrating with a friend who had been offered a scholarship to study for a doctorate. The hangover was dramatic. Persistent pain behind the eyes, nausea, dizziness and the linger of stale cognac on my breath. Yes, I was pleased for my friend, but I was also jealous and brooded on why I had not also pursued an academic career. Matters had been made worse that morning when I picked up the post. It had contained one of those maddeningly phrased rejection letters, that leave one feeling worse than a more honest and direct approach: 'Yours was a strong application and my colleague has asked me to thank you for finding the time to come in and meet him. But the quality of candidates for our graduate programme was especially impressive and I regret to say that you will not be called forward for a second interview.' What I took from this was: 'strong application' but not an 'impressive' candidate.

At least Mr George was pleased to see me. I found him in the library, where he was sucking humbugs and leafing through a week-old copy of *Le Figaro*. He stood up and offered me a sweet. I was glad of the minty fumes. They went some way towards banishing the reek of brandy about me. He shielded his eyes and looked up at my face.

'I don't think I need to ask about the weather up there today,' he said. 'Squally, eh?'

The bags under my bloodshot eyes likely gave me away.

'Let's just say that Michael Fish would have got it wrong.' I was referring to the former BBC weatherman who famously said in October 1987 'a woman rang the BBC and said she heard there was a hurricane on the way . . . well, if you're watching, don't worry, there isn't.' Hours later, a hurricane killed eighteen people in the UK and caused property damage running into the billions of pounds.

Mr George laughed, then apologised.

'I'm sorry, I shouldn't laugh. You are struggling today.' He sat down and gestured to a chair opposite him, before placing his paper bag of humbugs on the table between us. 'Tell me what's bugging you.' He looked at the sweets and emphasised 'bugging' so I couldn't help but snigger at the terrible pun. I sat down and prepared to unburden myself. Use of humour, empathy and the offer of a listening ear. Mr George was good at this.

I pulled my latest rejection letter from a jacket pocket, uncrumpled it and passed it over to him. 'This is what's bothering me.' Mr George adjusted his glasses and read carefully, before handing the letter back to me, voicelessly encouraging me to carry on. 'The latest of many. I've had so many rejections I'm losing the will to carry on. All my mates seemed to find jobs even before sitting finals. And here I am, with a hangover and a paint roller in my hand.'

'Are you telling me that a degree from Oxford and Winston Churchill as a reference aren't enough?' Mr George popped another candy into his mouth.

'It seems not.' I spread my hands. 'I just don't seem able to break through at the interview stage. I've sent out around fifty applications and had countless interviews. But it's always the same story after that. Apparently, I write a good application. But I always fluff it at interview.'

Mr George yielded to temptation and crunched what remained of his humbug. I waited, until he was able to speak without risking an eruption of hard-boiled splinters.

'Right then, young man,' he said. 'I am going to give you three pieces of advice and I want you to act on them. Do you understand?' I nodded. 'I mean, not just listen and nod. You must act on what I'm about to tell you. Do you promise me?'

I looked into the eyes of the diminutive Mr George, who squinted back at me through his NHS glasses. He seemed suddenly bigger and more authoritative. I wondered at the unexpected emergence of such steeliness. 'Sure,' I said, 'I promise.'

'Good,' he said. 'The first thing I want you to remember is advice from your Mr Churchill's grandfather. He said, "never, never, never give up".' A pause and a raised eyebrow. 'So, don't.'

Noted.

'Second – and I need you just to trust me on this one – is simple.' I waited as Mr George popped another humbug and parked it between gum and cheek. 'Whenever you are in an interview for any job, you need to make out to your interviewers that the job in question is the *only* one you want.'

'Really?'

'Yes, really.' Mr George leaned forward now, hands clasped on the table. 'Convince them that you have always wanted to be a sprocket-tester. You dreamed of it as a child. You have researched all sprocket-making companies in the UK and they are the best. The combination of your sprocket-testing enthusiasm and their sprocket-making skills will be irresistible to sprocket-buyers everywhere.' He sat back, smiling. 'This is your destiny. Sprockets.'

'I don't much care about sprockets,' I said.

Mr George smiled. 'Irrelevant,' he said. 'Your enthusiasm will bamboozle them and you will find yourself testing sprockets a-plenty within days.' He crunched on his humbug. 'But that is not the best advice I have to give you today.'

'Oh?'

'Oh, indeed. Now, tell me, what do you think is the most important question is in any interview?'

I thought for a moment, then shrugged. 'I don't know. Maybe the one when they ask you where you see yourself in five years' time.'

Mr George laughed. 'Nonsense. We've already answered that one. You see yourself working for the sprocket-makers, testing sprockets at a senior level, of course. No, no. There is a much more significant question than that.'

'Which is?'

'Which is "Do you have any questions for us?".'

'I always thought that was just standard interview guff.'

Mr George nodded. 'Indeed. And you may be right. The interviewer may think it guff too. And they expect you to answer "No, I think we have covered everything".'

'That's what I usually say.'

Mr George stood up now. I found myself in the unusual position of looking up at him. He seemed almost imperious.

'And that, dear boy, is where you are going wrong.'

'I can't see how.'

'Well, let me tell you. Throughout the whole interview, your questioners have been listening to you talk about you. And, forgive me, but that is not very interesting for them.'

Not what I wanted to hear.

'Nothing to do with you, you understand? You are perfectly fascinating, I know. But what most people want to talk about is themselves.'

This sounded promising.

'And that question is the opportunity you have to let them do so. So, ask them.'

'Ask them what?'

'About themselves, of course. Ask "What attracted you to this job? What do you get out of it? What do you think are the best parts of it? Why do you enjoy working here?". Any variation on those themes will do. Just make sure of one thing.'

'What's that?'

'Always use the word "you" in your questions.' Mr George sat back now and seemed once more to withdraw into himself. He reached distractedly for his copy of *Le Figaro*, almost whispering his final words of advice.

'Just make it all about *them*.'

I sat for a while, stunned at the change I had seen in Mr George. I felt stealing upon me the certainty that he was right.

'Thank you,' I said. 'That's fantastic advice.'

He was deep in his newspaper now, so I got up to leave, adding as I did so, 'I didn't know you read French.'

Mr George looked surprised. 'Oh, yes,' he said. 'And Spanish and German. A little Arabic, too.' He thought for a moment. 'Japanese once upon a time but I have forgotten much of that.'

I left him to his reading, puzzled but invigorated. And determined to act on his advice.

The following week, I travelled to London, for three interviews. One was with Cazenove. Another with one of the global management consulting firms. The third with a small political lobbying company. While I would have been happy with any of the three jobs on offer, I didn't feel specifically drawn to one of them.

But that was not the impression I gave the interviewers.

In all three cases, I followed Mr George's advice. Each interview was the one I had been hoping for. Each job was the only one that I wanted. Each company was the best in its field and I longed to work for it.

Each interviewer was fascinating and I wanted to know about *them*. 'Forget me,' I almost said, 'tell me about *you* and what brings *you* here.' I would listen carefully to the answers and ask follow-ups: 'Has this job been everything you expected?'; 'Where do you think this job will get you in the next ten years?'

The result was undeniable. After countless interviews and countless rejections, I had a new problem. Which of three jobs, offered to me in about as many days, should I accept? I thought about it for nearly a week and got as far as deciding to turn down the management consultancy. They were incredulous. Nobody turned them down.

The director of personnel phoned me, clearly in a foul temper. She said, 'But you told the interviewer that this was the only job you wanted.'

'I lied. Sorry.'

She hung up.

One down. But I still had to choose between two offers, each very attractive in their own different ways. I sought the views of friends and family. Some were all for the Cazenove job: it would offer a secure future, they said, with a great name. Others urged me to go for the lobbying role: much more interesting, they said, and at the heart of government. Not very helpful. So, I finally did what I should have done all along and sought out Mr George once again. As always, he listened carefully as I explained my dilemma, head cocked to one side.

Having laid out the pros and cons of each job, I asked him, 'Which do you think I should take?'

Mr George thought for a moment, looking grave and pensive.

'That's easy,' he said, finally. 'Take the one that pays the most.'

*   *   *

Mr George was, evidently, a pragmatist. I just don't know whether it was his innate pragmatism or undeclared professional training that led him to grasp the vital life lesson: that it is interest in others that cultivates their interest in you. Whatever the case, it certainly worked for me.

RECAP

- Cultivation follows targeting and the development of cover. It precedes formal agent recruitment, following a path of approach, acquaintanceship, friendship and trust.
- Spies engineer approaches through various means. Their aim at a first encounter is to secure a second, leading to a series of increasingly social meetings ('exposure').
- These meetings are used to move from acquaintanceship to friendship. Spies deploy tried and tested stratagems to persuade targets to like them.
- These ploys fall under three broad headings: being outward facing; being emotionally open; and displaying interest in the target.
- Spies also present gifts to their targets and buy them meals. This builds a sense of reciprocal obligation on the part of the cultivar.
- A deepening social relationship with a target leads gradually to the emergence of trust, which is an indispensable ingredient of any successful recruitment.

* * *

You have finished a targeting exercise and identified a target goals ally. And you have developed your personal brand: that combination of your personality Rubik's Cube that you want to display to your target. You would now like to build a relation-ship with the target and you understand the pathway: the approach, leading to acquaintanceship, friendship and, eventu-ally, trust. But now comes the tricky bit. How do you get that first meeting?

Try asking.

If this idea makes you feel uncomfortable, you are not alone. Asking for something can make us feel vulnerable. It hands power over to the person we are asking and invites in the fear of rejection. Perhaps the wait for a response triggers uncom-fortable emotions that we associate with anticipation of exam results or job interview outcomes. We are averse to uncertainty and ambiguity. Maybe asking for a favour from someone – which is what you will be doing – makes us feel out of control.

These are all natural and commonplace responses. You may have seen others hesitate to ask even relatively undemanding favours: 'Will you please watch my bag while I go to the buffet car?'; 'In which aisle can I find dog food?'; 'Is this seat taken?' You may have hesitated yourself, in similar situations. That is nothing to worry about. It is human nature.

It helps to know that many people are predisposed to be helpful, courteous and kind. The historian and writer Rutger Bregman even wrote a book celebrating this idea.[1] But it seems that we choose instead not to think well of our fellow humans. Psychologist Francis Flynn conducted studies in 2008, from which he concluded that 'people underestimated by as much as 50% the likelihood that others would agree to a direct request for help'.[2] Furthermore, according to Melissa de Witte of

1 Rutger Bregman, *Humankind: A Hopeful History*, Bloomsbury, 2021.
2 F. J. Flynn and V. K. B. Lake (2008). 'If you need help, just ask: Underestimating compliance with direct requests for help.' *Journal of Personality and Social Psychology*, 95(1), 128–143. https://psycnet.apa.org/record/2008-08084-009

Stanford University, 'the majority of help occurs only after a request has been made'. This may be because a 'direct request can remove [. . .] uncertainties, such that asking for help enables kindness and unlocks opportunities for positive social connections'.[1]

So, just ask.

Okay, there is a bit more to it than that. Not least because, most probably, your target doesn't even know who you are. This means that you will first need to establish a connection. The way *not* to do this is by finding a target's email address online and sending them an unsolicited message. This would likely result only in some indignation and the marking of your email address as 'junk'. At the other end of the spectrum, an introduction by a contact in common is ideal. But most approaches will lie somewhere between these two extremes. This is where smart use of social media can come in handy. A connection request, alongside a short note of introduction, can often pave the way towards more substantive contact. And don't forget the analogue approach: unsolicited emails may be unwelcome, but a well-written letter sent by snail mail to a publicly available business address has a novelty value that may well engage the reader. Just avoid sending such a letter to a private residence, an action that could be interpreted as sinister rather than engagingly unusual.

1 Melissa de Witte, 'Asking for help is hard, but people want to help more than we realize, Stanford scholar says', Stanford News, 8 September 2022. https://news.stanford.edu/2022/09/08/asking-help-hard-people-want -help-realize/

POSITIVE ASKING

Once an initial connection has been established, it is time to land that all-important first meeting, by asking for it. This stage needs careful consideration because, while asking for something is straightforward, asking in such a way as to maximise the chances of a positive response is a different matter. The challenge is to couch your request so that it achieves two things: first, to make it easy for the receiver to say yes; and second, to make it attractive for them to say yes. Six simple steps will help you to do this.

First, be clear in yourself what you are asking for. Vague requests are unlikely to elicit positive responses. When asking to meet, know first what the meeting is for.

Second, tell your target, in equally clear terms. Try a formula such as 'I would like to meet you to discuss how I could find employment in your field.' This is much more likely to meet with approval than a more general 'It would be great to meet one day.'

Third, be positive. Opening phrases such as 'I'm sorry to be a nuisance but . . .' or 'I know you are busy but . . .' serve no purpose. But they risk putting the recipient of a request in a negative frame of mind from the outset. Better to write something like 'I am a great admirer of your work and would appreciate an opportunity to learn from you.' If you doubt this, try putting yourself in your target's shoes. How would you feel about a message that begins with a negative sentiment? How would you respond to a message that begins with a positive sentiment?

Fourth, avoid conditionalities. Yes, reciprocity is vital to building a solid relationship but it is not helpful at this stage. A phrase such as 'If we meet, I will give you a positive plug on my social media channels' sounds presumptuous and is off-putting.

Remember, people are predisposed to help and you can appeal to this human trait. Conversely, overtly transactional exchanges can make some people feel uncomfortable.

Fifth, build in references to shared values or experiences. Try 'I share your enthusiasm for enhancing social mobility,' or 'I see that we attended the same school.' Much better than 'You don't know me, but . . .' Humans crave belonging, to a particular social group, to a political tribe, to a place, to whatever. I am a Brummie, for instance, and the hint of a Birmingham accent in an interlocutor draws me immediately closer to them. There is no shame in recognising this trait in oneself, nor in appealing to it in others, so long as it not done in a coercive manner (for example, by threatening to eject someone from a group unless they do as they are told). Such an appeal can set out why your target is so well placed to help, making it both easier and more attractive for them to do so.

Finally, show gratitude and humility. Explain clearly how much of an impact a meeting could have on you and thank them for it in advance. People like to feel they can make a difference, so tell them how they will. They crave, even more than the feeling that they *can* make a difference, acknowledgement and appreciation of their efforts to do so.

Control is an important consideration in all of this. It is vital that your target should feel in control of the situation. That they are empowered to help you. So, it is advisable to give them flexibility concerning their response to your request. This means providing various means of contacting you: a phone number, an email address, a postal address and social media account details if appropriate. It also means demonstrating willingness on your part to fit into their plans and schedule. Offer to meet them at their place of work or at another venue of their choice. When it comes to timing, however, it doesn't hurt to set some limits within which they can manoeuvre. You might tell them that you will be in their area on specific dates or certain days of the week. This will help to focus your target's mind on a date by which they should respond, to save your communication from falling to the bottom of their 'to do' list.

Of course, there are no guarantees of success, even with all the points above covered. You may therefore wish to build in a device that will allow you to contact them again: 'I look forward to hearing from you soon and will drop you a line in a couple of weeks to follow up' would meet the bill.

And, if they turn you down the first time, don't despair. It may be worth trying again in future, depending on the terms and tone of the initial refusal. Researchers at Stanford University claim that, if someone turns down a request for help, they are more likely to accept if asked again. It's certainly worth a try, once. Any more than once would make you a nuisance, so limit yourself.

CASE STUDY

You will remember that Tom's targeting exercise led him to Moussa, an actor from his hometown who frequently returns to give motivational talks at schools there. Tom now aims to meet Moussa, with a view to persuading him to post on social media images of himself wearing some of Tom's pieces.

Tom begins by researching on which social media platforms Moussa is active and following him on them. This deepens his understanding of Moussa's preferences, interests and attitudes, as well as opening possible lines of communication. He likes, reposts and comments on Moussa's social media activity, making sure to use his handle on each occasion. In time, Moussa starts to follow one of Tom's accounts, which enables him to send a short direct message, asking if Moussa would be open to receiving an email. Moussa replies that he would and sends Tom an email address.

Tom composes the following email:

'Dear Moussa,

Thank you so much for following me on X and for sending me your email address. It makes me proud to see someone from our hometown making such waves as an actor and I am thrilled to be in touch with you. As a struggling fashion designer, I love the fact that you take such good care of your appearance. And we share the same taste. You looked great in the Ozwald Boateng suit that you wore to your latest premiere. He is definitely one of my all-time favourite designers.

I read your interview with the local newspaper and think it is awesome that you spend time mentoring kids from the schools around here. It takes thought leaders like you to make social mobility a reality for some of the disadvantaged kids in our community.

Would you be happy to meet me for half an hour? I'd love to hear your thoughts on how I can better showcase my designs in Europe. I'm sure you have valuable advice to offer, drawing on your own experience of the journey from here to being a global name. A few minutes of your time could make a difference to my whole life!

I would be happy to come and see you in Paris. In fact, I have a trip there planned in a few weeks. If you will be around then, could I buy you an absinthe at a local bar? If not, please do let me know what would suit you, perhaps when you are next here on a school visit. I can be flexible.

Either way, I'll drop you another line when my travel plans have firmed up and I know where I will be staying.

Thanks for reading this and thanks in advance for any help you can give me. I would be thrilled to spend a bit of time getting to know the Moussa behind the fabulous image.

You can contact me by replying to this message, DM'ing me on X or calling/texting my mobile number below.

I can't wait to hear from you.

With my very best wishes, Tom.'

Tom took care to strike the right tone in his email. Enthusiastic without being effusive. Grateful without grovelling. Flexible but firm. He combined simplicity with clarity and honesty. He also used appropriate language, for a fashion designer writing to an actor. Words such as 'fabulous' and 'thrilled' might not work so well in a letter to a captain of industry, for example. This is the point of cover, or personal branding; showing yourself in the guise most likely to attract your target. The branding should be reflected in your opening letter or message to your target. Consistency of personal presentation is your goal.

Which brings us to the question of how best to handle yourself once a target has agreed to meet you for the first time.

THINK SENSE

Because your target is going to experience you using all of theirs. Except taste, one hopes.

Consider how to dress. If your personal brand is adventurer, desert boots and combat trousers may be in order. If businessperson, formal attire is never a bad idea. Artists can indulge their creative flair when selecting their outfits.

Think about how you sound. A would-be newsreader might be expected to enunciate clearly and slowly. An aspiring therapist or nurse will benefit from cultivating a soothing tone. Sound is also about the words you use, not just how you say them. Try to make sure that your vocabulary fits your brand (for more on this, see Chapter Two (p. 30)).

Take note of how you feel. A firm handshake is usually appreciated. If you are inclined to clamminess, carry a handkerchief to dry your hands before entering the meeting. If it is cold, take advantage of a moment of privacy to rub your hands together: better still, wash them with warm water as close as possible to the point that you will offer a handshake.

This should also create an aroma of soap, or perhaps you will wear a perfume or aftershave. Choose one to suit your personal brand.

Getting all of this in order before a first meeting will help you to relax and focus on your goals for the encounter. Turn up early, so you can get a sense of the meeting environment and take some time in front of a mirror and a wash basin, to put any necessary finishing touches to yourself. If you are meeting in a public place, have a dummy run the day before, dropping in to order a coffee and assess the best places to sit, to allow discreet conversation at an unforced volume. Spies call this a 'recce'. Try to conduct a recce at about the time of day your meeting will be. It won't cost you anything other than time and it will make you feel more in control of the environment (we'll come back to this in Chapter Nine (p. 270)). Control is good. It allows you to focus on what matters.

As for what does matter, be realistic about what you can achieve in one meeting. Decide on one or two ideas or thoughts about you that you would like your target to take away from the meeting. Lay the groundwork for establishing a friendship but don't fixate on it. Please don't try to throw at your target the whole suite of relationship-building techniques outlined above. You will get in a muddle and come across as insincere. Instead, choose one that suits you best – it may be speaking positively about acquaintances in common, displaying some vulnerability, or showing interest in your target – and stick with that for now.

Above all else, aim to secure a second meeting, because then you can bring other skills into play, enabling you to get under your target's skin and find out what really makes them tick. We'll explore how spies do this, and how you can too, in Part Two. But, first, I'll tell you about a time when making myself likeable gave me the edge over someone who really should have known better.

*   *   *

Adam the ex-Mossad man did not want me there. But he had no choice, so made sure that I knew my place. He sat me in the back of the car with our translator, while he rode up front with a former colleague, listening to music by Arik Einstein. I was happy enough with this arrangement, as it limited the amount of time that I was forced to spend talking to Adam. Samira was much more interesting.

The Republic of Guinea was still a volatile country in 2011, three years after a military coup orchestrated by Captain Moussa Dadis Camara. In September 2009, Camara's security forces killed more than 150 people and raped countless women at a pro-democracy rally in the capital, Conakry. Camara himself was shot in the head by an aide in December of that year. Then, elections in 2010 saw President Alpha Condé rise to power. Condé's victory in a second round of voting surprised many, as he had polled only 18 per cent in the first round, compared to the 40 per cent racked up by his opponent Cellou Dalein Diallo. Rumours abounded that Condé had accepted bribes and campaign funding from international mining companies, in return for promises of mining concessions. Mining is big business in Guinea, a country reputed to have the second biggest mining reserves in Africa.

In fact, mining is pretty much the only business in Guinea, aside from subsistence agriculture. It accounts for over 80 per cent of the country's exports. And it is safe to say that it attracts some shady characters. But Condé was making efforts to clean up the sector's image, working with George Soros and his Open Society Foundations. The idea was to revise the country's mining code, commit to the Extractive Industries Transparency Initiative (EITI) and put in place anti-corruption measures to ensure would-be bribe-payers were penalised. This plan was cause for some optimism, even in the year that the presidential palace was shelled, reportedly in a failed attempt to assassinate the president. That had taken place in July 2011, three months before I landed there with Adam.

I had George Soros to thank for my presence. Sort of. A hedge fund run by one of his former employees was encouraged by Soros's involvement in planned mining sector reforms. The fund was keen to get into Guinea's diamond industry, an important source of exports to Israel and a sector that was dominated by informal (artisanal) miners. They had identified for potential investment a company (which I shall call GD Co) that had been granted numerous mining licences by Condé and they wanted it checked out before committing funds. They had selected Adam to do the checking. He was a former Mossad officer, who now ran a business intelligence company out of Tel Aviv, specialising in Africa's mining operations.

I had met Alberto, one of the hedge fund's founders, at a dinner party in London two weeks before I boarded my flight to Conakry. He was excited about opportunities in Guinea and I asked if there was any way in which my intelligence consultancy could help unlock them. Alberto said they were already working with a risk management consultancy and told me enough that I was able to work out it was Adam's outfit. I was joking when I asked, 'Are you sure it's a good idea to send an

Israeli investigator to a Muslim country that cut ties with Tel
Aviv in 1967?' But Alberto seemed rattled. He said, 'Good point.
We had better send you out there with Adam. Just to balance
things out, you know.' I assumed he was joking, too. That idea
was dispelled when a courier arrived at my home the following
morning, to take my passport to the visa section of the Guinea
Embassy.

The courier left me with a note from Alberto, outlining the
mission. A contact in Guinea had tipped off the hedge fund that
Condé's mining minister had demanded a bribe from GD Co, in
return for granting mining permits. This sounded plausible and
in line with usual practice in Conakry. They wanted me to help
Adam find out if such a demand had been made and, if so,
whether GD Co had complied. All without alerting the target to
our investigations.

Quite a challenge. But there would be three of us on the case
and I was happy to play tag-along.

And that was what Adam was determined I would be. We
walked out of the airport together, into the steamy heat of
Conakry, to be met by Adam's accomplice Saul, who had arrived
a day earlier and found an old Peugeot 107 to rent. Adam made a
show of opening the back door and ushering me into the cramped
space next to a slim woman in her forties, who was wrapped in a
loose colourful headdress and smelled faintly of sandalwood. He
then climbed into the front passenger seat and set about ignoring
me and her. I twisted in my seat to offer a handshake to my travelling companion, who accepted with her gaze averted.

'I'm Jules,' I said. 'Here to help Adam.' I nodded towards the
two old Mossad friends, who were talking animatedly in
Hebrew. 'You can think of me as a spare wheel.'

She smiled. 'I thought that was my role,' she said. 'I was told
I shall translate from French to English, but Saul speaks fluent
French and tells me Adam does, too.'

'No problem. You can translate for me,' I smiled. 'But you haven't told me your name.'

'Oh, sorry. It is Samira Balamou.'

I recognised the surname, the same as that of a high-profile politician who had been 'disappeared' during the dictatorship of Ahmed Sékou Touré. It is estimated that Sékou Touré, Guinea's first post-Independence president, killed up to 50,000 opposition figures and one-time allies whom he considered a threat. Often, they were incarcerated in notorious prisons, such as Camp Boiro, where some were subjected to the so-called 'black diet': no food or water until death.

'Like Jean-Pierre Balamou,' I said. 'You share a name associated with greatness. Balamou was quite the hero in his day.'

Samira looked down and spoke quietly.

'He was my father,' she said.

This took me aback.

'I am so sorry. I didn't mean to make light. Please forgive me.'

Samira reached over and brushed my hand lightly with her fingertips. The hairs on my bare forearms rose to her touch and I hoped she wouldn't notice.

'Don't worry,' she said. 'I am pleased you know about him. And you are right. He was a great man. Though I only knew him until I was eleven.'

'I feel for you,' I said. 'I lost my sister when I was eleven, so perhaps I understand a little about your pain.'

Samira met my eyes now. 'Perhaps a little,' she said. 'I am sorry for your loss.'

'And I am sorry for yours.'

We rode on in silence, me leaving Samira to her private thoughts, Adam and Saul quite unaware of the small drama that had unfolded a few feet behind them. We had left the main airport road now, to avoid a protest that was blocking the highway. The old Peugeot's suspension springs creaked as we bumped over a dried mud track, Saul picking a careful route through a poverty-stricken township. Baleful dark eyes stared at us as we passed groups of men playing *mancala* with scooped-out barks and small stones, or dealing dirty playing cards for hands of poker. Outside one hut, a boy of about three stood naked in a bucket as his mother slopped soapy water over him and lathered his tight-curled hair. The woman saw me watching and smiled broadly. Her son waved, then saluted.

I leaned forward. 'So, what first?'

Adam had a plan.

Not a very good one, though. For the next two days, we drove around Conakry, calling on officials and businesspeople, seem-ingly at random. Each meeting followed the same pattern. Adam would introduce Saul, then me, leaving Samira to speak for herself. Then, after routine pleasantries, he would tell our hosts that we were conducting research into the diamond mining sector in Guinea. This would lead to a handful of general questions about reserves, locations, active mines and partici-pants in the sector. Neither Adam nor Saul even pretended to take notes of the answers. After about ten minutes of this, Adam would lean forward, clasped hands outstretched on the desk.

'As you know, we Israelis have a reputation for straight talk-ing. So, I'm going to tell you that GD Co was asked for a bribe by the minister of mines.' Dramatic pause. 'Do you know if this is true and if they paid it?'

For some reason, he always delivered these lines in English, despite conducting most of the interviews in French. Each time, Samira would translate. And, each time, she would glance at me and roll her eyes. The answers were equally predictable. From a government official, it would be a variation on the theme of 'There is no official corruption in the new Republic of Guinea.' From one of GD Co's competitors, it would be something like 'There is no smoke without fire.' But nobody was able and willing to provide genuine insight, one way or the other. Worse still, it would only be a matter of time before word got back to GD Co that we were asking awkward questions, which was something the client had asked us to avoid at all costs.

I tried raising my concerns with Adam but he was dismissive, telling me that he had conducted many such investigations in the past and his technique always paid off in the end. In any case, he argued, we already had enough to report to the client that they should not proceed, because so many of GD Co's competitors were certain they had paid a bribe. This seemed unfair to me, given the obvious bias of those sources. So, I decided to go it alone, through an invaluable resource that Adam and Saul had completely overlooked.

Samira.

I calculated that she must have met and befriended many officials and others over the years, in her role as translator. Amongst those, there would be some who were privy to dealings between the minister and GD Co. Perhaps someone who was familiar with the terms of their contract and would know if it contained suspicious line items for 'consulting fees' or 'security services', to be paid to offshore accounts. Or, better still, someone in the company who would be able to tell Samira the real story about the meeting in question. As it turned out, she could trump both these possibilities.

First off, I invited her to dinner, over which we talked about anything but work. I asked her about her infancy and invited her to share memories of her father. We discussed our shared experience of childhood grief and she told me, while raising a glass of imported pinot noir, about the religious crisis she had suffered after the loss of her father. She explained that she had struggled with her mother to be allowed to go to university, rather than be married off. And that it was a daily challenge for an educated, single mother to be taken seriously in Guinea. 'Many men', she said, 'just look straight through me. Like Adam.'

We talked about Guinea's future under Alpha Condé and she shared her dream that, one day, she could find employment in Europe, as she feared that little would change for her at home, whoever was president. I promised to circulate her CV among friends and former colleagues. She told me about her hopes for her daughter, who would soon be applying to study abroad. We agreed that I would dine at her house the following day, when I would be able to tell her daughter about colleges in the UK.

It was only as I was walking Samira back to her car that I broached the subject of GD Co's dealings with the ministry of mines.

'What do you think about GD Co?' I asked. 'Do you think you know anyone who might be able to tell us about how they secured their mining licences?'

'I can tell you about it,' Samira said. 'I was translating for their CEO when they were negotiating with the ministry.'

I stopped, laid a hand on her arm, and started laughing. 'So, you have known the answer to Adam's question all along?' She nodded.

'Yes. It wasn't the minister who asked for a bribe.' I shut up and let her speak. 'It was an official in the department responsible for environmental licensing.' She named the official. 'He told them he would be unable to grant them clearance without a *petit cadeau*. Except it wasn't so *petit*. He wanted twenty thousand dollars for what he called his facilitation services. In cash.'

'And he was happy to talk about that in front of you?'

'He had no choice, as he couldn't speak English and the CEO couldn't speak French. I translated it all.' I must have looked incredulous, for she added, 'I told you, men just look straight through women like me. Except you, maybe.'

I was shaking my head in disbelief.

'What did the CEO say?'

'He was very good. He refused. Told the official that he would report the request to the minister himself and to the president, if necessary.'

'And that worked?'

'Like a dream. The official said there had been a misunderstanding. He blamed me for mis-translating his words.'

'Extraordinary,' I said.

Samira shrugged. 'That's the way it goes. He would have forgotten all about me as soon as the meeting was over. The CEO didn't believe him. He thanked me for playing the scapegoat. Told me I had given the official a ladder to climb down. Whatever that means.'

We had reached Samira's car by now and she slid behind the wheel, as I held the door open.

'That is all fascinating, thank you so much,' I said. 'But why didn't you tell Adam?'

Samira laughed. 'Maybe because there would have been no need for him to pay me for the full week, if he had got the answer he wanted on the first day.'

'Fair point.'

Samira pulled the door closed and dropped the window.

'Besides,' she said, as the ignition caught, 'I only told you because I like you.' She revved the engine and pressed the button to raise the window.

Her parting words were 'And I don't like Adam.'

* * *

We are surrounded by people who have insights and knowledge we don't. Showing respect towards and interest in others, whatever their position in life, is not only the right thing to do.

It can also unlock a willingness in them to share the benefits of their experience with you. I hope this is something that Samira's daughter found to her advantage, during her studies in the UK.

RECAP

- Asking a target goals ally for a meeting can be daunting. But remember that most people are predisposed to help.
- Establish a connection first: through a friendly intermediary, on social media or even by sending an old-fashioned letter in the post. Be sure only to use legitimate means.
- When asking for a meeting, be clear what it's for, appeal to common ground with your target, offer them flexibility and thank them in advance.
- If possible, recce a meeting place before the big day. Try to go there at about the same time of day as the meeting will be held.
- Remember that your target will use multiple senses in forming a first impression. Align your look, sound, smell and feel with your personal brand.
- Likeability is key to building successful alliances. But limit your ambitions in a first encounter. Securing a second meeting is a win.

PART 2

Getting Together (Recruitment)

'If you go looking for a friend, you're going to find they're very scarce. If you go out to be a friend, you'll find them everywhere.'
Attributed to Zig Ziglar

CHAPTER FOUR

The Paradoxical Power of Elicitation

Spies are excellent listeners.

This is partly because they are in the business of gathering intelligence from human sources. Listening is a great way of doing that. But it is also because, first, they need to find out as much as possible about their targets, to assess their readiness for formal recruitment. They aim to explore in detail a target's existing or potential access to intelligence of interest and what might persuade them to share that intelligence. So, they need to make the target comfortable with being open about themselves: to talk about their unspoken fears and hopes, their family lives, their attitudes to work, and their relationships with co-workers and management.

Crucially, they try to do this without asking too many questions. Without being obvious about their intentions. They have a word for this process: elicitation.

Why do spies use elicitation techniques? It's not only because they are sneaky by nature or nurture, though habit almost certainly comes into it. It is also because overt questioning automatically raises barriers in the mind of the person questioned. Repeated questions are interrogative and most people feel uncomfortable with being interrogated. It causes them to ponder 'What is this person [the questioner] after?

What is their hidden agenda?' In response, they become wary and evasive, if not intentionally misleading. You have probably experienced this yourself, from both sides. Think of a time when you have asked yourself why someone is pushing you so hard for information and how that made you react. Did you withdraw from them, conversationally or physically? I'll bet you did. Then think of a time when you have, perhaps thoughtlessly, aimed rapid-fire questions at someone else. Did they say something like, 'My goodness, you ask a lot of questions' or 'This feels like an interview'? Bet they did. If so, you probably realised at the time that their comment was polite code for 'Back off, buster.'

In an effort to overcome this natural human suspicion, spies use elicitation techniques to disguise the fact that they are soliciting information. The word has its roots in the Latin verb *elicere*, which means 'to draw forth'. The FBI describes elicitation as 'a technique used to discreetly gather information. It is a conversation with a specific purpose: to collect information that is not readily available and do so without raising suspicion that specific facts are being sought.' The agency adds that elicitation is 'usually non-threatening, easy to disguise, deniable and effective'.[1] We'll unpack what all this means later. The former FBI officer and author John Nolan puts it more succinctly. He describes elicitation as gathering information without asking questions.[2] This is a memorable summary but a little misleading. It is possible – indeed, likely – that questions will form part of an elicitation. But spies will be mindful about the way in which they frame them and deploy them.

1 FBI, *Elicitation*. https://www.fbi.gov/file-repository/elicitation-brochure.pdf/view
2 Social Engineer podcast, Episode 35: Mastering Elicitation with John Nolan. https://www.social-engineer.org/podcasts/episode-035-mastering-elicitation-with-john-nolan/

Either way, the following should by now be obvious: on the one hand, direct questions sometimes prompt their target to suspect a hidden agenda where there is probably not one; on the other hand, the use of elicitation techniques to hide an agenda is less likely to make the target suspicious.

That is the paradoxical power of elicitation.

This paradox explains why government agencies are so keen to alert US citizens, particularly those privy to classified or commercial-in-confidence material, to the risk of hostile third parties using elicitation techniques against them. A simple Google search will throw up warnings from the FBI, the Department of Homeland Security and NASA, amongst other government departments. However, if done well, elicitation can work even with individuals who have been sensitised to it. Another paradox.

So, how does it work?

The answer to that is, there is no simple answer. But we can outline some basic principles, the start-point being in the FBI description above. The description mentions a conversation with a 'specific purpose'. This is key. One thing that sets spies apart from civilians is the role of detailed planning in their human interactions. Nearly every aspect of a spy's dealings with a target will be thought through, played out and second-guessed in advance. For many of us, this *modus operandi* is alien. Our interpersonal style tends to be *ex tempore* and subject to whim in the moment. Many believe that such a free-wheeling approach makes for more enjoyable social occasions; they won't find any objection to that view here.

But not every encounter is social. In formal business meetings, for example, there is often an agenda to lend structure. Within this, some attendees will have no specific aims to achieve in the meeting and will make unprepared contributions. Others – fewer – will decide in advance exactly what outcomes they desire and how to set about getting them. You will doubtless have seen both approaches in action and, while there are advantages and disadvantages in each, it is likely that the attendee with a structure in mind will be more effective than his or her colleagues.

Spies bring planning and structure even into the most apparently social of occasions. (At least, they do so when they are at work. The fortunate ones don't carry the habit with them into their personal lives.) Included in this is knowing exactly what information they would like to discover by the end of a specific encounter. In addition, they will have in mind a framework that they will use to elicit that information. This is not to say that they won't allow room for flexibility. Humans are sometimes predictable but, equally often, can act in an unforeseen manner. Consequently, spies will *prepare* to be *flexible*. Yet another paradox.

Look again at the FBI description of elicitation. It is 'non-threatening, easy to disguise, deniable and effective'. What does 'non-threatening' mean? A behaviour that is threatening to me may be water off a duck's back to you. And *vice versa*. Psychologists have identified five major personality traits and each one of them might affect how threatening an individual finds another person's behaviour. These are: extroversion/introversion; agreeableness; openness; conscientiousness; and neuroticism. Spies adapt the suite of elicitation techniques according to their assessment of these five personality dimensions in their target. But, as you will have realised, part of the elicitation process is aimed precisely at assessing a target's personality in the first place. Paradoxes abound. The solution to this one is to maintain flexibility on the way to reaching well-defined goals.

Which brings us to a review of some of the elicitation techniques that a good spy will have in their quiver, ready to draw or to replace as a specific situation unfolds. One thing that all of them have in common, as per the FBI description, is that they are 'easy to disguise.' Or, perhaps more correctly, they are useful in disguising the true purpose of an interaction.

ELICITATION TECHNIQUES

We can group elicitation techniques under four broad headings: commonality; reciprocity; appeal to ego; and provocation. You will note that some of these headings align with the techniques outlined under the cultivation skill. And some align with the techniques for engaging with motivation, as you will learn in the next chapter (p. 138). Very skilled and experienced spies can combine these skills, running them alongside one another, to create a smoother and sometimes faster path to recruitment. But it takes a very high degree of confidence to pull this off undetected. Often, it is cleaner and easier to think about each stage in isolation.

Commonality

These techniques are, arguably, the softest of the four types. They are used to position spy and target in a similar zone, thereby enhancing the latter's willingness to share information. It can't be too problematic to share information with someone who is already expert in a particular field, or who has experienced similar life events. Can it? Another way of thinking about commonality techniques is that they seek actively to remove a sense of threat in the conversational sphere. For this reason, they may be more effective with targets who tend towards introversion, are relatively high in agreeableness, are less open, high in conscientiousness and who display signs of neuroticism.

A couple of examples. First: establishment of mutual interest. This might sound obvious but it can sometimes be tempting to highlight differences and seek conflict in conversations, even with relatively new acquaintances. If you doubt that, I invite you to think about how the topics of the War on Terror, the Trump presidency and Covid-19 non-pharmaceutical interventions shaped personal interactions. For the spy, it is important to put aside strong feelings about any such matters and instead to emphasise what they have in common (real or imagined) with a target. Shared cultural interests, political orientation, religious faith, experiences (pleasurable, challenging or traumatic), pastimes and hobbies are all fair game in this respect. The possibilities are legion.

A second, related, technique, is establishment of associations in common. Shared associates might be friends, colleagues, comrades-in-arms, clients, service providers, or any other group that works in a specific context. These are more difficult to feign than mutual interests but it is possible with a little imagination. And it is a very powerful technique. Nearly every meeting I have had in recent years has kicked off with recitations of common associates active in the private intelligence and security fields. At the end of this, all involved have greater confidence in their interlocutors and are more relaxed about sharing information with 'one of us'. Me included. None of us is immune to elicitation, though the effectiveness of specific techniques will vary from person to person.

Reciprocity

These tactics are also great confidence builders. At their simplest, they involve a straightforward exchange. The spy offers up some apparently sensitive information, unbidden, to gauge whether this triggers the human response of perceived obligation. If the target has a developed sense of fair play and is not constrained in that moment by their wider obligations (to their employer, to their family, to king and country) they may naturally offer up some confidential information in return. This can be chalked up as a win by the spy without further ado. It would set the tone for future exchanges. Alas, life is rarely so straightforward but it does happen. At the less dramatic end of the scale, reciprocity may involve simply volunteering a confidence about one's emotional self. This tactic may help the target to open up about themselves in turn, especially if they score high on the agreeableness and openness scales. But perhaps it would trigger someone who is highly neurotic or fail to land with someone who is particularly introverted, leaving the user of the tactic stranded in a conversational no-man's land. Such calls are made on the hoof and mark out the real pro at work.

Ego

We get into riskier territory when using tactics that appeal to a target's ego. Relatively benign, but still capable of backfiring, is the ploy of displaying ignorance. The idea is to tell someone that you could do with their help to understand a topic better. That topic might be the target, of course, suggesting phrases such as 'I can't read you at all' or 'You sure are a complicated character.' The target may respond with a chuckle and some insights into their personality but they also might reply 'I'm not very interesting,' or 'There's not much to understand.' The outcome will be dependent in part on the target's personality type. An extrovert is much more likely to respond positively than an introvert. Be careful trying it with someone who is highly neurotic, though: you may get more than you have time for.

Another approach under this heading is straightforward: flattery. Most people like to feel that they are expert in a subject or have special insights. This ploy might be considered a variant of displaying ignorance, as it is designed to place the target in a seeming position of superiority to the spy, capable of dispensing valuable wisdom to them. Again, it is worth noting that, for many people, their specialist subject is themselves. A spy might say to their target, 'You seem to have great self-awareness, so I'd be interested to hear how you would respond to [insert imagined scenario].' But some targets will see through this stratagem very quickly, especially those who are genuinely self-aware. In certain circumstances, this approach would fail the FBI's elicitation definition, as it is not 'easily disguised'. Handle with care.

Provocation

Handle provocation techniques with even greater care. These are highest risk and would-be users are well-advised to try them in benign settings before going 'into battle' with a real target. First up is the use of deliberately false statements, delivered in an attempt to provoke the target into setting the record straight. This is a close relative of the display of ignorance but can be more powerful. Equally, it runs the risk of the target writing off the spy as a charlatan. Targets may be particularly sensitive about false statements involving themselves, depending on their personality type. Take, for example, a statement such as 'I gather that you aren't enjoying your job right now', made to someone that the spy knows is quite content in their current role. A highly agreeable target may reply, 'Oh, I don't know where you got that idea. I have just been promoted to human resources manager and I'm really enjoying using my people skills to deal with personnel problems.' Great. That would reveal a lot about the target in one go. However, a target who scores low on agreeableness might come back with 'Who the hell told you that pack of lies? I'll wring their neck.' Granted,

THE PARADOXICAL POWER OF ELICITATION

this would tell the spy something potentially valuable but the gambit would be unlikely to advance her relationship with the target.

USE OF QUESTIONS

So much for the methods of seeking information without asking. But questions can be part of the elicitation armoury. For a start, there is a whole suite of questions that are in common social use and are helpful to kick-start conversations: 'What do you do?'; 'How do you know the host?'; 'Do you live nearby?'. A spy will be comfortable using these niceties as springboards for more inventive exploration of a target. Indeed, in certain circumstances, avoidance of their use could raise suspicions. Spies pay attention to what is expected of them, as well as to the unexpected. Beyond these icebreakers, there is even room for some closed-ended questions: that is, questions that can be answered with a simple 'yes' or 'no'. Amateur spies may avoid closed-ended questions, perhaps because they mix up elicitation with debriefing (we'll come back to the latter in Chapter Eight, p. 244). But, used sparingly and with self-awareness (there are few situations in which it is helpful to come across as a member of the Spanish Inquisition), they can short-circuit a lot of otherwise exploratory discussion. Why mess about when establishing whether someone is vegetarian or teetotal, for example? This information seems trivial but can be of great help in building a holistic picture of an individual. And the yes or no answer leads easily to more open-ended questions, which invite the target to bare their soul. Furthermore, if the questioner allows a short silence after a monosyllabic response, the target is likely to fill the conversational vacuum by offering up additional information unprompted.

At a certain point, once a good degree of rapport has been established, even leading questions can be useful. 'The prime minister is a corrupt fool, isn't he?' can draw the target into an unguarded reprise of everything that they think is wrong with the government of the day. Or cause them to spring to the prime minister's defence. Revealing, either way.

Closed-ended or open-ended, leading or neutral, the crucial thing is that the spy will listen to the target's responses to their questions. Actively.

HOW TO LISTEN

Active listening is a skill and it takes practice. You have probably noticed that many people's idea of a conversation is to wait their turn, politely or otherwise, so that they can then express their views on the subject under discussion. Or to steer it in another direction of their preference. Spies, like therapists and natural empaths, take a different approach. They listen patiently, reflect their understanding of a target's comments back to them and ask them to expand, if appropriate. They will validate their target's opinions and thoughts. This means more than cocking one's head and saying, 'That's fascinating.' Much better to say something like 'I hadn't thought of it like that but I think you may be onto something. If I understand you correctly, you are suggesting . . .' This serves the dual purposes of flattering a target's ego through validation and inviting them to expand on their thoughts, without expressly asking them to do so.

Of course, the techniques described above are not exhaustive. But they are a good review of the *types* of techniques available to the spy. And to you. There is plenty of room for use of imagination in developing other techniques. To which end, it is useful to have some understanding of what drives people to share information. Where better to turn for this than to the US Defense Counterintelligence and Security Agency (DCSA), whose stated role is to 'protect America's trusted workforce, trusted workspaces, and classified information'? This agency lists the following as 'human factors that enable elicitation':

'• Desire to seem polite and helpful, even to strangers.
'• Desire to seem knowledgeable or well informed.
'• Desire to seem competent.
'• Desire to feel appreciated and believe we are contributing to something important.
'• Tendency to gossip.
'• Tendency to correct others.
'• Tendency to underestimate the information's value.
'• Tendency to believe others are honest.
'• Tendency to complain.
'• Tendency to show empathy toward others.
'• Tendency to be indiscrete [sic], especially when emotionally charged.'[1]

Of the above, I would highlight 'tendency to believe others are honest' because this is the closest the DCSA's document gets to discussing what I believe to be the most important aspect of elicitation: building trust.

The late Judith E. Glaser wrote and talked extensively about the neuroscience of conversations. She developed the concept of conversational intelligence,[2] highlighting the chemical effects of different styles of interaction. According to Glaser, well-handled conversations can stimulate production of 'feel-good'

1 DCSA, *Elicitation*. https://www.dcsa.mil/Portals/91/Documents/CI/DCSA-CI_Elicitation_2021.pdf
2 Judith E. Glaser, *Conversational Intelligence: How Great Leaders Build Trust and Get Extraordinary Results*, Bibliomotion, Inc, 2014.

biochemicals such as dopamine, oxytocin and endorphins. Release of the neurotransmitter oxytocin is associated with feelings of wellbeing, safety and trust.[1] Glaser asserts that trust 'primes the pump so that people can get intimate and feel open enough to be inclusive, interactive, and intentional'.[2] I couldn't agree more.

So, trust is central to elicitation. Furthermore, in a final paradox, elicitation through trust-building can benefit the target of this skill, not just the person doing the eliciting. As the following story illustrates.

* * *

I met Maria in a strip joint in Roppongi, Tokyo's red-light district.

It was an upmarket joint, if such a thing exists, full of suited salarymen and their international guests. The décor was bare and scrubbed clean. Leather banquettes that smelled faintly of disinfectant were arranged around a square stage clad in black and white marble tiles. On the stage, young women – all of them undeniably beautiful, and from all over the world – writhed around polished steel dancing poles. Glassy-eyed men sipped on astronomically priced martinis and leered or pretended to look away. The soundtrack was 'Closer' by Nine Inch Nails, on repeat: I may have been the only person who noticed, at that surreal hour sometime after 1am.

Overhead, rows of air-conditioning units whirred away the smoke of a hundred cigarettes, replacing it with a slight chill. Somehow, this heightened the inhumanity of the place and left

1 Interview with Glaser in *Psychology Today*, 2019. https://www.psychologytoday.com/us/blog/conversational-intelligence/201905/the-neuroscience-of-conversations
2 Glaser, *Conversational Intelligence*, p. 158.

me feeling more unsettled than I had been when my hosts insisted on taking me there after buying me dinner. I had read somewhere that it would be considered rude not to accept such hospitality when a guest of corporate Japan. Or maybe that was the excuse I gave my twenty-six-year-old self, in 1996.

My hosts were senior clients of the Japanese stockbroking company I was working for then. Well-off, educated and sophisticated. Also, red-faced with drink, garrulous and lavishly generous. They bought me cocktails faster than I could drink them, packets of cigarettes, cigars, and the companionship of the young woman sat to my left. A stripped-back companionship, it must be said. 'Closer' was playing too loud for any conversation between us, even as Maria pressed herself closer.

This was maybe a good thing. Maria – tall, slim, with waist-length black hair that matched a figure-hugging sheer dress – was not a conversationalist. Instead, she spent her time sipping champagne, forcing a smile and trying to slip her hand into mine. In between these efforts, she made regular visits to the toilets, reappearing each time a little enlivened. One of my companions – Kimura-san to me and Kim to his friends – shouted questions in her repeated absences. Was I having a good time? Was Maria the 'right girl' for me? I would nod and smile, which emboldened Kimura-san to up the ante in the hospitality battle with his two colleagues. He pressed a wad of yen into Maria's hand. She secured the cash in a fake Louis Vuitton crossbody bag, stood up and took my hand, to tug me to my feet. Kimura-san and company smiled and nodded vigorously, pointing to a red door behind us.

I followed Maria through the door, into a narrow hallway. There were three cubicles on each side, covered with red damask curtains. A menacingly large Japanese man stood at the end of the hallway. He pointed Maria towards one of the cubicles and she led me in. It was a square space, with a small leather bench set against a gold-painted back wall and bare wood floors except for a soft mat in front of the bench: I could imagine what that was for. She pulled the curtain closed behind us and pushed me onto the bench. Standing in front of me, she writhed her hips and ran her hands across her body. Then, with experienced fluidity and lack of self-consciousness, she began to inch her dress upwards, over her thighs.

I felt my face redden.

'Please don't do that,' I said. Maria looked confused, so I said again, 'Please don't do that. I don't want it.'

'You don't want it?' She straightened her skirt. 'What's wrong? Don't you like my body?'

Oh, God, I had insulted her without intending to.

'It's not that.'

'Well, there is something wrong,' she said. 'I had better go and give your friend his money back.'

Now, as well as insulting Maria, I was going to insult my hosts. This was getting out of hand. I groped for something to explain away my awkwardness. 'It's just that I recently got married. It wouldn't feel right.'

That seemed to do the trick. Maria sat down beside me and pointed at my left hand.

'You are not wearing a ring.' True.

'No. It was too tight, so I have sent it to be adjusted.' False.

She fished a carton of cigarettes out of her bag and waved it in front of me. It was only then that I noticed the cinema-style ashtrays set into the wall. I took a cigarette and covered my embarrassment with the ritual of patting my pockets to find a lighter. She beat me to it and held up a lacquered Dupont to me. I was grateful. If I had been forced to light her cigarette, I would not have been able to disguise my shaking hands.

'Okay then,' she said. 'But we have ten minutes. What do you want to do instead?'

'How about we just chat? At least we can hear each other here. Why don't you tell me about yourself?'

She shook her head. 'I don't want to talk about me.'

She was the uncomfortable one now. The idea of revealing anything about herself other than her body seemed to frighten her. I took a step back, instinctively.

'Of course. We don't need to do that. I don't like to talk about my background, either.'

'Why not?'

'It's upsetting,' I said. 'I lost someone very close to me when I was young and it made me suicidal.'

Maria laid a hand on my knee and turned her head to blow cigarette smoke away from me. I noticed for the first time that her musky perfume went well with the smell of tobacco. 'I'm sorry,' she said. 'I have also thought about suicide.'

'There are many reasons why people do,' I said.

'Yes. Especially in this game.'

'Can't comment on that,' I said. 'I know next to nothing about this game. As you can probably guess.' I smiled at her and stretched out a hand to show that the nicotine had done nothing to calm my jitters. Maria laughed. 'I don't know why women choose to get into it.'

Her smile faded. 'They don't choose.' She took a long draw on her cigarette and spoke as she exhaled, the smoke obscuring her pain. 'At least, I didn't.'

I changed the subject then, telling Maria about my imagined wife's work as an imagined therapist. I said, 'She has taught me the importance of respecting boundaries. I can see you don't really want to talk about all this, so we shan't.' I led Maria back to our table, where Kimura-san received us with winks, nudges and giggles. I guessed that his colleagues would soon be paying for me to enjoy more 'private dances'.

They did. Several. It was nearly 5am when we left the bar, by when the three men had each paid for two sessions. In total, I spent an hour with Maria in the privacy of our booth. I didn't ask her another question after my initial misstep. I didn't need to. We spent the following five 'dances' holding hands, both fully clothed, as she slowly revealed her harrowing story.

Maria's mother was Brazilian. Her father, whom she had never met, Dutch. She had been raised in Amsterdam, where her mother taught at a senior school. As a young girl, she had dreamed of going to university, in Antwerp for some reason, and becoming an academic. Her school grades justified the dream. Amsterdam's permissive drugs culture destroyed it. Experiments with cannabis and mushrooms led to dabbling in harder drugs, straining her relationship with her mother. She was desperate to get away from home by the time she was sixteen and took work in the red-light district, initially as a wait-ress. Nobody was inclined to check her age and, soon enough, she drifted into sex work, to fund an increasingly vice-like cocaine habit. A familiar story amongst her fellow sex workers, she told me. But at least she had access to clinics and charitable support in Amsterdam.

Some years before I met her, a Japanese client handed her his business card, which said that he was a modelling agent. Spies aren't the only people to use cover. He persuaded her to travel to Tokyo, at her own expense, where he promised to fund a photographer who would produce a portfolio that would cata-pult her onto the catwalks. All nonsense, of course.

After a twelve-hour flight, and battling a seven-hour time difference, Maria found herself lodged in a cheap hostel with other young women from around the world. She was yet to leave that accommodation. Over the coming weeks, her 'agent' supplied her and her cohabitees with drugs, took their pass-ports for 'safekeeping' and sold their bodies. Maria turned tricks for clients in business hotels, on the nights that she wasn't working as a hostess in Roppongi. A minder was assigned to her twenty-four hours a day, robbing her of privacy and dignity. She lived with the risk of disease and violence every day but she was denied medical or emotional support by her tormentors, who controlled all the money she earned.

No wonder Maria found it difficult to trust men.

I felt sick as we left the club, my hosts boasting about their own exploits behind the damask curtains. Maria was in the lobby, accompanied by a pinched-looking man I took to be her minder. I smiled but she refused to acknowledge me. Impulse seized me and I approached her with all the bank-notes I had in my wallet. Sterling, dollars and yen. As she took the 'tip' from me, the minder pretended to be interested in a flyer he was holding. I leaned towards her and risked a whispered question. At that stage, neither she nor I had anything to lose.

'Will you tell me your real name, please?'

Startled, she stared at the pinched man for a second. He remained bent over the flyer. Music was still playing loud enough to drown anything she said. She reached up and pretended to kiss my cheek, whispering her full name as she did so.

Nils thanked me for this information, when I met him at his embassy a couple of days later. He told me that the Netherlands was committed to working against people traffickers and took seriously the rights of its citizens in other countries. He promised to take up Maria's case and let her know, somehow, that she could find support at the embassy. It would not be a problem to issue her with a fresh passport, if she could provide them with details about her family in Amsterdam.

It was all I could do. I had no proof of criminality, only Maria's word for what had happened to her. It was for the embassy to decide whether the Japanese police should be involved. So, I thanked Nils and turned to go.

'Thank you again,' he said. 'But I must say I am very surprised.'

I hesitated. 'What do you mean?'

'Well, in my experience, the most difficult thing is getting victims like this to talk in the first place. They are usually terrified. Why should she trust you, a stranger who was in a strip bar, after everything she has been through?'

I gestured to my slim build and glasses. 'Maybe I don't look threatening.'

Nils smiled. 'No, it's more than that,' he said. 'What do you do?'

'I'm a stockbroker.'

'Sorry to hear that,' he said. 'Maybe you should change career. You could become a social worker.'

I smiled back. 'That really doesn't sound like me.'

'Or a spy,' he said.

* * *

RECAP

- Elicitation is a set of techniques used to obtain information subtly, without the target being aware that information is being sought.
- Paradoxically, use of elicitation is less likely to produce a defensive reaction than transparent and direct questioning, so long as it is done well.
- Planning is essential for successful elicitation. Spies know what information they seek and how they will set about it. But they remain flexible in the moment.
- Elicitation techniques can be grouped under four broad headings: commonality; reciprocity; appeal to ego; and provocation. Provocation is the riskiest gambit.

- Techniques can be tailored to – and exploratory of – the Big Five personality traits: extroversion; agreeableness; openness; conscientiousness; and neuroticism.
- Questions have a place in elicitation, too. Avoidance of questions altogether could appear suspect in many social and professional settings.
- It is important to develop the skill of active listening. Becoming a good conversationalist helps win targets' trust. Trust helps other open up.

*   *   *

We are all citizens of the world. We all have responsibilities to our fellow citizens. It is not only that we should handle encounters with people like Maria sensitively. I implore you to use the skill of elicitation only for positive ends. There is a tendency to think of elicitation as being only for the benefit of the elicitor. But it can also play an important part in building collaborative alliances, which is where it comes in for you.

The difference between elicitation and commonplace conversations is that the former is preceded by an element of planning. Planning to meet certain ends. There is nothing inherently wrong in that. Arguably, this approach introduces efficiency into our dealings with others, which may save everyone time in the long run. We have all experienced the occasional frustrating conversation, perhaps with an ill-prepared salesperson, in which our interlocutor seems to take forever to get to the point. Furthermore, use of elicitation techniques should create a more comfortable environment for your target goals allies. As noted above, few of us like to feel that we are being interrogated. Conversely, many of us like to feel that we are part of a meaningful dialogue, in which our views are heard and given careful consideration.

This is about becoming a good conversationalist. If it wins you new allies along the way, so much the better. Allow me, then, to lay out a roadmap for use of elicitation once you have established repeated contact with a goals ally.

STEP ONE

Make a plan. Know what you want from an encounter. This should be a familiar refrain by now. In this case, it means being clear in your own mind about what information you would ideally like from your target.

STEP TWO

When you have defined your desired outcomes – the information that you need – stop and ask yourself, 'Is this realistic?' It is important not to overreach. Just as your objective in a first meeting is to secure a follow-up, the goal in subsequent meetings should be SMART. Remember that? Specific, Measurable, Achievable, Relevant and Time-bound.

Working backwards, the time limit is set. It is the duration of your meeting, which is often predictable, especially during the working day. Relevance will be determined by how you see a goals ally helping you to achieve a broader objective. This will be different in every case and is likely to evolve, so allow yourself some flexibility on this matter. Just make sure you set out to seek information that will align with your evolving goals. We have covered achievable: keep checking in with yourself that your objective is realistic. If you doubt that it is, adapt and make it so. Measurable is obvious: you will either find out what you want to know or you won't. Finally, specific takes a bit of thinking about. It is tempting to set an objective such as 'to find out about my target's philanthropic activities'. There is value in that, for sure. But think how much more value there would be in 'identifying two philanthropic programmes to which my target has contributed'. You might add 'and how'. But think carefully before you do that. Ask yourself again if it would be realistic.

STEP THREE

Part of the answer to that is contained in this step. Write a character sketch of your target. Yes, write it down. But preferably not in a way that identifies the target and not on an accessible database. Respect your target's right to privacy and be careful not to transgress any data protection laws. In general, it is safer to avoid recording any sensitive data about a target, as defined by the GDPR,[1] even though you are not acting as an organisation.

Writing a character sketch may be a daunting prospect but it needn't be. Nobody expects you to be a professional psychologist. Most spies aren't either but they routinely make character assessments, mentally and in writing. It is also likely that you will have only limited information on which to base your assessment, following one meeting and a remote targeting exercise. But you will have some and a little often goes a long way, once you start to think about it. It may help to use a model when producing your assessment. This might be the Big Five personality traits outlined on p. 106. Or you may want to dive a little deeper and use the Myers–Briggs model of sixteen personality

1 ICO, Special Category Data. https://ico.org.uk/for-organisations/uk -gdpr-guidance-and-resources/lawful-basis/a-guide-to-lawful-basis/ lawful-basis-for-processing/special-category-data/#scd1

types.[1] You could always test your own personality first, using one of the many free resources to be found online. This would help you to start thinking about how personality assessments work from the outset.

STEP FOUR

Think again about specific elicitation techniques and consider which ones are most likely to work with your target. Whichever model of personality assessment you have chosen, you now have a system against which to make such assessments. Cross-reference your thinking against the DCSA's list of 'human factors that enable elicitation' (p. 113). Do all this rigorously and as objectively as possible. A stratagem won't work just because you like it and think you would be good at it. As in so much else that we cover in this book, this is not about you. Cultivate that aspect of yourself that is outward looking and empathetic. Try to imagine how you would feel in your target's place, when faced with various ploys. Trust your instincts.

STEP FIVE

Select one of the techniques you think might work. Just one, unless you are already well experienced in elicitation. To try more than one – maybe two, at a stretch – as a novice is asking for trouble. You are likely to come across as forced, insincere or, worse, annoying. If you discover in a meeting that you are not making headway towards the information you seek, relax and revert to relationship building. There will often be a next time.

1 https://eu.themyersbriggs.com/en/tools/MBTI

Better to err on the side of caution, practise patience and be ready to accept a soft landing rather than risk a crash and burn.

Throughout, consciously guide yourself back to the idea of collaboration. Is what you are setting out to achieve about building an alliance in a collaborative way? Or is it about exploiting your target? Always make it the former. This will be to your advantage in the longer term. Part of this is thinking about what you can offer your target in return for their help. An element of your offer might simply be providing a listening ear, without judgement. You may be surprised to find out how much a target values something so simple.

Then, get out there and give it a go, like Tom.

CASE STUDY

Tom was delighted to receive a call from Moussa, a week after sending his email. Moussa was in town, visiting his mother, and suggested they meet for coffee. Tom checked out the venue the day before they were due to meet and identified a quiet table in a booth of its own. He arrived early the following day, to make sure he could nab the table, where Moussa joined him later, saying that he had only half an hour to spare.

Following the meeting, Tom opened a folder on his PC called 'Moussa', being careful not to include his surname or other identifying details. He saved a new document to the file and made the following notes:

'I met Moussa on 2nd June at High Roller Coffee. The meeting lasted forty minutes, most of which we spent discussing his career. He told me that he had been a very shy teenager, partly because he had been bullied by racists in his class, who made fun of his accent. Stung by this, he found free elocution lessons online and turned to acting to express himself, appearing in various school plays. It wasn't long before he was regularly playing the lead in productions of Shakespeare and Arthur Miller. His family was not well off, so he was lucky to win a scholarship to a major acting school. After that, he auditioned for both screen and stage until his breakthrough, when he was cast in a middling role for a TV detective series set in London. His performances on that show led to approaches from high-profile agents and he was able to take his pick. His choice of agent suggested that he should move away from TV and opened doors for him in Europe, as he speaks fluent French. A Parisian filmmaker took Moussa under his wing and his career on the continent took off.

Moussa said that he misses his hometown and finds Parisians difficult. He intends to return home soon, to be nearer his elderly parents. Interestingly, he hopes one day to establish his own fashion brand.

I spoke only a little about myself, mentioning that I had also been bullied at school because of my sexuality. I said that I felt I was facing similar challenges to Moussa, as a member of a minority group. I asked him to expand on his experiences of racism and he said that, ultimately, they had made him stronger and more determined.

We got on well and he agreed to meet me again before he returns to Paris, so that I can show him my portfolio. We shall meet at the Grey Eagle pub at 7pm on 8th June.

Moussa is surprisingly introverted, for an actor. He speaks quietly and with humility, often apologising if he feels he is dominating the conversation. He has a very agreeable personality, seemingly averse to conflict, and he puts others first. He is clearly open to new ideas and experiences, willing even to live in a city that he finds difficult and to change course in his career at the suggestion of others. He demonstrates high conscientiousness, making sure his family is looked after. He arrived bang on time and, before we left, he gathered up our coffee cups and returned them to the counter, with a tip for the barista. She asked for his autograph and he wrote a sweet message for her on the side of a paper cup. He is clearly sensitive and thoughtful but not neurotic. He has taken time to appraise himself and understand his place in the world.

At our meeting on 8th June, I will aim to find out whether Moussa has offered mentoring support to individual youngsters in the past and, if so, what form it took and what led him to do it. I think he will respond well if I tell him about my voluntary work at the Saplings Children's Hospice and what drives me to give up my time for it. I also get the sense that he would like to be appreciated for his contributions to the world away from acting.'

What is Tom up to? He practised active listening during his time with Moussa and spent considerable time reflecting on their interaction, analysing Moussa's actions and words. This is because he next aims to find out what makes Moussa tick, before asking him for specific support. In other words, he is planning to explore Moussa's motivations. The role of motivations is pivotal for agent recruitment in the espionage world. It is equally important in our personal and professional interactions, especially when we ask something of someone. We shall examine this topic in the next chapter (p. 138).

But, first, a footnote. Elicitation is an art. Even the most skilful practitioner sometimes draws a blank. It is not possible to work out in advance which of the various possible approaches will work. And, sometimes, a gamble pays off, as the following story illustrates.

* * *

I have met many lieutenant colonels over the years. None more aptly named than 'Colonel Attack'.

Rumbek, South Sudan, 2010. A year before independence. After over twenty years of ruinous civil war, the Southern People's Liberation Army (SPLA) – a guerrilla movement – was close to its objective of separating the broadly Christian-animist south from Islamist Khartoum. In preparation for an independent future, President Salva Kiir had decided that some of his militiamen should be transferred to a civilian intelligence agency that would later become the National Security Service (NSS). I was head of a private team stationed in Rumbek for three months to train twenty of them in skills necessary for service in the NSS.

It was not going well for me.

The training was heavy going. The recruits were good students, despite many of them having little formal education. They were curious, avid and attentive learners and it was a pleasure working with them. But it was difficult to take the bush fighter out of the would-be intelligence officer. Each morning, rather than jackets, they would sling AK47s and belts of ammunition across the backs of their chairs. During interrogation exercises, their instinct was to bully and shout rather than coax information out of their targets. The threat of violence was never far away. I couldn't shake the feeling that I was wasting my time. Years later, as I read accounts of the NSS's evolution into an organ of repressive control, that feeling returns to me.

The terrain was also challenging. The temperature was often above 35°C and rarely below 25°C, even at night. Our compound was basic, with limited air conditioning hit by frequent power outages. There was a pool on-site, if I ever fancied a dip in untreated tepid water luminous with a layer of green algae. There was a smell of death about it. Our meals – thrown together by a cheerful Malaysian man who picked his nose and was never seen to wash his hands – were bland but unhealthy; hunks of meat from dubious sources swimming in oil, accompanied by a stiff maize meal porridge. It was unwise to step outside the secure compound, where groups of lawless youths infested streets that lacked much else. Inside the gates, dangerous snakes and other creatures crawled between – and sometimes inside – our standalone rooms. One day, I felt an unusual weight under the lapel of my jacket – Heaven only knows why I wore a jacket in that heat – and flipped it inside out to find a scorpion nesting there. After that, I checked my shoes and clothes before dressing every morning.

There was little to do in the evenings, as my team and I digested the gristle from dinner. We could buy bottled beer from a rudimentary bar, staffed by the smiling Malaysian. But one was enough to cause a banging hangover. Otherwise, it was a case of heading back to our rooms, to read, though I had run out of reading material. There were no televisions. And no WiFi or cell phone coverage, so no calls home. This compounded the homesickness I felt because I was missing my partner's birthday.

I was also physically unwell, from the heat, poor diet, lack of exercise and an attack of sciatica, from which I suffer periodically. Anyone who has experienced sciatica knows that it is a relentless, tears-inducing pain that radiates from the lower back, down one leg to the sole of the foot, making it very difficult to focus on anything else. Few positions, standing, sitting or lying, offer relief from it. The nearest useable clinic was probably in Juba, a day's drive away on mud roads to the south. I had no option but to put up with the pain. We were six weeks into the three months of the deployment and I was considering requesting a rotation out of it. In other words, I was considering giving up. Few would have blamed me.

But I felt passionately about South Sudan. I had heard harrowing tales of maltreatment of its people by Khartoum-sponsored militia: of systematic rape, torture and murder. One Juba resident told me that he had witnessed soldiers tie up his civilian neighbours in hessian sacks, before laughing as they threw them into the Nile. I admired the perseverance and resilience of the SPLA's fighters, who set out to avenge these injustices and protect their countrymen. I believed theirs was a just cause that deserved to be more widely known about. I was incensed that the British government, amongst others, refused to acknowledge what was happening and remained wedded to a policy of pursuing a united Sudan.

My time running the intelligence course offered me unrivalled access to current and former soldiers, all with extraordinary tales to tell. All burning with the injustices of oppression by their northern masters. So, I resolved to stay put and to spend my spare time recording their experiences. Later, I would write formal accounts of their struggles, their ideals and the values that drove them, to share with western diplomats and journalists. I would do my bit to support a people that I felt had been denied a fair hearing, whose voices were only heard in the west if on the basketball court (South Sudanese people are strikingly tall). If that meant pushing on in the heat, wincing with the pain of sciatica, so be it. What was that discomfort compared with the plight of my hosts?

I spent breaks, lunchtimes and evenings with my students, listening to them describe their time with the SPLA. The drills and the dramas, the camaraderie and the camouflage, the boredom and the bombs, the hand grenades and the hand-to-hand combat. It was thrilling stuff but I struggled to connect emotionally. They were all reserved, refusing to explore beyond the strictly factual. Reluctant to reveal the man behind the uniform. And, when I pressed them to explain what drove them, what they felt about their experiences, they all said one thing. 'You should talk to Colonel Attack.' Why?

Because he had been a child soldier.

Colonel Ajak Gai Atak was born in 1983, the year that the second war of independence started in South Sudan. It was to continue until 2005, so Atak was more than a war baby. He was a war child, war adolescent and war adult. Atak was formed by, steeped in, the horror of armed conflict. War defined him.

He was now opposite me in my convent-like room, he sitting on an upright wooden chair that creaked under his weight, me perched on the bed, twisting to find any angle that would allevi-ate my sciatic agony. Atak had laid his rifle between us on the stained lino floor. My air-conditioning unit had packed up and the smell of sweat in that room was powerful. I had thrown open the windows and we could hear jackals howling in the background. Every so often, a thud and a manic fluttering of wings. Unidentified flying bugs – some the size of walnuts – would collide with the metal gauze mosquito screens, disorien-tated by the flickering light from an uncovered, low-wattage bulb that swung above us from a grimy cord.

He was a magnificent man, six foot eight and heavy with muscle, his face etched with the ritual scars of the Dinka ethnic group. He sat immobile, other than chewing the kola nuts held in his left hand. He fixed dark, unblinking eyes on me. Not distrustful, exactly. More bemused. I was the first person ever to ask him to tell his story. Bemused, and obstinate. And impa-tient. He was scheduled to leave the course early the following day, to take up a position in the president's office. He had been offered promotion and now had little reason to indulge his head of training. But he had agreed to speak to me out of politeness.

Our discussion so far had proved frustratingly minimal throughout, circular at times. One typical exchange was:

'Please tell me about how you came to join the army.'

'My father said I must.'

'Must?'

'Yes. It was my duty.'

'Your duty? That's a powerful word. What do you think your father meant by that?'

'He meant that it was my duty to join the army.'

Our conversation was not meant to be an elicitation exercise but it became one and I was struggling. In part, this was because Atak was a difficult man to read. He was neither notably extroverted nor introverted, of middling agreeability, open in some ways and not in others, conscientious up to a point, not neurotic but with some evidence of paranoid thinking (unsurprisingly).

As with the others, there was no problem getting Atak to tell me the bare facts. I had learned that his father had gone away to fight while he was a baby and had returned on crutches. That Khartoum's militia men had invaded his village soon after and that he, his family and his neighbours had been forced out of their homes. They had trekked to find refuge over the border in Ethiopia. There, aged twelve, his father had cajoled him into joining an SPLA training camp. He had been a fast learner and was soon back in South Sudan, where he ran what he called 'spoiling errands' for his battalion: sabotage operations behind enemy lines, in which groups of boy soldiers dressed in civilian clothes planted explosives to blow up supply lines. Suicidal stuff.

After an hour or so of our interview, I had a handle on events and their chronology. But I had no clue about the truly interesting aspects of those events. How did they make Atak feel? What drove him to put his young life in danger, blowing up supply lines when he should have been kicking a football around with his mates? What did he and his fellow child soldiers talk about as they snuck behind enemy lines or ate around campfires as night fell? What was the long-term impact on him of militaristic life? How did he feel about it now? Was it worth it? Would he tell his own pre-teen son that he had a duty to join the SPLA?

I had tried numerous stratagems under the headings of commonality, reciprocity and appeal to ego. None had got me very far. For a start, it was difficult to find common ground between someone brought up in a developed country in peace time and someone born into conflict and strife. Conversationally, I had little to offer to invite reciprocity: Atak was not very interested in my emotions or feelings about anything. Why should he be? And Atak's ego was grounded, not in how his time as a child soldier had made him feel, but in his pride that he had served his country.

I could feel any control I had of the encounter slipping away from me and a sense of uselessness replacing it. I was an impostor. I had no place teaching these men how to elicit information from unwilling interlocutors. Obviously I wasn't up to that job myself. I was beginning to understand why they preferred breaking seats over people's backs to drawing them into shared confidences. Not that I was capable of that. I couldn't help but compare my slim frame and skinny arms with Atak's imposing physique. At that point, I felt so sapped of energy and in such pain that I doubted I would even be able to lift his AK47 from the floor.

I suggested a comfort break. Atak took himself outside to smoke, I went to the bathroom. I stayed there a long time, thinking. Atak would be leaving tomorrow, so I had no more time to build trust with him. But perhaps there was another way of getting him to talk. He was a proud man. Very proud. I needed to work with that, if I was to progress our conversation from facts to feelings. And the best way I could think of to do that was to use provocation: that most risky of techniques.

Did I dare?

Atak came back into my room as I left the bathroom. A cockroach scuttled across his path and I heard the crunch of cartilage as he flattened the pest with a size-thirteen army boot. I limped back to my bed, Atak watching me wordlessly, as he wiped his boot carefully on the almost-smooth door mat.

He retook his seat, yawned and looked at his watch with exaggeration.

'I need to sleep before I travel to see the president in Juba in the morning,' he said. 'Maybe we can finish this now?'

Part of me wanted nothing more. I had so far eked out the paracetamol in my med-kit, so I had a handful left. Maybe now I could bid Atak good night, take a double dose and snaffle some sleep, before getting on the satellite phone and asking to be airlifted out of there. Game over.

I reminded myself that I admired Atak and his compatriots. I was determined to tell their stories and my gut told me his was fascinating; the sort of human-interest story that can transform an audience's view of a conflict. If I stopped now, I would be letting him and the others down. I would be doing so because, to be brutally honest, I was scared. Of him. Of how he might react to what I had planned to say, while I brooded in my bathroom. I looked at the rifle for a few seconds, thinking of everything it represented in South Sudan's struggle for nationhood. Then I raised my head and met Atak's unrevealing eyes.

Fuck it, I thought.

Deep breath.

'Okay,' I said. 'I understand. Thank you for your time this evening. But, before we finish, I'd just like to hear what you think about something a contact of mine in Khartoum said. He is a military man and he said he was part of the group that came to your village.'

Atak looked unnerved, for the first time.

'What did he say, this *cockroach*?' He spat the word.

'He told me that the army had not come to fight you. They had come on a humanitarian mission. That they brought food, water and medical supplies to your village.'

'He is a liar,' said Atak. He lit another cigarette, not bothering to go outside this time.

'He is a decent man. I don't think he has ever lied to me.' Atak dragged deeply on his fag and stared at me as I shifted position, searching for relief in my lower back. I went on: 'My friend told me that he and his colleagues came to help you, with a message of peace from Khartoum and that you all ran away because . . .' I hesitated.

Atak broke in, 'Because what?'

I spoke low and slow, trying not to shrink from Atak's unrelenting gaze.

'Because you were all cowards.'

Atak sat, stunned, for several seconds. His eyes, so inexpressive until now, flashed with indignation, anger and resentment. Towards my Sudanese 'contact'? Or towards me, the messenger?

Suddenly, he stood up. Towered above me. Pointing at me.

'Why would you listen to what that cur said?' he demanded, voice low and menacing. I tried to keep the shake out of mine.

'I'm not saying he was right. But that is what Khartoum is saying. I can help you set the record straight.'

'You can help me?' Atak sounded incredulous. 'But you westerners know nothing. You sit in your houses in London with your TVs and your cars, while we fight for our freedom and see our loved ones murdered. You know nothing.'

'I know that, Colonel,' I said. 'That is why I asked to speak to you. Please tell me. Then I can tell the others.'

He hesitated a while and then, slowly, sat himself down. He wiped his brow, and his eyes, with his sleeve and his shoulders slumped.

Then the dam broke.

For the next two hours, Atak spoke and I listened. There was no opportunity for me to direct the flow of conversation, no chance of absorbing everything he had to say. So, I let the voice recorder do its job, with occasional nods and grunts of encouragement. Once, we stopped for me to fetch him water. Once, he bellowed with rage. Another time, recalling how his mother had used a wheelbarrow as a makeshift wheelchair to push his father to the safety of the refugee camp, he cried. This was more unsettling than his anger. He told me about the emotional pain that had driven him to fight, his commitment to his family, his community, his nation, his ideals. He told me what those ideals were. He cursed the Khartoum government and its agents but vowed to seek reconciliation with his perse-cutors, once his country was free. He spoke. And spoke. And I listened.

Finally, when he was spent, I clicked off the recorder and thanked Atak for his time and his honesty. I told him that I was humbled he had chosen to share such painful experiences with me and promised that I would do my best to tell South Sudan's story to the world.

He sat for a while, as though contemplating whether to say what was on his mind. He decided to speak, as he gathered up his AK47.

'You know what, Fisher? You are right. My country needs allies like you.' He nodded towards the recorder. 'I trust you to handle what I have said carefully. The world needs to know what we have suffered.' Heaving his rifle across his back, he added, 'And I am sorry to be leaving your course. What you are teaching us is vital for our new nation. I shall speak to the others before I go and tell them to learn from you. I know that they respect you, as I do.'

I stood up to see Atak out and was surprised to feel the pain in my back beginning to ease. Maybe I would stay on, after all.

* * *

RECAP

- Be careful to ensure you use the skill of elicitation only for positive ends, to build collaborative alliances. To do this, you will need to plan your encounters.
- Set objectives for the information you wish to recover and make sure they are SMART: Specific, Measurable, Achievable, Relevant and Time-bound.
- Develop a character assessment of your target goals ally, perhaps using the Big Five personality traits or the Myers–Briggs model of sixteen personality types.
- Don't be afraid to keep records of your encounters with targets, while developing an assessment of them.
- Respect targets' right to privacy and your legal obligations concerning data handling. Never record any sensitive data about an individual.
- Decide which of the elicitation techniques will work best with your target's personality and select one – or two at most – to use at your next encounter.
- Remind yourself that you seek collaboration. What can you offer to your target to make encounters enjoyable or useful for them too? A listening ear might be enough.

CHAPTER FIVE

The Enabling Power of Identifying Motivations

I wrote in Chapter 2 (p. 30) that cover is 'arguably the most important of a spy's repertoire of skills'. Fine, but cover for its own sake is pointless. We have learned that good cover is only ever in the service of something else. Its use provides an excuse for the spy to engage with a target in the first place. It establishes interests in common that become the soil for successful cultivation of that target. It sets a framework within which the techniques of elicitation are deployed. All this works towards the pivotal aspect of any agent recruitment: an appeal to motivations. In fact, if I were pushed to describe in one phrase a spy's job, that phrase would be: 'To identify and engage the motivations of intelligence targets.'

If the elicitation skill is used to get a target to SAY something, the motivations-engagement skill is used to get a target to DO something. In the case of the spy-target relationship, it is used by the spy to persuade the target to become an agent. In other words, to betray their country or their cause. To become a traitor.

Be in no doubt. Nobody would become an agent if they were not already strongly motivated to do so. The stakes are simply too high.

This brings us to the truth at the heart of espionage. The truth that makes it possible for spies to achieve the extraordinary, the unthinkable. It is that, in making a successful recruitment, a spy is only tapping into a willingness – maybe even a longing – that was in the target before they came along. The spy's brilliance is their ability to identify a target's dormant or semi-dormant motivations and create conditions in which the target feels able to realise them. In other words, identifying a target's motivations *enables* the spy to fulfil them. In turn, fulfilment of their motivations enables recruitment of the target as an agent.

Put another way, a good spy is fully aware that the trade is not about them. It is *all about the target*. A good spy will think of themselves as super-facilitator of a target's aspirations. Because good motivations come from within.

The KGB grasped the connection between a target's motivations and the spy's role as facilitator, noting that, 'In finding the target's dominant motives for behaviour, his wishes and his problems, the operative [the spy] must draw attention to himself as a person able to help the target fulfil his wishes and solve his problems [. . .] This is where the operative's creative thinking is manifested, and his art as a recruiter and an intelligence officer.'[1]

As the KGB's training notes make clear, there are two distinct stages involved in engaging a target's motivations. First is identifying what they are. Second is making clear to the target how the spy can help to satisfy them. We shall examine the all-important first stage here and turn to the second stage in the next chapter: 'The Pulling Power of the Perfect Pitch' (p. 175).

Spies are systematic thinkers. They tend to think about motivations in a systematic way. This frequently involves a model referred to as MICE.

1 KGB, 'Some Aspects of Training the Operative for Psychological Influence of Foreigners During Cultivation'. https://www.4freerussia. org/wp-content/uploads/sites/3/2019/11/Some-Aspects-of-Training-the-Operative.pdf

'MICE' is an acronym. It stands for Money, Ideology, Coercion and Ego. Some spies might tell you that all the possible motivations for a target to accept a recruitment pitch will fall neatly under one of those four headings. I disagree to a degree, but we'll come back to that.

MONEY

A fellow trainer of mine in South Sudan was fond of quoting the old business saying that 'Turnover is vanity, profit is sanity, but cash is king.' I am tempted to rephrase it for intelligence purposes: 'Coercion is irrationality, ego is vanity, ideology is sanity but cash is king.'

In the TV series *Succession*, Kendall Roy says during the eulogy to his father that money is 'the lifeblood, the oxygen of this wonderful civilisation that we have built from the mud'. Admittedly, this is florid language, but his point is undeniable. However distasteful it may be to some, money is what holds us together, both in body and soul and as a society. Often, those who rail against this fact are those who have the most of it. I have never met anyone stuck in poverty who expresses a distaste for money, even as they decry the inequalities of its distribution. Those who have no money long for some, those who have some strive for more, those who have the most hoard it jealously (with the occasional conscience-salving gesture presented as philanthropy). This is understandable for, as my father is fond of saying, 'Money may not buy you happiness, but it sure buys you a more comfortable form of misery.'

Money is unique in that it has a potential role to play at every level of Abraham Maslow's Hierarchy of Needs, which he postulates as applying to all humans. For those unfamiliar with this concept, it was first laid out by Maslow in 1943, in an article called

'A Theory of Human Motivation'.[1] The article was published in the journal *Psychological Review* and has been widely reproduced since, often diagrammatically in the form of a pyramid. At the base of the pyramid are 'physiological needs', such as for food, shelter and sleep. Above those come 'safety needs', or the search for defence from insecurity and danger. Then come 'love needs'; the longing for 'friends, or a sweetheart, or a wife, or children'. Below the apex of the triangle are 'esteem needs'; the desire for 'self-respect, or self-esteem, and for the esteem of others'; and, at the apex, 'the need for self-actualisation'. In Maslow's words, 'a musician must make music, an artist must paint, a poet must write, if he is to be ultimately happy. What a man *can* be, he *must* be. This need, we may call self-actualisation.'

The role of money in meeting physiological and safety needs is self-evident. Its place in realising love needs is less clear cut. But it is safe to say that wealthier people probably find it easier to attract friends and mates than their impoverished neighbours. They also, at least in western societies, tend to win esteem as if by right. Finally, financial security is very helpful in freeing up time for the would-be artist, writer or musician. We can't all be like T. S. Eliot, piecing together *The Waste Land* during breaks as a bank clerk.[2] But we could probably all be a bit like Gilbert Kaplan – a non-musician who went on to conduct international performances of Mahler's Second Symphony – if only we too had first 'amassed a fortune on Wall Street'.[3]

1 A. H. Maslow, 'A Theory of Human Motivation', 1943, *Psychological Review*, 50, 370–96. http://psychclassics.yorku.ca/Maslow/motivation.htm
2 Tristram Fane Saunders, 'A broken-down bank clerk and a month in Margate – how T. S. Eliot wrote The Waste Land', The Telegraph, 21 April 2022. https://www.telegraph.co.uk/books/what-to-read/broken-down -bank-clerk-three-months-margate-ts-eliot-wrote/
3 Mahler Foundation, Gilbert Kaplan. https://mahlerfoundation.org/mahler/contemporaries/gilbert-kaplan/

Furthermore, money is addictive. Some studies suggest that the optimal amount of money for human happiness is relatively modest: an annual income of about £120,000, according to Jan-Emmanuel De Neve, professor of Economics and Behavioural Science at the University of Oxford.[1] However, we all know that those who can generate significant amounts of money rarely give themselves a break from doing so, even when they are worth many billions of pounds. Warren Buffett, estimated net worth $122 billion,[2] continues to invest, despite turning 93 on the day I write these words.

It turns out that we quickly get used to a higher level of income and, of course, 'he who pays the piper calls the tune'. No wonder, then, that spies around the world explore their targets' financial vulnerabilities and seek to draw them into financial relationships at an early stage. As the KGB puts it, 'One of the CIA's documents on recruitment of agents puts great stress on drawing the target into a recruitment situation by offering him help at the initial stage of the relationship.' Of the 'various methods' cited by the KGB, two jump out: 'offering medical assistance' and 'offering financial aid'.

Unsurprisingly, it doesn't take much research to find high-profile cases of espionage in which money was the prime or a major motivation. Furnham and Taylor[3] describe the recently deceased Robert Hanssen as 'a senior FBI officer [who] provided extremely damaging intelligence to the Russians, mostly for cash'. Perhaps ironically, Hanssen was identified as the source of these leaks by Alexandr Shcherbakov, 'a down-on-his-luck

1 BBC Radio 4, Money Box: How much money do you need to be happy? https://www.bbc.co.uk/programmes/articles/1yxp6zSJHfjQh9T-Mx0j8LPL/how-much-money-do-you-need-to-be-happy
2 Bloomberg Billionaires Index, Warren Buffett. https://www.bloomberg.com/billionaires/profiles/warren-e-buffett/?leadSource=uverify%20wall
3 Furnham and Taylor, *The Psychology of Spies and Spying*, p. 64.

former KGB officer,' reportedly in return for a multi-million-dollar payout.[1] Money talks, on both sides of a divide.

The problem is that money tells many tales. In fact, it can be a bit of a traitor itself, its sudden presence revealing that a previously hard-up civil servant or corporate IT worker may be up to no good. Consequently, a good spy will be on the alert for any target that appears to be driven solely by financial gain. It is unlikely that such a person would be able to resist flaunting their new-found wealth, to somebody, somewhere, thus endangering their own security and that of their handler.

Another problem with money as a sole motivator is that it provides an agent with every incentive to make up intelligence that he judges his handler wants to hear. This appears to have been the case with a former Iraqi intelligence officer, Maj. Muhammad Harith. Harith reportedly fabricated intelligence about Baghdad's supposed weapons of mass destruction that contributed to the case for war made by the US and UK in 2003. His fantasies were initially considered corroboration of reporting from the notorious agent codenamed CURVEBALL, whose case we examine in Chapter Eight (p. 244), where we look at detection of deception. Between them, Harith and CURVEBALL caused immeasurable damage, not to Iraq (that war would probably have been waged regardless) but to the reputation of the western intelligence community. It has been reported that Harith acted as he did because 'he wanted a new home'.[2]

---

1 Jeff Stein, 'Riddle resolved: Who dimed out American traitor and super-spy, Robert Hanssen?', Newsweek, 1 November 2018. https://www.newsweek.com/who-dimed-out-american-traitor-super-spy-robert-hanssen-1196080
2 Peter Taylor, 'Iraq: The spies who fooled the world', BBC News, 18 March 2013. https://www.bbc.co.uk/news/uk-21786506

IDEOLOGY

Evidently, it is desirable that some other motivation should drive the would-be agent. Ideology is ideal.

It is difficult to think of anything so noble as risking one's life or liberty in the service of a political ideal. So long as it is the 'right' ideal, of course. We are not inclined to ascribe nobility to such British officials as Kim Philby, Donald Maclean and Guy Burgess, who all defected to the ideological sunlit uplands of the Soviet Union. As an aside, it is interesting to note that all three repudiated the principles of capitalism, yet all three were from wealthy families – as noted above, a moneyless person decrying money is a unicorn indeed. It is not easy to admire these three and their comrades Blunt and Cairncross, especially as their actions may have cost others their lives. But it is also not difficult to understand why they were prized by their Soviet handlers. Ideological commitment can be a powerful motivation. If it aligns with a spy's, it makes the latter's job very much easier.

EGO

A little bit of ego helps, too. After money, it might be the next biggest human driver. There is a fascinating scene in the movie *Schindler's List*, in which Oskar Schindler (played by Liam Neeson) tells the psychotic Amon Goeth (Ralph Fiennes) that 'power is when we have every justification to kill, and we don't [. . .] That's what the Emperor said. A man steals something, he's brought in before the Emperor, he throws himself down on the ground. He begs for his life, he knows he's going to die. And the Emperor . . . pardons him. This worthless man, he lets him go [. . .] That's power, Amon. That is power.' In a following scene, Goeth is enraged by a slave-boy's failure to clean his bathtub but, instead of following his instinct to shoot the boy, Goeth places two fingers on his forehead and says, 'I pardon you.'

Schindler has appealed to Goeth's ego. Specifically, in this case, to what he has identified as Goeth's God Complex. It doesn't last long. As the boy scurries away across the yard in front of Goeth's villa, his psychopathic tendencies prevail, and he raises his rifle to shoot the boy in the back of his head. But it was worth a try, and it is a neat illustration of the ego's role in motivations.

In typical espionage settings, egotistical motivations tend to be less dramatic. It may be that a civil servant in mid-life feels she has been passed over for promotion and desires some recognition of her talents. A narcissist may seek the thrill of 'specialness' that comes with his initiation into the world of spying. A frustrated academic wants to prove the rightness of their world view, in a case of ego and ideology fusing. A records-clerk in a government department may have been stung by the attitudes of his superiors and thirsts for revenge, as well as a few extra quid. In some instances, would-be agents just want to be *seen*. By someone, maybe anyone. In all cases, a good spy will use elicitation techniques to reveal these sometimes latent drivers on the journey towards recruitment.

COERCION

Finally, with apologies for disrupting the natural order of the MICE acronym, a brief word on coercion: the imposition of motivation from without, to help the target avoid harm, hurt or embarrassment. Whether it takes the form of blackmail, deprivation, threatening behaviour, or torture, it is rarely a good idea.

In fact, I would argue that anyone who provides intelligence in response to such tactics should not be considered an 'intelligence agent'. An agent is someone who works willingly with their handler, over an extended period. The victim of coercive techniques is more likely to seek an early way out of their 'relationship' with a handler, if not a means of exacting revenge. To reiterate, the best motivations come from within.

Recently, the MICE model has become a little unfashionable. Some experts consider it to be simplistic or incomplete and they present alternative schemas. Michael Smith, a former military intelligence officer turned journalist,[1] throws sex, tribal loyalty, revenge, patriotism and adventure into the mix.[2] Harry Ferguson lists, in addition to MICE, love, guilt, the need for help, revenge and boredom.[3] Furnham and Taylor bracket motivations under the headings of ideology and belief, money, excitement and friendship.[4] It may be that the MICE model has gained traction mainly because it is a handy mnemonic. But I would also posit that many other lists are simply expansions of, or variations on, the MICE theme. Tribal loyalty and patriotism, for example, could come under the Ideology heading. Revenge, adventure and excitement, under Ego. The need for help may be a variant of the Money motive, though not always.

It is more difficult to categorise sex, love and friendship within MICE. However, rather than simply junk a framework that has stood the test of time, I would suggest a small modification that may capture these strong emotional connections between two people. I would add 'Desire to Please' as a fifth category, thereby forming MICED.

1 https://www.michaelsmithauthor.com/index.html
2 Michael Smith, *The Anatomy of a Spy: A History of Espionage and Betrayal*, The History Press, 2019.
3 Ferguson, *Spy*, p. 100.
4 Furnham and Taylor, *The Psychology of Spies and Spying*, p. 56.

DESIRE TO PLEASE

A spy will certainly play on a target's desire to please, usually stopping short of offering sexual gratification in return. We have already explored how important the bonds of friendship and trust are in developing a relationship between a spy and their target. And there have doubtless been many cases over the years in which agent and handler have fallen in love, or there has been unrequited love on the part of one or the other. After all, the process of cultivation and recruitment is a form of courtship. But a desire to please is not usually enough to persuade a target to become a long-term agent. This is because they will, at some point, be handed over to another case officer and desire to please is not something that is easily transferred.

Conversely, when it comes to analysing and engaging the motivations of target goals allies, significant parts of the MICED model will not be in play. Money and Coercion can be ruled out and, if Ideology plays any part, it will only be in a very narrow sense. For your purposes, Ego and Desire to Please will come into their own. We shall explore this further below, and I shall propose a new way of thinking about motivation, with the acronym GRADE. But first, a tale about how I identified and appealed to Ego, to win over a recalcitrant border guard, long before I ever consciously applied this skill.

* * *

Many people are surprised to learn that I was twenty years old before I travelled abroad. What's more, I wasn't very good at it, first time round.

Money was tight during my childhood and family holidays were domestic affairs, staying at a friend's house, nearby in the country, while they jetted off on adventures around the world.

They were wonderful vacations but did little to equip me with the personal resources to negotiate airports and aeroplanes, border formalities, foreign currency management, language barriers and cultural differences. Money also prevented me from joining the annual school skiing trips. I would be one of a handful that stayed behind, sat in a classroom reading, under the resentful eye of the teacher who didn't get to go to the slopes that year. I tried to broaden my horizons in my gap year but, again, lack of money thwarted my plans, as described elsewhere.

So, by the time I got to university, I had rarely ventured far from the Midlands. I had spent one New Year's Eve in London and made it to the pebble beach of Aberystwyth a few times on day trips. Well-travelled, I was not. I remember being impressed during Freshers' Week, when one of my course-mates pulled a handful of change from his pocket and sorted through francs, Deutschmarks and Italian lire to find some ten-pence pieces for the Coke machine in our common room. Oh, to be so sophisticated.

My opportunity to join the globe-trotting grown-ups came in the long summer vacation between first and second years. I had joined a university society that aimed to support students from the former Soviet Union, following the fall of the Berlin Wall. The following academic year, I would be starting a course called 'The Economies of Former Communist Countries'. My interest in this area helped me win a scholarship to attend a semi-academic conference on the challenges of the transition from communism to capitalism. It was to run for a week in the magnificent Szirak Castle Hotel, an hour's drive away from Hungary's capital, Budapest. The scholarship covered accom-modation and catering for the full week, so all I needed to do was find money for the journey there and back as well as for the odd beer. That, and get hold of my passport.

The passport was straightforward enough. I collected it from the passport office in Victoria a few weeks after submitting my application. It was one of those old-fashioned UK documents, hard- back, stern black, and slightly too big to fit comfortably in the inside breast pocket of a jacket. A photo of me looking young, pallid and startled was glued onto the third page and there was a space for me to sign it, in black ink. It had a weighty importance about it, to go with the pomposity of the wording on the inside of its cover: 'Her Britannic Majesty requests and requires, etc.' I was very proud of it. But I forgot to sign it.

Getting hold of the money was a bit more difficult. I saved some from casual jobs: a tenner cash-in-hand for washing glasses behind the bar of my local rugby club; a little more for designing adverts for a local free paper, using QuarkXpress. My then-girlfriend, who was better with money than me, lent me some and my mum made up the balance with a loan from a small inheritance she had recently received. I decided to travel by ferry and train, which was much cheaper than flying. After paying for my tickets, I had about £150 at my disposal, which felt like a lot back then. It wasn't.

It was with clammy hands that I showed my passport to the immigration officer at Dover. He waved me through but called after me, 'Don't forget to sign your passport when you have a moment.' I felt a bit foolish, revealed as a rookie on my first international outing. But there was much to distract me, figuring out how to board a ferry to Calais and, from there, a train to Paris, with a change to get me to Zurich: exotic destinations, with confusing train stations to navigate. I still forgot to sign my passport, but none of the border officials in France or Switzerland noticed or cared.

The final leg of my epic journey was by night train from Zurich to Budapest, on a direct service run by the Hungarian railway company MÁV. The connection time at Zurich was tight and I struggled with the unfamiliar look and sound of the Magyar language. It took me a while to find the right train and carriage to board and I didn't have time to eat dinner. As I hoisted my case into the carriage, I realised that I had also skipped lunch, in the excitement of my first continental adventure. I told myself that I would be able to buy food and drink on board.

Stepping into my sleeper berth was like stepping into an Agatha Christie novel. The décor was from the 1930s: laminated surfaces in drab brown and yellow; a leather cord to pull open the window a few inches; the type of rugged upholstery that would scratch short-trousered legs; a musty smell, mixed with the tang of diesel. It was basic but thrilling.

It was hot, that August day. No air conditioning and only the narrow window opening to stir the air. Beads of sweat tracked slowly down my back. I tried to create a through-draft, by sliding open the door to my compartment. But it slid closed again, so I wedged it with my case. The train guard – red-faced in his woollen uniform and peaked cap – didn't like that. He remonstrated with me in Magyar and I shrugged, so he picked up my case and shoved it onto the ropes of the overhead luggage-holder. He held out his hand for my ticket, snipped a corner off it and stomped away. I kept the door closed.

A loud whistle and the train jerked into action. I made my way to the buffet car, in search of food and cold water, bumping off the sides of the narrow corridor as the train swayed on its way. A large, grumpy woman in a maroon headscarf and matching lipstick sat behind the counter. She dragged on a cigarette as I pointed to a salami sandwich and a can of fizzy drink with a name I didn't recognise. Plonking them down, she tapped the counter to demand payment. I fished out some French francs from my wallet and handed the notes to her. She handed them back, shaking her head. I tried sterling but she tutted and wagged a finger at me. She jabbed at a button on a till from *Open All Hours* and rubbed some forint between fat finger and thumb. It hadn't occurred to me that MÁV would only accept Hungarian currency. I retreated. The woman and I hadn't exchanged a single word, let alone food or drink.

I was suddenly acutely aware of my thirst and panic rose in me. Of course, there would be water in the toilets, so I headed there. A sign above the sink featured a stylised image of a glass with a red circle around it and a red line through it. I took this to mean that the water was not safe to drink. For a few seconds, I debated whether I should risk it anyway. But I decided against dysentery and went back to my baking berth. The red-faced guard had returned in my absence and lowered the overhead bed. I had ten hours to pass without food or water, so I undressed and slid between the sheets.

I really had to get better at this travelling lark.

It was an uncomfortable night, my first time sleeping on a train. The service made frequent stops, at which doors would slam, lights would pierce through the inadequate blinds, people would shout, and whistles would be blown. Progress between stops was slow and jerky. Frequently, I was aware of the train braking and the carriages shunting up against each other in domino succession. When I did sleep, it was to dream of eating bacon and eggs and drinking from a tinkling spring of bright, clear water. The more to disappoint me when I awoke with an empty stomach, a parched mouth and a headache.

The heat became more oppressive as the night went on, so I threw off my sheets. I was naked when the door slid open, and a Hungarian border guard walked in. He must have had a universal key because I was sure I had locked the door. The guard had command of one English word: 'passport'. I wrapped the sheet around me and retrieved mine from my jacket, where it hung from a peg opposite. Perhaps flustered at being confronted with a naked, pale, skinny Englishman, he flicked quickly through the pages to find the visa, pasted into my passport by the Hungarian Embassy a few weeks earlier. Satisfied, he handed it back to me, without bothering to issue me with an entry stamp.

At least his appearance meant that I was now in Hungary and could look forward to breakfast and something to drink in the next few hours. My relief as we rolled into the cavernous Keleti station eclipsed any excitement I might have felt. I checked again the letter from the conference organisers. A coach would collect arrivals from Keleti station at set hours. But, first, food. I queued at a *bureau de change* to cash my travellers' cheques: a slow process, of communistic bureaucracy. Then, forint in hand, I headed to a kiosk in the departures hall, to buy an open sandwich and a bottle with a picture of apricots on the side. I downed half the bottle, before realising that it was alcoholic. I headed back for water. Thirst sated, I emerged into the sunshine of the station forecourt, just in time to see my coach turning out into the traffic.

I guess I could have spent the morning looking around Budapest and returned to catch the next coach four hours later. But I was exhausted, dishevelled, hot, lugging a heavy suitcase, and a bit pissed from the schnapps. A cab to Szirak Castle was the more attractive option, so I collapsed into the passenger seat of a waiting yellow cab, showed the driver the address of the hotel and fell asleep, neglecting to check whether he had set the meter.

He hadn't.

An hour or so later, parked in front of the steps up to the castle entrance, he wrote down the amount he demanded from me. It is difficult to argue with a cab driver at the best of times, let alone in a language you don't understand. So, I emerged from that cab 14,000 forint poorer, equivalent to about £115. That would be expensive for the journey today. Thirty-two years ago, it was extortionate. And it left me with a painfully small amount of money for the week.

Thankfully, food and non-alcoholic drinks were covered, so I didn't suffer too much. But there was no sitting up with my compatriots late into the night, downing beers and debating capitalism. There was a rest day halfway through, on which we were to be ferried to Budapest for a day's sightseeing and a slap-up lunch. Fearing that I would not be able to pay my way, I feigned a stomach-ache that morning and spent the day reading and walking in the hotel gardens, accompanied by the tweeting of birds and the familiar pangs of hunger: no lunch was served, as all the other guests were in Budapest. But I got dinner, so didn't go to bed hungry, and the rest of the week passed by unremarkably.

It was on the journey home that my various travelling errors formed a perfect storm.

The border guard who got on at a tiny station just outside Austria was far more belligerent than his colleague who had woken me on the way into Hungary. According to his badge, his name was Ámon. He was blond and muscular and I judged him to be in his early twenties. But worry lines scored his face and stale beer soured his breath. He had two days of stubble and the short temper to go with it. Also, in contrast with his colleague, he had excellent command of English, which he was determined to use on me. He filled the door to my berth with his bulk and looked disgustedly at my passport.

'Where is your entry stamp?'

'Your colleague forgot to give me one.' Ámon looked me up and down and returned his attention to my passport, leafing slowly through it, examining each empty page in turn. He waved it at me.

'Where is your signature?'

'Oh,' I said, reaching for the passport. 'I forgot to sign it. I'll do it now.' He snatched it away from me.

'You will not. This passport is invalid.' He slipped it into one of his side pockets, moving a holstered pistol out of the way to do so. 'Come with me.'

'But the train is about to leave,' I said.

'Your problem,' he said. 'Not mine.'

As Ámon led me across the platform, I could see my fellow conference attendees staring out of the windows and whispering to each other. *Maybe they think I'm a spy*, I thought, *rather than just a hapless first-time traveller.*

My captor left me in a bare concrete room that stank of urine and cigarette smoke. It was furnished with a table and two chairs, the only thing missing from the classic interrogation scene being a bright angle-lamp to glare into my eyes. There was also a once-white plastic wall clock, yellowed with nicotine. I watched the time tick down to my train's departure. If I missed it, I had no money for a replacement ticket back to the UK and no credit card to tide me over. I wondered if there was a word for the nervous involuntary movement of my right leg, as it bounced on the ball of my foot. *Nimming*, perhaps?

I heard a key turn. Ámon flung the door open and plonked himself into the chair opposite me. It creaked.

'We have a problem,' he said.

'Oh, yes? What's that?'

'My superior has taken your passport and he will not release it until you have paid a fine.'

'How much is the fine?'

Ámon looked away. 'Twenty thousand forint. Ten thousand for the lack of signature, ten for the lack of stamp.'

£165, or so.

I pulled out my wallet and produced the small amount of money I had left. Maybe 1,000 forint, some francs and a twenty-pound note. I put it all on the table.

'That's it,' I said. 'Everything I have. You can take it if you want.'

I thought I saw some embarrassment cross his eyes. 'But the fine is twenty thousand.'

'I know, but that is all I have.'

'We have a problem,' he said again.

He's cornered, I thought. What do you do when you are after a bribe and your victim has no money? Let them go? Or escalate it and make them miss their train? Admit defeat? Or fight? I feared the latter. After all, there was a genuine problem with my passport. Problems, even. Ámon could easily give me up to the system, whatever that was in those days following communism's collapse. I needed to give him a reason to take my side.

I needed to work out what motivated him, other than money.

He wasn't much older than me and I sensed his frustration. Obviously educated, Ámon was fluent in English, which was rare in Hungary at that time. The system that he had known throughout his childhood had collapsed in the past two years, the collapse delivering promises and opportunities. But they had come to nothing. He was still in a lowly uniform, bullying travellers at a remote crossing point during the day, drinking to forget the pointlessness of it at night. This man wanted to be *seen*. He wanted someone to recognise his importance, his place in a confusing world. I saw some of his longing in myself.

My next words surprised myself.

'You know, Ámon, I think you are more important than you are admitting to me.'

He looked up, sharply, perhaps irritated that I had used his name. 'What do you mean?'

'I mean, you speak great English. You are educated.' I gestured around me. 'You could be running this place and I bet your boss knows that. You could be at Oxford University with me, not here.'

He stared for a while. Then nodded.

'So,' I said, 'I bet you could help me out here.' I pointed out of the window. 'That train is about to leave, and I have to be on it. Otherwise, I am trapped here, with no money.' I gathered up the few bank notes that lay on the table between us. 'You can have all this, or you can let me keep it and buy myself some food. That is your choice. But I bet you can go to your boss and get my passport back.' There was a moment of silence between us. I pushed my nimming knee down. If *Schindler's List* had been released by then, I might have been tempted to add 'that's power, Ámon. That is power' and asked him to pardon me.

There was no need.

Ámon stood up abruptly, scraping away his chair with the backs of his knees. 'Wait here,' he said, as though I had a choice. This time, he was gone for less than a minute, probably no longer than it took to pull my passport out of his pocket, out of sight. He came back into the room, waving it in triumph. 'Come on,' he said, 'Let's get you on that train.'

He held up a hand to me as the train pulled out. I was immediately surrounded by conference delegates, who demanded to know the story. Someone bought me a glass of sparkling wine and I sat down amongst friends. The wine was warm, overly sweet, flat and disgusting. But it didn't matter. My spirits were bubbling.

Yes, I had proven myself useless at travel. I didn't know how to use a passport. I neglected to carry water with me on long train journeys in summer. Foreign currencies bamboozled me. I accidentally downed booze to quench my thirst, first thing in the morning. I missed coaches, got ripped off by taxi drivers. Whiled away time reading and walking alone rather than admit my penury. I got myself into trouble at borders and had to talk my way out of it. I was the ultimate clueless Englishman abroad.

And I loved it.

* * *

Ámon was bored and frustrated with his life. Maybe he was also in genuine financial need. But I doubt that is what motivated him to seek bribes. What he really yearned for was recognition of his authority and power. Luckily for me, I could identify with that. So, I was able to pinpoint a powerful motivation and engage with it. He wanted to be seen and I let him know I saw him.

RECAP

- A spy has no chance if their target lacks motivation to become an agent. A good spy will think of themselves as super-facilitator of a target's aspirations.
- There are two stages to engaging a target's motivations. First is identifying what they are. Second is making clear to the target how the spy how can help to satisfy them.
- Traditionally, spies have thought about MICE: Money, Ideology, Coercion and Ego. Ignore coercion. It has no place in decent spying.
- Money may be the most powerful motivator. But it has drawbacks and ideological drivers are highly desirable in addition. Ego helps, if properly managed.
- The MICE model is outdated but can be modified with 'Desire to Please' as a fifth category, thereby forming MICED.
- Desire to Please is also relevant to the motivations of target goals allies. It forms part of a revised model, GRADE, that we shall examine next.

* * *

MICE are fascinating creatures and the acronym is very useful when assessing the motivations of espionage targets. However, the model needs to be adapted when examining motivations for someone to become a goals ally. The drivers for a successful or high-profile person to mentor, endorse, sponsor or otherwise assist someone else are different from the motivations for someone to become an intelligence agent, though there is some crossover in the Venn diagram of these two sets of impulses.

In the case of target goals allies, money is unlikely to feature. It is, of course, conceivable that you are in a position to pay a social media influencer a large sum to give you a shout out on their channels, for example. If so, good for you, but you probably don't need to be reading this book. Alternatively, there are circumstances in which an influential person may expend effort supporting you, on the assumption that they will reap a financial reward later. This is the case with agents representing writers, actors and public speakers. Again, though, if you are at the stage of being able to attract an agent, you are likely already to have made the breakthrough that this book is designed to help you achieve.

Also, commitment to an ideology is unlikely to be of much help, at least in the dictionary definition sense of 'a set of beliefs or principles, especially one on which a political system, party, or organization is based'.[1] Religious conviction may play a part. As will ideals (or values), as opposed to ideology. But we can find a better way of modelling those.

Coercion can be safely ignored, for obvious reasons. It would not only be morally objectionable to strongarm someone into supporting your objectives. It would also, most probably, backfire. Nobody likes a bully or a blackmailer and these types are frequently rumbled. We shall not waste further time on them here.

1 Cambridge Dictionary. https://dictionary.cambridge.org/dictionary/english/ideology

The main area of the MICE model that is relevant to motivations in target goals allies is Ego. We'll come back to why, but Ego takes its place in our own motivations model, specifically adapted for building life-changing alliances. From now on, instead of thinking about rodents, ask yourself the following question about your target goals allies: do they make the GRADE?

GRADE is a mnemonic for: Gratitude; Responsibility; Altruism; Desire to Please; and Ego.

This model is based on a phenomenon that psychologists call 'prosocial behaviour', which can be defined as 'any act we willingly take that is meant to help others, whether the "others" are a group of people or just one person. The key is that these acts are voluntary and not forced upon the helper.'[1] Let's look at the GRADE motivations for prosocial behaviour in turn.

GRATITUDE

A successful person might realise they have benefited from a privileged social position (such as, for example, being part of an ethnic group that has traditionally enjoyed advantages over others, or being part of a class that has access to private education or networks of influence). As a result, they may feel they have a debt of gratitude to society, which they seek to 'repay' through acts of generosity or support for people less fortunate than themselves. In fact, this phenomenon is not limited to those who have benefited from social privileges. I know one successful entrepreneur who was born into underprivileged circumstances and became wealthy through imagination, quick-wittedness, determination and hard work. He habitually

1 Lee W. Daffin Jr., Ph.D. and Carrie Lane, Ph.D., *Principles of Social Psychology*, Washington State University, 2021. https://opentext.wsu.edu /social-psychology/chapter/module-11-helping-others/

describes himself as 'extremely lucky' and spends considerable time mentoring others. For him, his intellect and character traits are 'innate privileges' and he feels no less keen a sense of gratitude than others whose advancement is due to external privileges. His modesty forbids me from naming him.

Whatever the source of an individual's gratitude, it can be a strong motivation to support others – particularly young people and people from marginalised groups – to become successes themselves. Such people can become valuable and enduring goals allies.

RESPONSIBILITY

This motivation is closely related to gratitude, in that gratefulness may give rise to feelings of responsibility to do good in the world. The phrase *noblesse oblige* sums it up: 'privilege entails responsibility'.[1] But the responsibility motivator can (and does) extend beyond the reciprocal. Religious conviction is one obvious driver of prosocial behaviour. But even non-religious people may feel a nebulous responsibility to support and assist others. When pressed, they might be able to articulate a philosophical case for their prosocial acts. Perhaps by turning to Sophocles, who said that 'to be doing good deeds is man's most glorious task'. To the Dalai Lama: 'Our prime purpose in this life is to help others and if you can't help them, at least don't hurt them.' Or, maybe, to Immanuel Kant, who declared that 'an action, to have moral worth, must be done from duty'. Alternatively, they may just spread their hands and say, 'It is the right thing to do.'

It doesn't really matter, at least when it comes to assessing the motivations of a target goals ally. The important consideration

1 *Concise Oxford English Dictionary.*

is *if* the target has a sense of responsibility, not *why*, though a broader discussion about moral imperatives may be used as a means of elicitation (see Chapter 4 above).

It may be, though, that they don't carry a burden of responsibility. Instead, they are motivated to do good for its own sake, out of selflessness, or altruism.

ALTRUISM

This is a tricky concept. Philosophical debate about the possibility of genuinely selfless actions continues to rage, with some thinkers claiming that even Aristotle, in his *Nichomachean Ethics*, 'accepts a form of psychological egoism, namely that each person acts ultimately for the sake of his own happiness'.[1] This view is also referred to by psychologists as 'psychological hedonism', which posits that 'only pleasure or pain motivates us'.[2] Fascinating as this debate may be, we are more interested in the 'empathy-altruism hypothesis', which holds that the emotions of sympathy and compassion 'create motivation where the ultimate goal is improving the welfare of the other person who ignited these feelings, hence the behaviour is altruistic'.[3] Such emotions often arise in relationships that involve some emotional engagement, such as a kinship or friendship. However, these cases might better be captured by the next category of motivation in the GRADE model.

---

1 Guy Schuh, 'Aristotle on the impossibility of altruism', 2017. https://open.bu.edu/handle/2144/20871
2 Stanford Encyclopedia of Philosophy, Hedonism. https://plato.stanford.edu/entries/hedonism/
3 Arto Klemola, 'Motivations Behind Prosocial Behaviour', 2013. https://core.ac.uk/download/pdf/38094767.pdf

DESIRE TO PLEASE

Given disagreements about the possibility or impossibility of altruism, the concept of desire to please is more helpful when assessing the motivations of a target goals ally. Ask yourself if they have demonstrated – either through direct expression or through elicitation – any desire to please in their interactions with you. If you have done your job of cultivation well, they will have come to like and trust you. In this case, it is likely that they will indeed be motivated by a desire to please you.

EGO

If not, you might want to examine the role of egoism, arguably the most powerful of all non-financial motivations. Spies may be interested in an ego that wants to change the world, that thirsts for revenge on unworthy colleagues, or that seeks the recognition it lacks from peers. The would-be recruiter of goals allies is looking for something less dramatic. At the most basic level, reciprocity may play a part: if your target helps you, you may be able to repay the favour later. This is a valid motivation but possibly not the most desirable, from your perspective. Better is the target who derives satisfaction from express gratitude on the part of a recipient of their support. Or who believes that being seen to do good deeds enhances their public image: look for the person who posts prolifically on social media about their charitable activities.

Some targets may adhere to the Buddhist notion of karma. The Buddha said 'All living beings have actions (Karma) as their own, their inheritance, their congenital cause, their kinsman, their refuge. It is Karma that differentiates beings into low and high states.'[1] Perhaps your target is not familiar with this saying but has a more general sense that 'the universe will deliver' or that 'we get back what we give'. Again, these are valid motivations to explore and may act as elicitation 'keys'.

Mood enhancement may be relevant. Doing good, helping others, being supportive may improve a target's mental state. According to the National Institutes of Health,[2] a 'study found that the brain's pleasure centres became activated as people decided to donate part of a new stash of money to charity, rather than keeping it all for themselves'. The same study used functional magnetic resonance imaging (fMRI) 'to classify people as either egoists or altruists, depending on whether their brains responded more to a money influx to themselves or to [. . .] charity'. They found that 'altruists, with their stronger responses to charitable donations, gave money to [a] food bank nearly twice as often as the egoists'.

It appears that there is such a thing as 'the helper's high', leading to 'positive emotions following selfless service to others'.[3] As Tom discovered.

CASE STUDY

The day before their planned meeting on 8th June, Tom sent Moussa an SMS, to check that the agreed time still worked for him. He included a link to a meme about fashion, as he didn't want the message to be too businesslike. Moussa replied quickly, liking the meme and

---

1 Ven. Masahi Sayadaw, 'The theory of Karma', BDEA/BuddhaNet. https://www.buddhanet.net/e-learning/karma.htm
2 Vickie Contie, 'Brain imaging reveals joys of giving', NIH, 22 June 2007. https://www.nih.gov/news-events/nih-research-matters/brain-imaging-reveals-joys-giving
3 Larry Dossey, 'The Helper's High', Science Direct, Vol. 14, Issue 6, pp. 393–399, November 2018. https://www.sciencedirect.com/science/article/pii/S1550830718304178

confirming that he would be at the Grey Eagle pub at the agreed time. As before, Tom conducted a recce of the pub, to gauge how busy it would be at the time of his meeting with Moussa and to spy out good places to sit where they could hear one another comfortably. On the day, he reviewed his previous notes about Moussa and made a mental plan about how he would approach the evening. He wanted to be able to 'switch on' quickly when they got together. In other words, he wanted to engage Moussa with intention.

Afterwards, Tom wrote the following short contact note.

'Moussa said that he was impressed by my designs: they reminded him of Michael Kors' work. Such a compliment!

I put my designs away and told him that, while I love designing, I am realistic that there are many young design-ers around and no good reason why I should make a success of it. Sometimes, this gets me down, so I try to keep myself grounded by volunteering at the Saplings Children's Hospice. I said that I had mixed feelings after spending time with the patients there.

Moussa said that he knew what I meant. He told me that, sometimes, he offers mentoring services to kids who have emotional problems, all the way from autism to abuse survival. His work with them saddens him but, at the same time, it enlivens him. His exact wording was 'I get a proper high from making life better for them, which makes me feel guilty sometimes.' I said that there was no need for guilt and that we all help others for different reasons. Moussa thought for a while about that. He eventually replied: 'I think you are right. It obviously makes me feel good to do something worthwhile. But I also know that I have been lucky. I met people along the way who supported me, when they didn't have any reason to do so. I want to give something back.'

I said that he must enjoy the gratitude he gets for his work. But he shook his head. 'It's not about that at all. The kids have little to be grateful for and I don't want them to see me as some sort of saviour. I just want them to thrive.' I previously thought that Moussa was after appreciation. I was wrong.

We agreed to meet in Paris when I visit next month. The Grey Eagle meeting was raw and emotional. It won't be appropriate to repeat that when we see each other in Paris. Instead, I think it will be the perfect time for me to make my pitch.'

At the beginning of this chapter, I summarised a spy's job as being 'to identify and engage the motivations of intelligence targets'. We have outlined the first of this two-stage process above, reworked the model for the purposes of recruiting goals allies, and seen how Tom successfully set about identifying Moussa's motivations. Moussa is undoubtedly grateful for the success he has enjoyed in life and this motivates him to help others. But it is also evident that he would feel a sense of responsibility to help others, even in the absence of personal success. Furthermore, he is not looking for anything specific in return for the assistance he gives to others. His sense of responsibility drives him to do good for its own sake. Gratitude and Desire to Please play a part, but Responsibility and Altruism are more important. Ego doesn't come into it.

Next, in Chapter Six, 'The Pulling Power of the Perfect Pitch', we'll look at how spies handle the second stage: that is, how they appeal to a target's motivations to recruit them as agents. And we'll explore how you can work with the motivations of target goals allies to persuade them to back your cause. But, before that, I'd like to tell you about Susan, a police officer, and what motivated her to help a wanted man flee her country.

* * *

Susan was the smartest police officer I ever met. She had a first-class degree in Linguistics and spoke three languages fluently. In her spare time, she studied engineering and had qualified for a private pilot's licence before she was twenty-five. She wanted to be an undercover officer, in the equivalent of the UK's Special Branch. In my opinion, this would have been a waste of Susan's intellect, but she was a natural actor and would have been brilliant at it. Or at anything else she turned her formidable mind to.

Her male superiors had her directing traffic.

Susan was married to Sam, who was the smartest taxi driver I had ever met. They had got together at university, where Sam had studied Philosophy. He was recommended to me as a driver and general fixer in an African country that I visited frequently in the 2010s: it is better that I don't say which one, for Susan's sake. Sam's favourite thinkers were the Stoics, and we passed time discussing Eudaimonia, while choking on petrol fumes in stand-still traffic. That is, when we weren't talking about Susan, to whom Sam was devoted. He worked extra hours to pay for Susan's flying hours, to ensure her licence remained valid. I found excuses to hire him, even when I was renting my own vehicle, because I wanted to support them both and because I thoroughly enjoyed his company. Over various trips, we had become close friends and I was a regular visitor to their home. There they would air frustrations with the government and its inability to kickstart the country's moribund economy. This failure meant that there were few career opportunities suitable for people with their qualifications.

In particular, they were angry with the president. Furious, in fact. And they weren't the only ones.

The president had been elected in a supposedly democratic poll, but few believed the outcome reflected the will of the people. The electoral playing field was, in the parlance of international observers, uneven. The military was known to back the ruling party and opposition candidates had been harassed throughout their campaigns. On election day, there were insufficient polling stations in opposition-supporting areas and many voters had been disenfranchised. Others felt that they had been bullied into voting for the president, with reports of 'observers' entering polling booths with them. It had been impossible to verify the announced results, with opposition officials, journalists and independent observers barred from regional counting centres. The international community had grumbled about the result but had taken no action. So far, so typical.

Since his election, the president had set about enriching himself and his family and was implicated in numerous corruption scandals. The government regularly flouted global human rights norms, criminalising and persecuting minority groups. Still, the international community stood by, offering little but finger-wagging in support of the oppressed. Then the government came for the journalists, persecuting and intimidating those who dared to criticise the ruling junta. One such was Ali, who told me over dinner that he was scared for his life.

Ali had asked to meet me at a casino, which had an outside dining area with widely spaced tables. Humid, languid night air wafted the smell of woodsmoke and barbecued meat to us, as we selected a table underneath a speaker that was blasting music by the South African legend Brenda Fassie. 'Nakupenda', she sang: I love you. Ali and I smiled at each other across the table, pretending not to notice the two goons in ill-fitting jackets who took the next table along from us and ordered a couple of sodas. Classic surveillance behaviour in that part of the world. We ordered mutton chops and local beers, sitting back and affecting nonchalance. Ali kept his voice light and airy as he described the events of the past two days, under the cover of Brenda Fassie's husky singing. She had moved on now to 'Ngizobuya': I will come back.

The previous day, Ali had noticed an unusual car parked outside his small house. There were two men sat in the front of the car: the same two who now sat twenty feet from us, fiddling with their soda bottles. They had kept him company for over twenty-four hours, and he was scared. The previous month, a colleague of his at the opposition-leaning daily newspaper had told him that two men were following him. A few days later, that colleague was found dead in his car, which had crashed into a tree on a remote stretch of road, just outside town. Ali was unable to prove foul play, but he believed firmly that his fellow journalist had been murdered. He was terrified that he was next in the firing line and had decided to flee the country. If only he could shake off his followers and get over the border without having to use an official crossing.

It was understandable that Ali drank far more than I did that evening. I refused to let him drive home. If an accident was planned for him, his intoxication would provide the perfect cover. He saw the sense of that, through the alcohol, and agreed that I should drive him back to the apartment I was renting, where he could sleep it off. I pulled out of the parking lot onto a dual carriageway and made a U-turn at a gap where the metal of the road's central reservation had rusted away. It was a prohibited manoeuvre, but everyone did it, to save driving half a mile to the next turning point. For some reason, Ali's followers had lingered as we set off, and there were no other cars around. So, I felt it was safe to swing my hired Land Rover Defender around. But my heart sank as a police officer stepped out of the shadows and raised a hand to stop me. I was only thankful that Ali was too drunk to care. In his state of heightened paranoia, a police stop might have sent him over the edge.

I pulled the jeep onto a patch of gravel by the side of the road and lowered the driver's window, to find Susan smiling at me.

'Hi, Jules,' she said. 'I wasn't expecting it to be you. Why isn't Sam driving you this evening?'

'He's on an airport run,' I said. Susan shone her torch at Ali and wrinkled her nose at the smell of booze.

'I hope you haven't been drinking as much as he has,' she laughed. 'Otherwise, I'd have no option but to arrest you.'

A flash of headlight beams caught my eye and I turned to see the surveillance team leaving the casino in a white Toyota Land Cruiser. They slowed at the gap where I had turned but, perhaps seeing that I was busy with a police officer, decided to drive on rather than swing round. They no doubt thought I would be held up for long enough that they could catch up after circling the roundabout half a mile down the road.

I spoke quickly. 'I need a favour from you, Susan. I have to go, now. Immediately.' I pointed to Ali. 'This man is in danger. Can I take him to your place, please?'

She waved her torch forward. 'Sure,' she said. 'Get going. Was that other car following you?'

'Yes.'

'Okay. I'll flag them down for a routine stop. Give you some time.'

'Thanks, Susan. You might literally be a lifesaver.' I floored the accelerator and swung into the next turning. A few more random turns satisfied me that there was no Land Cruiser behind us, so I drove to Sam and Susan's house, where I was able to park in a covered garage, out of view from the road. There, we waited for an hour or so, until I heard Susan arriving in her police vehicle. She hurried us into the house, and we got Ali to bed.

'What's going on?' Susan poured me a Scotch and we sat in her living room, where the air-conditioning unit hummed and whirred. It was chilly and the hairs on my bare forearms stood to attention. I explained Ali's situation, as briefly as I could, then asked the killer question.

'Can you help get him out of the country?'

Susan took a sharp breath in and held it for several seconds, holding a crooked forefinger to her lips.

'But, Jules,' she said, finally. 'I am a policewoman. You are asking me to break the law.'

I shook my head. 'No, I am asking you to save a man's life. All he has done is write articles about the president's corruption. Now he is being followed. He doesn't know why or by who, but he fears they will try to kill him.' Susan was silent, her brow furrowed. 'There is no arrest warrant out for him, is there?'

She shook her head.

'So, it is simply a case of protecting a man who is scared for his life. Surely that is part of a police officer's job.'

'If he wants our protection, he can ask for it formally.'

'And you really believe that will work? You don't think the president's men can take him off the street, even under your noses?'

'Of course, they do it all the time.' Susan was up and pacing the room now. I pressed on.

'You don't owe this government anything. You know they are illegitimate and you know they are killers. You don't owe the police force anything. They have ignored your talents. They have refused your requests for transfers. They've got you issuing parking tickets.'

'They pay my salary.'

I looked around at the threadbare furniture and the old cath-ode-ray TV set. 'Barely. And, in any case, you do the job they pay you for. You even nearly issued me with a ticket this even-ing.' Susan laughed at this and sat down again. 'I am asking you to save a man's life. Surely that is the important thing.'

I waited. A clock ticked. Ten seconds, fifteen, twenty.

Finally, Susan's brow smoothed, and she spoke. 'You are right. The president is a monster. He probably would have your friend killed. I can't allow that.'

'Thank you, Susan. I knew you would do the right thing.'

'But you can't be involved,' she said, sharply. 'I don't want you breaking the law here. I'll let you get away with an illegal U-turn but that's it. So, get out of here and I'll make a plan with Ali in the morning.'

She hugged me as she threw me out.

It was a few days before I met Susan again. I dined with her and Sam at one of the city's better hotels. My treat, as thanks for her help. Her eyes were sparkling, and she accepted a glass of champagne, even though she rarely drank. As the alcohol hit its mark, she became more and more talkative, keen to spill the details of her adventure.

'We knew they'd be watching Ali's house,' she said. 'So our first problem was getting his passport and some personal belongings to take with him.'

Sam piped up. 'I was the decoy.' He looked absurdly pleased with himself. 'I drove to Ali's place and saw the car waiting for him. I walked around the back and just waited there for five minutes. When I came back round to the front, I was carrying an envelope I had in my pocket, so it looked like I had picked something up. Sure enough, they followed me as I drove away.'

'How long did they follow you?'

'All morning. I had three fares and they tailed me for each one. Eventually, they got tired of it, so they came up to me at lunch and started questioning me. I told them I'd had a call to go to Ali's address and pick up a passenger but there was nobody there. I waited a while and then left.'

'Did they ask you about the envelope?'

'They did. I gave it to them. It had a shopping list on it. Told them I'd passed the time making the list while I waited for the non-existent passenger.'

I laughed. 'Brilliant.' Turning to Susan, I said, 'What were you doing in the meantime?'

'I drove Ali to his house, and he collected what he needed. I warned him he could only bring a medium-sized bag, because it would need to fit in the back of a Cessna 152 and not unbalance us.'

I raised an eyebrow. 'You flew him out of the country?'

'It seemed the easiest way. We drove to my usual airfield, and I filed a flight plan to take us on a circular trip. Part of my flying hours. But I know of a landing strip at a game reserve, just over the border. No problems with radar and no need for clearance to land. It's all done with visuals at those places.'

'Genius. But did the people at your flying school ask why you had someone with you?'

'I often do. There's no rules against it and they don't much care. But we had a different problem.'

'What was that?'

'Ali is scared of flying. It took me a while to get him onto the plane. And, when we were up, he passed out.' She drained her glass. 'I thought he'd had a heart attack at first and there was nothing I could do until I got the plane down. We were about half an hour from the border, so I had to decide whether to make an emergency landing on this side or just keep on going.'

'Hard call,' I said. 'What did you do?'

'I kept going. Made sure the plane was straight and level and did a basic check on him. He wasn't fibrillating and he was breathing. I reckoned he had just fainted from the stress of it all. Leaving the country and flying in a rackety old Cessna can do that to a man.' Her eyes twinkled.

'So, you got him out?' She reached for the champagne bottle and refilled her glass.

'I did. We landed at the airstrip, and I managed to revive him.' She raised her glass. 'Let's drink to my first aid training. About the only useful thing the police ever did for me.' We all clinked glasses and Sam took his wife's hand, gazing at her with awe.

'What a woman,' he said.

'I'll drink to that,' I said.

'Don't make me blush,' said Susan. 'But thank you, Jules, for getting me involved.'

This surprised me. 'You're thanking me. Why? I thought you had reservations?'

'I did. But I realise now that I needed a way of venting my frustration at this useless government. I felt so exhilarated after handing over Ali to the care of the reserve managers. Taking off again felt like I was taking off into a new life. It satisfied some longing in me. And it gave me an idea about a career change.'

'That's great,' I said. 'What's the idea?'

'I won't tell you right now. I don't want to jinx it.'

I nodded, sipped at my champagne, and let the matter drop.

Sadly, I haven't seen Sam or Susan since that evening, as they moved country soon after, to follow Susan's new career. But I rang her a few years later to catch up. We reminisced for a while, then I asked how she and Sam were getting on as expats.

She told me that she was loving her new life, working as a pilot for an air ambulance charity.

* * *

RECAP

- MICE is not quite the right model for assessing motivations of target goals allies. Think GRADE instead: Gratitude; Responsibility; Altruism; Desire to Please; and Ego.
- The GRADE model applies to individual motivations for prosocial actions; those taken voluntarily to help others, whether a group or an individual.
- Gratitude applies when a successful individual recognises that they have benefited from privilege and desires to repay a perceived debt to society.
- Responsibility may be religious or secular in nature, arising from a sense of obligation to do good in the world, through helping others.
- Altruism is a contentious concept but Desire to Please is a form of it. This is particularly powerful where bonds of friendship have developed, through cultivation.
- Ego is a powerful motivator for prosocial actions. Reciprocity may be involved, or a target goals ally might simply seek a 'helper's high'.

CHAPTER SIX

The Pulling Power of the Perfect Pitch

The time has come. This is what it has all been leading to. The recruitment pitch. The moment that our spy reveals her true purpose to her target and invites him to become an agent. There's no turning back from here.

That is why preparation is vital. Before reaching this moment, the spy has been meticulous with hers.

Throughout the targeting and cultivation stages, she has kept a formal written record of every interaction with the target and her developing assessment of him. And before the big day, the spy and her support team undertake a rigorous and systematic review of the resulting file. They form an assessment of the target covering three vital matters.

ACCESS

First, did the targeting exercise get it right? Can the target retrieve information relevant to the requirements set out in the first stage of the intelligence cycle? Can he retrieve information that could become intelligence, in the defined sense of its being 'of military or political value'?[1] If so, is that information privileged, or could

1 *Concise Oxford English Dictionary.*

it be retrieved by other, more straightforward, means? In other words, is it secret? Law Insider defines 'Intelligence Secret' as 'intelligence information [. . .] protected by confidentiality to prevent access, knowledge, or possession by parties that have no right to them'.[1] This is the typical standard applied when deciding whether or not a target is worth the risk of a recruitment pitch. Analysis of the reward to risk equation is central to gaining clearance to attempt a recruitment: risk management is a vital part of a spy's job, as we shall examine in Chapter Nine (p. 270).

SUITABILITY

The second area of assessment relates to risk. Would the target make a good agent? Does he have the wit and creativity to retrieve secret information without attracting suspicion? Few of us are conscious of our 'tells'. But a good spy will have observed her target closely, to ascertain whether he is able to lie convincingly and retain composure when under pressure. It is not only an agent's potential behaviour when at work that is of interest. The team will also want reassurance that he won't brag about being involved in intelligence work or speak recklessly when under the influence of alcohol. If money is a significant motivation, is he the sort of person who will flaunt his newfound wealth? If so, he is likely to attract unwanted attention: it was, in part, unexplained wealth that led the FBI to investigate Aldrich Ames, the CIA officer arrested in 1994 for supplying classified material to Russia.[2] All these considerations will be weighed in the balance.

1 Law Insider, Intelligence Secret. https://www.lawinsider.com/diction-ary/intelligence-secret#:~:text=Intelligence%20Secret%20means%20Intelligence%20information,have%20no%20right%20to%20them
2 FBI, Aldrich Ames. https://www.fbi.gov/history/famous-cases/aldrich-ames

MOTIVATION

Third, of course, is the question of motivation. Why would he betray his country and work for us? As we have seen, a considerable part of the spy's work during the cultivation stage is to identify and explore a target's motivations. Now is the time to work out if those motivations are sufficient to win the target over.

*　*　*

Does the target have the right access? Is he suited to the life of an agent? Does he have motivation to become one? Once these three questions have been answered to the satisfaction of headquarters, clearance will be given for the spy to make her approach. She will begin developing a plan for how that will be done. A good plan will cover setting, mood, language, contingencies ('what-ifs?') and extrication ('get-outs').

There are no specific restrictions on the setting for a recruitment pitch. It could be made in a quiet corner of a restaurant or bar, in a hotel lobby or private room, in a rented office space, or on a walk, through woods or along a seashore. You will be able to think of many alternatives. Wherever is chosen, though, it must afford privacy to the spy and her target. As far as possible, the spy must ensure that they will not be overheard. It is also important that the two do not look out of place in the chosen setting, to avoid provoking curiosity. And there will need to be a plausible excuse for them to be there together, if challenged. It is also desirable that the target feels relaxed in that setting, a consideration that plays into mood.

Ideally, the target will be in a relaxed and receptive frame of mind when the pitch is put to them. Again, potential means to achieve this state are many and varied. The spy will consider what she knows of the target when selecting a venue and time, and in deciding how to set the tone. It would be better to pitch a convivial night-owl over dinner than over breakfast, for instance. A power-dressing go-getter might prefer the breakfast. A workaholic is not apt to thank the spy for interrupting their day with a long lunch. An introvert is likely to prefer a quiet drink in a private hotel room to an encounter in the bustling lobby downstairs. A teetotaller might prefer a tearoom or coffee shop to a bar. And so on. The good spy will have visited various possible venues at different times of the day to help her tailor the setting for the needs of the target.

But this isn't all she has to do to relax her target, of course. She will need to set the tone once they are together. It is not usually a good idea to make a pitch from the get-go. Better to spend time discussing personal matters and lending a sympathetic ear to any worries the target may have. Some humour does not go amiss, either. If the meeting is over a meal, it is advisable to wait until coffees and liqueurs have been served before getting down to business. That is, so long as the target has time to spare and is not in a hurry to get away. There will be much to discuss if they agree to be recruited. Not all of this is susceptible to planning; we all know that personal encounters have a habit of going their own way. But it is better for the spy to go into the meeting with a basic architecture in mind, albeit prepared for flexibility.

The segue from social chitchat to formal is difficult to manage and needs careful choice of language. Agent recruitment is not comparable to a business meeting, a sales pitch or a job interview. It is vital that it *sounds* different and less structured. But it is just as vital that the spy is clear about their intentions. As Ferguson puts it, 'The key point about any recruitment pitch is that it must make clear that this is an intelligence operation and exactly what the target is being asked to do.'[1] Getting the balance right between these two competing forces can be challenging. A few rules of thumb can help.

First, the spy should reiterate the strength of their personal relationship with the target. This can provide a neat (not to say seamless) ushering in of the pitch. For example, she might say, as she leans over to refill her target's wineglass, 'I have so enjoyed this evening. It has reminded me of how much I value our friendship. So much so, that I really want to be honest with you. There is something that I think you should know about me.' These words might preface her coming out as an intelligence officer, without making an overt pitch at that stage. A target's response to this revelation can be most revealing. It might even help to guide the next step. If the target reacts in horror and rails against her for having not been straight with him, she will reconsider the advisability of pitching him on that occasion. He may need some time to get used to the idea. Conversely, a chuckling response along the lines of 'Worst kept secret ever,' or a more sober 'I always suspected you were', could be seen as an implicit invitation to proceed: equivalent to 'We both know what's going on here. Let's seal the deal.'

Second, the spy should use the language of teamwork, collaboration and reciprocity, rather than recruitment, even if that is what it is. Decide for yourself which phrases sound better, out of the following three pairs:

- 'I would like us to work together' or 'I would like you to work for me'?

---

1 Ferguson, *Spy*, p. 113.

- 'I think we can find a way to work against the system here' or 'I need you to pass me information to support my country's national interests'?
- 'I'd like to find a way to help you pay for your child's medical fees' or 'I'll pay you for passing me secrets'?

You will have noticed that the first of each of these formulations also mirrors different motivations: desire to please, ideology and money. This is the third consideration for a spy when deciding the language to use during a recruitment. Remember, this is the second part of my summary of a spy's job: to engage a target's motivations. This is better done with some subtlety, albeit without leaving room for doubt. The spy might say, 'I heard you when you said you are struggling with money, so I have a proposal that may help you', or 'I think you have a fascinating take on what is happening here and I'd like to share some of what you say with my government. I know they would appreciate it.' Whatever the precise form of language, though, the target must be left in no doubt that they are being invited to become an intelligence agent.

Without that much being clear, the spy would find it tricky to address a vital aspect of the spy-agent relationship: security. We shall come back to this in Chapter Nine (p. 270). For now, it is enough to note that the spy should make it clear that their number one priority is the target's security. She should offer reassurances about how many people will know the target's identity and the nature of his work. She might explain what measures are in place at her agency to ensure secure handling of information. And she could begin to broach the subject of tradecraft, described by Furnham and Taylor as a process to 'ensure that potentially hostile people or technical devices do not observe their [handler and agent's] meetings'.[1]

1 Furnham and Taylor, *The Psychology of Spies and Spying*, p. 114.

Part of tradecraft is planning for contingencies. This is also something the spy must do when preparing for her recruitment pitch. It involves anticipating a series of 'what-ifs?' What if the target goes into a form of denial and simply refuses to believe the spy when she tells him she is an intelligence officer? What if he accepts the pitch but demands an outrageous sum for his services? What if he responds that he is also an intelligence officer and makes a counteroffer (it's not unknown for each of two officers from opposing sides to think they are the cultivator rather than the cultivar)? What if he declares his love for the spy? Or offers to trade secrets for sex? All of these questions and more must be pre-empted and prepared for.

And then there is the big one. What if the target says no? In this case, there is not only the blow to the spy's self-esteem to consider. There is also the small matter of her safety. Is she in a hostile operating environment? Is there a chance that the target could report her to the authorities? If the answers to these questions are yes, she will need an extrication plan in place. If not, her get-out will be more about saving face and keeping options open for the target, should he change his mind. A breezy 'Forget I ever mentioned it' is unlikely to do the trick. A more considered line might be 'I'm sorry, I seem to have misjudged something here. Please forgive me. Of course, I fully respect your decision but, if you do ever change your mind, you know how to get hold of me.'

The most important part of that response is 'I fully respect your decision'. As I have already stressed, the best motivations come from within. Empowering a target is the name of the game, not robbing them of their autonomy or placing undue pressure on them. The same applies when it comes to asking a target goals ally to give up their time to support you, in whatever way. We'll look at how best to do that next, after

I tell you about one of my earliest attempts at recruiting a goals ally.

I didn't even know that was what I was doing.

* * *

Why *should* Peter agree to mentor me? This was the question churning in my mind, as I made my way to our meeting in his lord mayor's parlour. I was walking there, both to save the bus fare, which I could ill afford, and to give myself time to think. I had completed my Finals the previous week and just about shaken off the hangover from extended celebrations. Now, it was time to start the serious work of winning over allies to help me land a job. I was taking a shortcut through Summerfield Park, down the road from home. Kids were playing impromptu games of football in the weak June sun. Their shouts of encouragement, triumphal roars, groans of disappointment and the thuds of boot on leather were the soundtrack to my trudging progress. But I was deep in thought and hardly noticed them.

Why *should* he agree to mentor me?

I had known Peter Barwell for a few years, but not well. He was councillor for a nearby ward and we had done a bit of canvassing or leafleting together, during the odd local election campaign. I had chatted to him at constituency events. He knew who I was. I was confident that he liked me. But that was about it. I hadn't consciously cultivated him. I wouldn't have known what that meant, back then. It wasn't much of a basis for my asking him to champion my personal cause. Nonetheless, I was going to ask him. I just needed an angle.

A stray football scudded across the path in front of me. I tried to get it back to the burly teenager who was running after it, but fluffed the kick, sending the ball wide and short of him. I pressed on, face burning, trying to ignore the taunts and laughter: 'Nice shot, geezer'; 'Come and join the game. I want you on the other side.' Not a great omen. The embarrassment stayed with me, all the way to the Council House, distracting me from planning my pitch to Peter. I didn't want to think about pitches, football or otherwise, after that.

The lord mayor was gracious and polite, as always. He took me on a personal tour of Birmingham's beautiful Victorian Council House, before settling us into his parlour, where he had tea and cakes brought in. He congratulated me on completing my Finals and asked about my career plans. I was still unsure about how to ask him to support me onto the professional ladder, so that cue passed. Then we moved onto general discussions about politics. John Major had won an unexpected victory over Labour earlier that year and Ireland was about to vote in a referendum on the controversial Maastricht Treaty, so there was plenty for us to talk about. At that time, I was considering a career in political lobbying. But, again, I missed my cue. We talked about a young relative of his, with whom I had discussed the idea of establishing a lobbying firm that would focus on local government. I missed that opportunity, too. Another open goal missed.

The hour ticked by, and I felt the situation slipping away from me. The more I fixated on the rapidly approaching end of our meeting, the more unfocused on my task I became. We were going to run out of time and Peter was going to wonder why I had asked to see him in the first place. He was going to think I was wasting his time. I *was* wasting his time.

But still the words wouldn't come.

The problem was my obsession with reciprocity. I naively thought then that all interpersonal dealings needed a transactional element of some sort. So, I mentally scrolled through ideas about what I could offer to Peter in return for his support. More campaigning assistance? He didn't need any, in his capacity as lord mayor. Refer potential clients to his printing business? I didn't know any. Offer to buy him dinner? I didn't have any money. I was stuck in a thought loop: 'I would like to ask for support from him, but I have nothing to offer in return. I will only be able to offer him something in return when I have progressed in life. I won't progress much in life without support from someone like Peter . . .'

It didn't occur to me that someone like Peter could have other motivations to help his youngers. But the clues were all around me. Photos of him awarding prizes at school sports days, framed letters of thanks from various charities for fundraising efforts, the fact that he had unquestioningly given up an hour of his precious time for me. His having been a councillor for nearly thirty years and being lord mayor were also clues. Peter was a public servant through and through, committed to bettering the lives of others.

Finally, he resolved my anguish for me.

'I have another meeting in five minutes,' he said, offering me the final slice of cake. 'It has been lovely to see you, Jules, and thank you for your thoughts on the current state of our politics.' He brushed a crumb off his jacket lapel. 'But I am sure you didn't come here only to pass the time of day. What is it that I can do for you?'

He had seen my discomfort and hesitation and decided to force the issue for me. It was a relief, but the pressure was really on. Now I needed to pitch him and I had not properly prepared for this moment, thanks to a stray soccer ball. I looked around me and my eyes came to rest on a photo of Peter on stage at his old school, Bloxham, giving a speech to the pupils. I gestured towards it.

'You are right, of course,' I said. 'Sorry for not coming to the point earlier.'

Peter shook his head. 'Not at all. It has been a pleasure.'

'I can't help noticing that you give up a great deal of your time supporting others. Especially younger people.'

Peter nodded. 'Of course. I have been very fortunate in life. I went to a fabulous school, and I had the support of a wonderful family and many friends. I'm always keen to give something back.'

'Well, in that case,' I said, 'I wonder if I could throw myself on your generous spirit?'

'What do you have in mind?'

'It's a tough job market out there and I could really do with a mentor, to help me navigate it. You know, someone with wisdom and experience. Someone who is successful and respected.'

Peter said nothing.

'Someone like you,' I added. Just to leave him in no doubt.

'I've always enjoyed your company and thought you an interesting young man. I'd be delighted to help you,' he said. 'What does that mean in practice, though?'

I was back on firmer ground. I had already rehearsed my answer to that question.

'You could make introductions to the senior people you know with graduate vacancies to fill. Put in a good word for me, provide a character reference. You could help me improve my CV, talk me through what successful businesspeople look for in candidates. Maybe act as a sounding board when I have inter-views coming up, so I can try out ideas on you.'

Peter nodded thoughtfully. He got up and went to his desk, to leaf through cards on a Rolodex (for younger readers, a Rolodex was a revolving card holder and was the main means by which businesspeople kept track of their contacts in the analogue age).

Pulling a card from the deck, he bent over to scribble a number on a page of headed notepaper. He said, 'An old friend of mine runs a public relations company here. I'm sure he will be happy to meet you and discuss some work experience. He'd value someone with some political knowledge. I'll call him this afternoon.' Handing the note to me, he added, 'Call David tomorrow morning.'

'Thank you, Peter, that's exactly the sort of help I need. Your help will make a huge difference to my job search, and I am hugely grateful.'

'Delighted to hear it.' He frowned in thought. 'What else can I do for you?' He leafed through his desk-diary, then snapped his fingers. 'I have an idea. I could do with a little bit of help here, now and again. Just a couple of hours a week, helping me write speeches and do some research. I could pay you expenses. But, more important, the work could go on your CV. Then I could provide work-references for you, as well as character references.' This was going better than I had expected. Peter picked up his phone and asked his secretary to move his next meeting back by half an hour. Hanging up, he said to me, 'Right, now let's talk about your CV.'

As it happened, I had a copy with me, in case he asked to see it. Peter took a pen to it, talking me through the structure, tone, language and content most likely to catch a recruiter's eye. He taught me a great deal in those thirty minutes but, if I had to pick one piece of advice that was most valuable, it would be this: 'Check, double-check and triple-check the spelling and grammar. After all, if you can't do the recruiter the courtesy of getting it right, why should he do you the courtesy of getting you in?'

This was not to be a one-off. Peter stayed in touch with me over that summer, as my job search went on. His friend David gave me two weeks of valuable work experience. I spent a few hours a week helping Peter with research, and he provided me with numerous references in return. He sent other leads my way, all of which led to interviews. I wasn't so good at those, and it took advice from another quarter to crack that problem, but that's another story, told elsewhere in this book. He gave me words of encouragement when I stumbled and was generous in his praise when I finally got a job.

In short, he was a valuable and generous goals ally.

It was many years before I would come to realise that I had subconsciously engaged directly with his motivations.

Gratitude: 'I've been very fortunate in my life.'

Responsibility: the *noblesse oblige* of a lord mayor.

Altruism: 'I'm always keen to give something back.'

Desire to Please: 'I'd be delighted to help you.'

And Ego: 'Someone with wisdom and experience. Someone who is successful and respected.'

I don't think I needed to appeal to Peter's ego, though. His instinct to help others was powerful enough without it. That much was made clear after his death on 4 March 2020, aged 84, in a fulsome tribute from his *alma mater,* Bloxham School. It read, in part, 'Peter's philanthropy set an example to the school community: through presenting books to the Liddon Library, providing the gift of a crucifix for the Confessional and donating to the Centenary Appeal Fund all within just a few years of leaving. The desire to give back to the school that had given him so much never waned.' I also learned, from the same source, that in 1985 Peter 'was awarded the Golden Cross of Merit for special services to the Polish community'.[1] I have no idea what earned him that distinction, but it does not surprise me that he did.

The website Bloxham Online, which chronicles events in the village of his former school and to where he retired, also paid tribute to Peter's generosity and sense of civic responsibility. It noted that 'In 1992, he was appointed lord mayor of Birmingham

1 Bloxham School, Obituaries. https://www.bloxhamschool.com/ob-news/sad-passing-of-distinguished-alumnus-peter-barwell-mbe-csm/?doing_wp_cron=1695324335.5874309539794921875000

and is remembered during his term of office for his generosity to the village at that time. On one occasion [he transported] a coach full of villagers to an evening dinner in the Council House before, later in the year, finding time to open the Bloxham Village Fete, wearing his full lord mayor's regalia.' The article described Peter as 'a very active member of the community, undertaking a variety of voluntary positions'.[1]

Peter Barwell MBE CSM, former lord mayor of Birmingham, is obviously remembered by his old school and by his fellow villagers in Bloxham with great affection, gratitude and admiration.

That is how I remember him, too.

* * *

RECAP

- Planning is vital before a recruitment pitch. The spy and her team will start with a thorough review of a target's file to assess if he is ready for an approach.
- They will ask three questions. Can the target get the required information? Would he make a good and discreet agent? Does he have motivations to become one?
- The spy will then plan for the recruitment meeting itself. The plan will cover setting, mood, language, contingencies and extrication. But she will be ready to be flexible.
- The pitch must be unmistakeable in its intent. The target needs to know who the spy really is and what she is asking of him. There is no room for ambiguity.

1 Bloxham Online, 'Tribute to Peter Barwell', 2 April 2020. https://bloxham.info/broadsheet/tribute-to-peter-barwell-mar-2020/

- The spy might discuss tradecraft: how she will keep the agent safe, assuming he has accepted the pitch. If he hasn't, she may need to enact her extrication plan.
- She will respect the target's decision. Recruitment is about empowering a target, not putting them under pressure. The same applies to recruiting goals allies.

* * *

Let's think about the verb 'recruit'.

It has a very specific formal meaning, according to the *Concise Oxford English Dictionary*: 'enlist (someone) in the armed forces' or 'enrol (someone) as a member or worker in an organisation'. Neither of these definitions quite applies to a spy's 'recruitment' of an agent, as the latter will not be joining the armed forces or becoming a member or worker 'in' the spy's organisation. However, the dictionary offers another, informal, definition: 'persuade to do or help with something'. It is this informal meaning that links the act of recruitment in espionage with the task of winning over a goals ally. Both set out to persuade someone to do something or help with something. So, it makes sense to approach both with similar, rigorous planning.

Before launching a formal planning process, though, there is some vital mental work to do, in both cases: getting into the right headspace.

Read again the opening words of this chapter: 'The time has come. This is what it has all been leading to.' Ironically – for me – it is a bit like a shot at goal. A lot of effort and planning has gone into getting you and the ball into position. Hit the back of the net, bask in the glory. Sail over the crossbar, feel the shame of failure. And you might not get another shot in this match. Thankfully, I am better at the metaphor than I am at the game.

So, before starting assessment of whether your target is ready, ask yourself if *you* are ready. Are you emotionally prepared to handle the stress of making a pitch? Would you be comfortable with your target rejecting your approach? You will be much better equipped for the task if you start from the strongest mental position you can manage. It is better to avoid high-stress events like attempted recruitments when you are feeling emotionally vulnerable. Or physically frail. The two often go together, so you may benefit from a programme of workouts in the run-up to the big day. If you have someone willing to discuss your plans with you, that is also a good idea. An honest friend or family member will be able to tell you if you are not mentally ready to go for it, even where you might find it hard to admit to yourself.

On which note, try to foster self-awareness, so that you can be honest with yourself. People who are self-aware can understand how others see them (preferably without becoming self-conscious). They are better able to be objective about themselves, hold themselves to their personal values, and manage their emotions. Self-awareness is a great muscle to work on. There are many online resources that will help you strengthen it, but here are a few exercises that I have found effective over the years.

1: Articulate your values

What do you stand for? Honestly. Don't adopt a set of values that you think might be socially acceptable. Instead, work out what genuinely matters to you. Physical health? Financial well-being? Freedom of self-expression? Being family-orientated? Compassion? Sociability? Conflict avoidance? There are no right or wrong answers here, just honest ones. When you have worked out the honest answers, affirm them, give them life.

Repeat them to yourself; say them out loud; write them down. Whatever works for you.

2: Align your actions with your values

Ever have that undefinable awkward feeling about yourself? A sense that something is not sitting right? Concerned that you are not a good or likeable person? It could be that your actions are out of kilter with your values. Misalignments can arise when we are in jobs that don't suit us, or when we submit to peer pressure to act contrary to our natures. Or it could just be that we haven't checked in with ourselves for a while. Develop the habit of occasional self-reflection, ensuring that what you do, say and value is in accord and consistent.

3: Get to know yourself by taking a personality test

I like the Myers–Briggs Type Indicator (MBTI®) assessment.[1] It is not the only one, but it is a resource you can easily take advantage of online. The assessment comes in the form of a questionnaire that measures responses to similar situations from different perspectives, thereby reducing the risk of the user pushing the results in a desired direction. The answers are analysed to assign a 'code' to the respondent, indicating where they lie on four psychological scales: introversion (I) – extroversion (E); sensing (S) – intuition (N); thinking (T) – feeling (F); and judging (J) – perceiving (P). You may be surprised by the outcome. I was. I had expected to come out as ENTJ; my results (re-confirmed a couple of times) showed me to be INFJ.

1 https://www.mbtionline.com/

4: Practise being consciously true to your personality

You may think this piece of advice unnecessary. After all, how can we betray our personalities? All I can say in response is that it took me over a year to reconcile myself to the idea of being introverted. I had always considered myself – and sought to behave like – an extrovert. Little did I know this was causing me emotional damage, and perhaps physical damage, as I tended to rely on alcohol to get me through social occasions that I didn't really want to be at.

It's not that I am particularly shy, though I can be at times. It is more that I, like all introverts, need to withdraw from the world occasionally, for solitude and private reflection. This is the way in which I restore my energy, whereas extroverts draw energy from being around others. Once I had accepted this, and consciously made time for myself, I became emotionally calmer and loosened my reliance on alcohol as a social prop. In turn, this enabled me to become more empathetic and sensitive to the needs of others. Confucius reportedly said, 'Respect yourself and others will respect you.' Maybe. I prefer, 'Respect yourself and you will respect others.'

BE MINDFUL

I'm not suggesting you take up meditation, though there are very good reasons to do that, if you are so inclined. Rather, I am inviting you to 'drop in on yourself' from time to time. Ask yourself, where am I and what am I doing? Then be there and do that. This technique is related to active listening, which we explored in Chapter Four (p. 103). For example, if you are talking to a loved one about their day at work, engage actively and in the moment with what they are saying. Rather than, say, allowing yourself to be distracted with ideas for the next chapter of the book you are writing. This is not as easy as it sounds, as I am sure my fiancée would confirm.

If you would like to explore mindfulness and meditation in more depth, I can't recommend highly enough the work of Jon Kabat-Zinn.[1]

But, for now, that's enough about you. Now that you are in a robust and confident frame of mind, ready to transmit your pitch clearly and articulately, it is time to consider the other side of the equation. Will your target be receptive? It is time to review your dealings with them to date and assess whether they are ready for 'recruitment'. To do this, you need to think like a spy.

As you read back through your goals ally file, ask yourself three questions.

POSITIONING

First, did you get the targeting exercise right? Is your target in the right position to become a champion for you? This isn't just about how successful they are, their public profile and the relevance of their occupation to your goals. You should also satisfy yourself that they have time available to spend assisting you.

SUITABILITY

Second, would your target make a good goals ally? Do they have a supportive character? Are they patient, empathetic and open-minded? Or are they impatient, introspective, and unreceptive? There is little point in trying to recruit someone who

1 https://jonkabat-zinn.com/

may say yes – with all good intentions – but then not have the emotional wherewithal to follow through in the longer term.

MOTIVATIONS

And third, what – if any – are your target's motivations for becoming your ally? Think this through systematically, using the GRADE model outlined in the previous chapter. A clear understanding of motivations is important because it will dictate the most effective language to use in your pitch.

Once you are satisfied that your target would make a valuable ally, who is both willing and able to commit to your cause, you can develop your 'plan of attack'. I suggest that you write down a plan, under the following headings: setting; mood; language; contingencies; and retreat. Note that this mirrors the spy's recruitment plan, except that 'extrication' has been swapped out for 'retreat'. This is because you will not have to flee the country if your target rejects your proposal. But you will need to bow out of your meeting graciously and with your self-respect intact. Forward planning can help you achieve this.

SETTING

As with a spy's recruitment pitch, there are countless possibilities for the right setting. The first consideration should be your target's likely preference, based perhaps on previous suggestions. They may have set a pattern of meeting in their office. If so, go with it. They may prefer to get together in restaurants, hotel lobbies, coffee shops or bars. Or at a private club, of which you or they are a member. Again, be guided by past experiences. Your second consideration should be whether the selected venue lends itself to a quiet conversation. Will you be able to find somewhere that you can sit with a reasonable degree of privacy? Will you be able to hold a conversation without either of you straining to hear the other?

Mood

Settings can also affect the overall mood of the encounter. Ask yourself what would be most appropriate for your specific case. Is your target brisk and businesslike? In this case, you may choose to meet at their office or in an office space that you have rented. If they are more easy-going, perhaps enjoying a drink and a meal when meeting others, you will not be short of appropriate venues. Thereafter, it is up to you to judge how you wish to shape the mood once in front of your target. In this case, formality may be more appropriate than for a spy's purposes. But not always. It is for you to work out the optimal tone to set.

LANGUAGE

Your desired tone, along with your assessment of the target's motivations, will also determine the language that you should use when making your pitch. Professional ('I really appreciate this opportunity to explore ways in which . . .')? Or matey ('it would be great to . . .)? Serious ('As you know, these are challenging economic times . . .')? Or jocular ('My career has stalled, and I could so with someone to help me jump-start it . . .')? Only you can assess the right language to use in your specific circumstances. But there are a few rules that should apply regardless.

First, be clear about what you are asking for. Consider 'It would be fantastic if you could give my first draft a read and advise me how I could develop my voice', as opposed to 'Could you take a look at my manuscript and tell me what you think?' Or 'I'd like you to be the first guest on my new podcast and put it out on your social media accounts', as opposed to 'It would be neat if you could help me launch my new podcast.'

Second, be concise. We are all tempted to ramble, especially if we are asking someone to do something for us. We want to get our justifications in first, or we simply keep talking to delay the moment of truth. Don't. It is much better to ask for what you want, after a certain amount of framing (we'll come back to this). Then shut up and listen to your target's response. You can have all the justifications and reasoning in reserve, to bring out as and when necessary. But don't get lost in them because, if you do, your target will too.

Third, preface your ask with an appeal to some aspect of their motivations. Think about a formulation such as 'I know you have given so much back to society through your foundation and I'd love to know if you could give some of your personal time to . . .' Then compare it to 'Your endorsement of my app idea could get Apple interested in it.' This is not to say that you shouldn't let your target know that their input will make a difference. You absolutely should. But lead with something that appeals to them first, before telling them how it will transform your life.

This is related to the fourth and final rule: get your gratitude in early. Everyone likes to be appreciated, so tell them they will be. Besides, if someone has just told you how thankful they will be for your help, it makes it that little bit more difficult to refuse.

CONTINGENCIES

Nonetheless, refusal remains a possibility. It could be partial refusal, for which you will need to plan some contingencies. Perhaps your target says, 'I don't think I have the time to read your whole manuscript.' It would be perfectly reasonable to come back with, 'Of course, I understand that. But could you look at the first two chapters, maybe?' Whatever you are asking for, have a couple of less demanding back-ups in mind, just in case. That said, don't push the 'yes, but' game too far. It can very quickly cause resentment. Sometimes, instead, you must accept defeat.

RETREAT

Which is where your planning for a retreat comes in. Don't overthink this. Dwelling on the idea of rejection may subconsciously lessen the impact of your pitch. But, also, don't risk leaving yourself lost for words if your target does decline your request. That could make the whole experience humiliating for you and there is no reason for it to be so. Decide in advance how you will – with grace, dignity and respect – respond to a refusal.

You may find it useful to rehearse a short form of words, such as 'Of course, I completely understand, and I hope you don't mind that I asked you. If you can think of anyone else who might be able to stand in for you, I'd be very grateful for an introduction. But only if it is off the top of your head. Please don't go to any effort.' You should also decide in advance whether to draw the meeting to an immediate close, if you are turned down. If you have other matters to discuss, there is no obvious reason to do so. Just have in mind what segue you will use to move from gracious acceptance of the refusal to those other matters.

The chances are, though, that you will not have to fall back either on your contingencies or your plan for retreat. If you have got the targeting, cultivation, and elicitation stages right, you are more likely to end up with a positive response, like Tom.

CASE STUDY

The sun was shining, so Tom selected a seat outside at *le Consulat Café* on rue Norvins, Montmartre. He had suggested the venue because it was easy to find, being a short walk from the Sacré-Cœur, but was also a distance away from the busy, touristy Place de Tertre. Besides, it was one of his favourite places for an *al fresco* lunch in Paris. He had arrived fifteen minutes ahead of the time agreed with Moussa. An opportunity to review his notes and mentally rehearse his pitch, one last time.

Moussa was flustered when he arrived a few minutes late.

'I am so sorry to be late, Tom,' he said. 'I was at a rehearsal all morning and then had to spend time with wardrobe for a fitting.'

Tom shook his head and smiled. 'No problem at all, my friend. I have been sitting here enjoying the sunshine. And it is very appropriate that you were detained at a wardrobe fitting.'

'Oh, yes? Why's that.'

'Let's come back to that.' He pushed a glass of chilled Chablis across the table towards Moussa. 'First, I expect you'll be needing this and to catch your breath.'

Moussa downed half his glass. 'Too right,' he said. 'I'm not usually a lunch-time drinker but I'll make an exception, just for today.'

The tone was set.

Their talk over lunch was light-hearted and friendly. Moussa told Tom about the movie he was filming and gossiped about the Paris fashion week, during which he had seen a handful of shows. Tom saw an opportunity. He told Moussa that he regretted not being able to afford Paris during that week, much as he would love to attend. 'This is where it's all at,' he said. 'This is the city I need to crack.' The conversation moved on, but Tom thought he saw Moussa register his comment.

Later, as the waiter cleared their coffee cups, Moussa said, 'You mentioned earlier that you need to "crack" Paris.'

Tom nodded. 'I think every would-be fashion designer feels the same way.'

'Of course,' said Moussa. 'It's a tough place though. Is there anything I can do to help you?'

The opening Tom had hoped for. He signalled to the waiter for the bill, before turning back to Moussa. 'Unless you'd like anything else?'

'To hell with it. Let's have another glass of wine. Now, tell me how I can help you.'

'Moussa, it is so kind of you to ask. But I'm not surprised. You do so much for others, already. Can you find the time to give a leg up to another of your townsfolk?'

Moussa waved the question away. 'I am an actor. I often have time on my hands. We call it resting between jobs.'

Tom laughed. 'Well, I said earlier it was appropriate you had been in wardrobe this morning because, to be honest, I wanted to ask you this all along. You have a reputation in the fashion world as a great dresser, so your endorsements matter. Will you be a champion for my work, please?'

Moussa spread his hands. 'Depends on what it takes, I guess.'

'Nothing onerous. And, maybe, something fun,' Tom said. 'You could wear a few of my pieces for photo shoots. Maybe one or two for each season. I would have them adjusted to your size and a friend of mine here is a great photographer. I'm sure they would be happy to help. Then it would be fantastic if you could post a few of them to your social media and hashtag me.'

Moussa nodded, enthusiastically. 'I like your designs,' he said. 'It's a great idea. When can we start?'

Tom chose his venue cleverly and set the tone for his encounter with Moussa from the outset, turning the focus on him and inviting him to kick back and relax. He was also skilful at 'framing' his later pitch. He let it be known, subtly, that he needed help and would likely be asking for some from Moussa. This way, he heightened the chances of his friend providing an opening for his pitch. He said it was appropriate that Moussa had been in a wardrobe fitting and encouraged discussion of the Paris fashion week. Consequently, Moussa was more likely to be receptive to the idea of being involved in fashion shoots.

Later, it was clever of Tom to signal the waiter for the bill before launching his pitch. This act of simple generosity would increase his likeability, most probably enhancing Moussa's desire to please him. His reference to Moussa's work with other youngsters from their hometown was an appeal to his sense of gratitude and social responsibility. Finally, he made an understated appeal to Moussa's ego, telling him that he has a reputation as a great dresser. In short, he covered the GRADE territory, without relying too heavily on any one aspect, in line with his assessment of Moussa's personality. He was clear that he was asking for a continued commitment from Moussa and spelled out exactly what the commitment would entail. He emphasised how thankful he would be for the help.

You might have noticed something else. Tom did most of his work – the framing and his appeals to motivations – ahead of the pitch itself. This is an example of what the renowned author-ity on influence, Robert Cialdini, has termed *pre-suasion*.[1] We'll look at what spies can learn from Cialdini in the next chapter (p. 215), after a story about how I pulled off a similar trick of pre-suasion, quite deliberately, in a professional setting.

But, before that, I have a few final thoughts on how to prepare for *your* recruitment pitch. Common-sense suggestions, really.

The day before, recce the venue where you will make the pitch. Make sure that it is appropriate, quiet and will be open at the time you have agreed to meet (you might be surprised how often even professional spies overlook this last point). The even-ing before, don't drink too much – if at all – and get a good night's sleep. It is always better to be sharp and rested for such encounters. On the day, review the notes you have made about previous meetings and rehearse again your lines. In the words of the inimitable Baz Luhrmann, 'stretch' and 'be kind to your knees'.[2] The best way to do this is to take a brisk walk to your meeting, if you can. It will clear your head, get the endorphins flowing, and prep you for the encounter.

Just don't kick any footballs on the way.

* * *

'Do you remember that first drive across Somalia?'

Magic chuckled. 'How could I forget?'

'I don't think I ever will,' I said. 'It is burned on my memory, mainly because I was terrified.'

'Let me tell you a secret,' Magic said, raising his glass of Coke to chink with my ice-cold Tusker beer. 'So was I.'

1 Robert Cialdini, *Pre-Suasion: A Revolutionary Way to Influence and Persuade*, Random House Business, 2017.
2 Baz Luhrmann, 'Sunscreen'. https://www.songlyrics.com/baz-luhr-mann/sunscreen-lyrics/

We were sitting in the lush, green gardens of the Karen Blixen Coffee House in Nairobi's wealthy suburb, Karen (which was not, as it happens, named after the famous Ms Blixen). It was February, Kenya's hottest, driest month. Mid-afternoon. We had eaten *nyama choma* (burned meat, in kiSwahili, usually much tastier than it sounds) on the terrace, before settling at a table on the lawn. Our bellies were pleasantly full, and I had a mild buzz from the Tusker. Magic, a sometimes-devout Muslim, contented himself with nicotine and caffeine for his high.

The lawn had been tended that morning and the smell of mown grass lay on the air. Birds were singing in the jacaranda tree which shaded us. It swayed in a gentle breeze, lulling us further with the shushing of its leaves. The mood could not have been more different from the time we had spent together in war-torn Somalia, back in 2007.

The previous year, an Islamist organisation calling itself the Islamic Courts Union (ICU) had seized power in Mogadishu, bringing some measure of control over the lawlessness and warlordism that had been Somalia's burden since the early 1990s. During that period, it was considered by many to be the most dangerous country in the world. Few westerners were to be found there, with even armies fearing the anarchy, vividly described in John Burnett's gripping memoir, *Where Soldiers Fear to Tread*.[1]

Whatever good the ICU had done, its imposition of strict Shariah law was unpopular with many Somalis. Its rise alarmed the international community, which was uncomfortable with overt Islamism so soon after 9/11. Instead, the west backed a hitherto toothless Transitional Federal Government (TFG). The TFG had established its base inland, in the second city of Baidoa, as it was unable to gain control over the capital, Mogadishu.

---

1 John S. Burnett, *Where Soldiers Fear to Tread: A Relief Worker's Tale of Survival*, Bantam Dell, 2006.

Most important, the ICU was opposed by Somalia's powerful western neighbour. In December 2006, the TFG launched a military offensive on Mogadishu, with decisive support from Ethiopia. The ICU was removed from power before the end of the year, with its leaders formally resigning on 27 December.

I was to be one of the first westerners to set foot on Somalian soil after that year of turmoil.

I was the G2 (Intelligence) component of a small private military team charged with assessing national security and presenting recommendations for its improvement to the TFG. Magic was an adviser to the TFG and had helped organise our itinerary. I had given him the nickname because of his apparently magical ability to get us out of danger. We spent much of that afternoon in the Karen Blixen Coffee House reminiscing about our escapades.

It had been four years since we had driven at dawn across Nairobi's national park to Wilson Airport. The morning had been chilly, even in February; it often was, given Nairobi's altitude. We were glad of our suits and ties. At Wilson we boarded a six-seater flight. The plane ferried consignments of *khat*, a plant with stimulating and addictive properties chewed by many East Africans, from Kenya to Somalia. I slept most of the way, to be woken by the thud of the plane's wheels hitting the runway at Baidoa Airport. More of an airstrip, really, surrounded by broken-down concrete shells that had once been airport buildings.

We were met at the foot of the plane's steps by two Toyota flat-bed jeeps mounted with Uzi 9mm submachine guns on metal tripods. 'Technicals', in military parlance. These whisked us to meet the prime minister of the TFG, Ali Mohammed Ghedi, bumping along cratered highways, scattering goats and pedestrians before them. My driver pressed on the motor horn for the entire journey. Following a short formal greeting over a breakfast of bananas and hardboiled eggs, we were treated to a tour of Baidoa, taking in an old school hall that doubled as the

TFG's parliament, and the remains of a car bombing outside its gates. There was little else to see.

Our accommodation for the night was in an army barracks that must once have been a prison, for my concrete room was more like a cell than anything else. I tossed and turned the night away, protected by a holey mosquito net that was slung from a hook in the ceiling and tucked under a mattress that stank of mould. The mosquitoes feasted themselves on me, but the net repelled some of the flying cockroaches, at least. I was relieved to rise again before dawn, joining a convoy of technicals that was to accompany Ghedi as he made his triumphant first entry to Mogadishu as prime minister.

Magic and I sat in the back of a double cab bakkie. Our security detail squatted around the Uzi tripod on the truck bed floor, carrying with them rolled-up mattresses, holdalls full of clothes, TVs, pots and pans. There were four of them, ranging in age from early teens to late twenties, all armed and all dressed in odd mixtures of camouflage and civilian clothing (Black Sabbath and Metallica t-shirts). They seemed excited to be moving to Mogadishu, chatting animatedly in Somali between heated arguments. Up front, the driver's child bride sat demurely in the passenger seat, wrapped in a colourful headscarf, as her husband got high on khat and floored the accelerator. He gave us a ride so terrifying that I remember it as a series of nightmarish flashbacks.

The moment he twisted round to face Magic, with whom he kept up a stream of conversation, without realising he was heading towards a bomb crater. I had visions of us hitting the lip of the crater and flipping. It occurred to me that I hadn't called my mum to say goodbye. Magic calmly but emphatically told the driver to 'accelerate, now'. An extra burst of speed gave us the momentum to clear the four-foot gap. The driver laughed, baring his teeth. His upper incisors were missing.

The moment we swung off the road, with the other cars, in pursuit of a gang of camel rustlers. The boys on the back were up and jumping, firing their pistols into the air and shouting obscenities. The driver's wife adjusted her headscarf. Magic leaned over to tap him on his shoulder. 'Let's get our guests back on the road,' he said. 'The others can deal with this.'

The moment we careered into Mogadishu's outskirts, a goat glancing off the side of the truck as it tried to get out of the way. The crunch, the howl and the sight of the poor creature dragging itself away with two broken legs haunt me still.

Mogadishu must once have been a beautiful city, of white Italianate villas looking out across the glittering blue Indian Ocean. What I remember, though, is a city as destroyed as it is possible to get without being razed. I saw not a single building without pockmarks from bullets. Many of them were missing roofs, some were missing side walls, so we could look in on families that eked out lives in the ruins. Others had been reduced to piles of smashed concrete and twisted metal. Everywhere, the smell of human shit, sewage running in rivulets through the cracked tarmac of the roads.

We stayed for a week, sleeping three of us to a room in the prime minister's residence, one of the few intact buildings the city could boast. By day, we drove to see the Mogadishu police chief in his bombed-out headquarters. Met the 'head' of intelligence who had no staff of which to be head. Discussed town planning with officials of a penniless council. Admired ragged army recruits while commanding officers boasted of 'their' successes in the war against the ICU. Or inspected institutions such as the city gaol, from which the prisoners could abscond simply by climbing through the holes in the walls of their cells.

One day, we went for an audience with President Abdullahi Yusuf Ahmed, in Villa Somalia, his residence. It was a brief meeting, with Magic escorting us out after only ten minutes. As we drove away, we heard the crump of a mortar bomb, fired by one of the various militia groups that remained loyal to the ICU (one day to coalesce into the much-feared terrorist organisation *al Shabaab*). Later, we learned that the bomb had struck Villa Somalia itself, damaging the room from which Magic had ushered us a few minutes previously.

That's Magic!

At the end of the week, I was able to produce a comprehensive assessment of the state of Somalia's national security. It is not mine to share. But no matter, because this story is really about how I recruited Magic, that summer's day at the Karen Blixen Coffee House.

I had recently founded a private intelligence boutique which specialises in African matters, and I was building a team of sources who could keep me updated on developments across the continent. Magic was one of my targets.

The purpose of our reminiscences was to remind Magic of our experiences together. We all know instinctively that friendships are strengthened by shared adventure, and I planned to orientate Magic's mind to our bonds. This is because I was sure I would need to overcome his financial motivations. I was proved right, as I steered our conversation away from the past and towards the future.

'I felt good being able to do something to help Somalia recover from the conflict,' I said. 'And now that I am running my own business, I hope to do more. Maybe we could work together to bring new investors into the country.'

'I would like to help you do that,' said Magic. 'What can I do?'

'You know what is going on there, on the ground. You have great insights into the politics. You know what is happening with the security situation. You know who's who and who can get things done.' Magic acknowledged the flattery with a small bow of his head. 'The best way that we can work together is for us to have a call once a month, during which we can discuss developments in Somalia. We can look at where the commercial opportunities are, and you could share with me interesting information that clients would find useful.'

'And you would pay me for my time?' This was what I had anticipated.

'I would love to do that, Magic, but there are three problems.' I counted them off on my fingers. 'One, I don't have any money yet. I started my business only a few months ago. Two, I don't have any clients intending to invest in Somalia yet. Your insights will help to win those clients. And three, you are classed as a government official, so I can't make payments to you under something called the UK Bribery Act. There are also laws in Somalia against bribing officials, so we need to work together to make sure neither of us does anything illegal.'

Magic frowned. 'That doesn't seem fair,' he said. 'I help you win clients. You get paid and I don't.'

'That's one way of looking at it,' I replied. 'Another way is that you will be serving your country better by bringing in investment. I am sure you want to do that, anyway, otherwise you wouldn't be working for the government. In addition, your bosses will recognise your efforts and it will help your career.'

He smiled and wagged a finger at me. 'You are very persuasive. But it still seems like you are the one who will be winning from this arrangement, Mr Fisher.'

'Of course, I shall benefit. I'm building a company, not a charity. But my business is about helping companies to do business in Africa with integrity. To avoid corruption and to be good corporate citizens, helping to develop the communities where they work.' I spread my hands. 'Surely you buy into that idea?'

'How can I not?' Magic lit another cigarette, angling his head to blow the smoke away from me. 'But it will take up my time and I will deserve some reward for that.'

I understood Magic's position. Somalia was a dirt-poor country. Most government workers were paid a pittance. If they were paid at all. It was not uncommon for the government to skip payroll. He was more fortunate than most, as a senior man, close to senior leaders. His salary was usually paid on time, and he had use of a government-owned apartment in Nairobi. The TFG paid his travel expenses and the all-important *per diems*, generous supplements to monthly income. But, by the standards of the diplomatic community in which he moved in Nairobi, Magic's lifestyle was unenviable. He would be in economy seats on flights while his international counterparts sipped champagne up front. The apartment he used was in a run-down part of Nairobi called Eastleigh, while his peers graced large houses with swimming pools in the upmarket neighbourhoods of Lavington, Upper Hill or Karen. I knew from previous discussions that he felt unable to accept hospitality at diplomats' homes because he could not reciprocate.

I couldn't blame him for seeking ways to improve his lot. However, I could not offer him any money. For legal reasons and also because I didn't have any. I had boot-strapped my business and was trying to square the circle of winning clients to generate income to create services that clients would pay for. I relied on Magic – and others like him – to pull off that trick.

He hadn't said no. Yet. However, I had played a couple of rounds of the 'yes, but' game. We were getting close to the point when I would have to show him the respect he deserved and admit defeat. I had one last hand to play before that.

'I get it, Magic, I really do,' I said. 'You will certainly deserve to be rewarded if you work with me to get this business moving and to bring investors into Somalia. Believe me, there is nothing I would like more than to be able to pay you for your input. But, as I have explained, that won't be possible in current circumstances.' I leaned over and gestured to his cigarettes, raising my eyebrows. He nodded, I took one and he held up a match to me. The comradeship of smoking. 'So, I guess there is only one reward I can offer you.'

'What's that?' He lit another cigarette for himself from the same match, shaking out the flame as he spoke.

'The satisfaction of knowing that you have helped an old friend when he needs you.'

There was a moment, as my comment hung in the exhaled smoke between us. Then, his smile broadened, as he pushed his packet of cigarettes across to me.

'Here,' he said. 'You might as well take these too.' He mimed stripping his top off. 'The shirt off my back any good to you?' We were both laughing by now. 'But, yes, I shall help you. We can have our monthly call, on two conditions.'

'You name them, Magic.'

'You pay for the calls.' He drained his glass of Coke. 'And you pay for lunch.'

I did both.

Magic was, as usual, magical. Month by month, he gave me penetrating insights into developments in Somalia, helping me understand at least a little about a country that has defied analysis for decades. He was always witty, gracious and generous on our calls. I shared his insights with clients but security conditions in Somalia continued to be challenging. I never did manage to persuade any investors to risk it. Then, eighteen months later, the calls stopped. I would ring and there would be no answer. I would text and there would be no reply. I feared that I had offended my friend or exhausted his patience.

The truth was much, much worse. A few months later, on another visit to Nairobi, a friend in common told me what had happened. Magic had been killed in a traffic accident.

On the road from Baidoa to Mogadishu.

* * *

RECAP

- At the right time, you will move to recruit your target goals ally, with a clear pitch for their continued support to you. This is best done after careful planning.
- First, get yourself into the right place. It's advisable to be in good physical and mental shape before a recruitment. Work out and develop self-awareness.
- Align your actions with your values. Take a personality assessment and be true to its findings. Practise being mindful and present in your encounters with others.
- When you are ready, write a formal assessment of your target. Are they able to become an ally? Would they make a good one? Are they motivated to do so?
- If the answer to all three questions is 'yes', then develop a recruitment plan, under the headings of setting, mood, language, contingencies and retreat.
- Basic principles should underpin your pitch: be clear and concise; appeal to your target's motivations; get your gratitude in early; know how to respond to a refusal.
- Don't forget to recce your venue the day before. Double-check opening hours. On the day, review your notes and rehearse the pitch one last time.

PART 3

Staying Together (Agent Handling)

'The secret of my influence has always been that it remained secret.'
Attributed to Salvador Dalí

CHAPTER SEVEN

The Keeping Power of Influence

The nature of influence means that the balance of power between any two people is not always obvious. This matters to spies.

Why? Because – let's face it – a recruit appears to have all the power. Sure, a recruitment is a big deal. But it is only a moment in time, in which a target agrees to *become* an agent. At any time after this moment, they could change their mind, shift the terms of trade, or betray the spy, perhaps putting their life or liberty at risk. Another undesirable possibility is that they could make up intelligence that the spy wants to hear, with potentially ruinous consequences. In Chapter Eight (p. 244), we'll look at a case of such deception, which was used to help justify the invasion of Iraq in 2003. We'll also examine some techniques for detection of deceit. These help but it is undoubtedly better to avoid the problem arising in the first place.

This requires ongoing use of influence techniques by the spy. So far, she has used *persuasion* to get her target to agree to something. Now, her job is to use influence to get him to follow through: to commit to staying in place, perhaps against his preferences; to retrieve useful, reliable intelligence, perhaps at risk to his freedom; and to transmit that intelligence to her, accurately and comprehensively, over the long term.

It is worth a quick detour here, to establish a distinction between the concepts of persuasion and influence, as the terms are often used interchangeably. One description of the difference, offered by the leadership consultant Nicole DeFalco, is: 'Persuasion can be used to spur someone to action or to make a decision without actually earning their sincere buy-in. With influence, dedicating time to win someone's heart or earn mindshare is, a prerequisite to the process of inspiring them to take action or make a particular decision.'[1] I have no quibble with any of that, but a concrete example helps.

Imagine visiting a used-car dealership with not much more in mind than browsing the stock. A persistent salesman – let's call him John – spots that you are taken by a handsome classic Jaguar. John locks on to you, badgering, wheedling and bargaining. He claims that he has another potential buyer waiting in the wings and offers you an apparently generous discount, on condition that you sign the paperwork there and then. You come away from the encounter as the not-so-proud owner of a car that is prohibitively expensive to insure, tax, maintain and drive through low-emissions zones. Buyer's remorse soon sets in and you begin to hate the vehicle. In this case, the salesman has *persuaded* you to take a particular course of action, perhaps even against your better judgement. You tell your friends and family to avoid John's dealership.

In a parallel universe, you are greeted by a thoughtful, intelligent and honest saleswoman. Let's call her Honest Jane. Jane explains the drawbacks of the model that you are looking at and takes time to listen to your specific automobile needs. She suggests two or three other cars that might meet your requirements better, all of which are less expensive than the Jag. You take one for a test drive while she attends to some paperwork. Over coffee, Jane describes the terms of a finance plan to spread

1 Nicole DeFalco, 'Influence vs. persuasion: A critical distinction for leaders', Social Media Today, 30 October 2009. https://www.socialmediatoday.com/content/influence-vs-persuasion-critical-distinction-leaders

the cost of your potential purchase. Then, quite unexpectedly, she suggests that you go away and think about it. You thank her, reach for a pen and buy the car. In this case, the saleswoman has *influenced* you to take a course of action. Furthermore, she has probably influenced you to recommend her dealership to friends and family.

The main difference between the two approaches – other than the second being in the best interests of all parties in the longer term – is that, in DeFalco's words, John has failed to earn your 'sincere buy-in', while Jane has won your 'heart' and earned 'mindshare'. This is what spies need to do, as they guide a newly recruited agent through the early stages of their rede-fined relationship.

Psychologists, anthropologists and consultants have made extensive studies of the role of influence in marketing and sales. Perhaps the most influential (ahem) of these is Dr Robert Cialdini, a Regents' professor emeritus of Psychology and Marketing at Arizona State University. In 2007, Dr Cialdini identified six principles – originally termed 'weapons' – of influence.[1] In a revised and expanded edition of his seminal work, *Influence: The Psychology of Persuasion*, he rebranded the 'weapons' as 'levers' and added a seventh. Taken together, the principles are: 'reciprocation, liking, social proof, authority, scarcity, commitment and consistency, and unity'.[2]

It is tempting to take these seven principles as a template for the exercise of influence by a spy over their agent. Furnham and Taylor make a good fist of this, providing examples of 'spycraft' under each of the first six categories.[3] For example, they explain under the heading of 'social proof,' that 'we use

1 Robert B. Cialdini, *Influence, The Psychology of Persuasion*, Harper Business, 2007 edition.
2 Ibid., p. xvii.
3 Furnham and Taylor, *The Psychology of Spies and Spying*, pp. 81–4.

others' behaviour to determine what is correct and accepted'. In the case of spycraft, they offer up the example that 'the handler has to pass the message that other courageous and far-sighted individuals are doing the same thing (providing secret information), while not implying that the handler is being indiscreet'. This is one example of how difficult it is to fit a spy's use of influence into Cialdini's 'model'. In fact, I don't think it works.

There are two reasons why not.

First, as is made clear by the title of Cialdini's book, he is not at pains to make a distinction between influence and persuasion, as we do above. In my view, the principles he espouses are a mix of the two. It follows that some of the principles will apply to the spy–agent relationship, while others won't.

Second, Cialdini was writing primarily about techniques used by commercial personnel: namely, people involved in marketing or selling goods and services. Spying often involves an exchange – of intelligence for money – but, in that trade, the spy is not akin to a salesperson. She is the one doing the buying. So, in fact, a spy is more like a highly specialised procurement officer than a salesperson. What's more, they are often buying from a provider who is understandably reluctant to sell, unlike commercial salespeople. Again, it follows that some of Cialdini's principles will not apply to the spy–agent relationship, while others will. Specifically, I would rule out the principles of scarcity, social proof and authority.

This still leaves four principles that are of potential use to a spy, as follows.

RECIPROCATION

This 'rule' – that 'we should try to repay what another person has provided us'[1] – is an easy one, especially if the agent is motivated by money. But a good spy will seek to elevate their relationship with an agent beyond the explicitly transactional. For instance, they may give their agent thoughtful gifts, do them small favours, give up their time to listen to the agent's worries, and offer them pertinent advice (which they may seek from professionals on their agent's behalf). The point of this is not to rack up some financial obligation to be repaid. Rather, it is to create an ongoing sense in the agent that they are seen, heard and appreciated by the spy. Done well, this in turn nurtures an obligation to demonstrate appreciation of the spy *by* the agent. What better way of doing this than giving them what they most obviously seek, useable intelligence?

LIKING

In the hands of a skilful spy, such solicitous behaviour elides the principle of reciprocation with the principle of liking: the uncontroversial observation that 'people prefer to say yes to individuals they like'.[2] It makes sense that a target will be more inclined to like someone who truly engages with them and demonstrates that engagement with well-thought-out gifts, favours and advice. In addition, the spy may make efforts to enhance their natural attractiveness, since this tends to increase their likeability. This isn't to say that they will take drastic steps, such as undergoing plastic surgery. Being well-groomed and well-turned-out is enough, since we like people who make an effort

1 Ibid., p. 23.
2 Ibid., p. 124.

with their appearance before they spend time with us. If you doubt that, ask yourself why we routinely clean, groom, scent and dress ourselves in our best outfits when going on dates.

Regular meetings between the spy and her agent help, as we grow to like those with whom we have repeated – especially positive – contact. The prevalence of workplace friendships and romances is testimony to this. At their encounters, the spy may lavish her agent with praise, flattery and approval. People like people who like them, and these gestures imply strong liking of the agent by the spy. The old saying that 'flattery will get you everywhere' is based on observable truth, as realised by the clothes-shop assistant who is quick to say, 'That jacket looks great on your slim frame.' The power of flattery was brought home to me when I asked a lothario friend of mine what he thought was his most successful chat-up line. His reply: 'I only have one. I walk up to her and say, "You are easily the most beautiful woman in this room".'

Furthermore, approval can be addictive, especially if that approval comes from someone we like and desire to please. Most of us can identify with the drive to win positive comments and good marks from our favourite schoolteachers. The espionage equivalent might be the spy telling her agent, 'The last piece of intelligence you produced was so powerful, it went straight to my president and he is reconsidering his policies based on it.' If he has heard this once, the agent will be strongly motivated to produce further valuable intelligence, because he will almost certainly want to hear it again. This is helpfully related to the next principle.

COMMITMENT AND CONSISTENCY

The ideal circumstances for a spy are: first, for their agent to decide to become a provider of high-quality intelligence; and second, to come to identify themselves as such a provider. This is because, in Cialdini's words, 'Once we make a choice or take a stand, we encounter personal and interpersonal pressures to think and behave consistently with that commitment.'[1] In other words, once a target has accepted – of their own volition – an invitation to become an agent, they are likely to seek self-justification for that decision and commit to being as good an agent as they can be. This becomes a self-reinforcing cycle, spun along by the spy's lavish validation of her agent's efforts. 'You are doing brilliantly, keep it up' is a powerful motivator. As for words that none of us wants to hear, what about, 'You've let me down, you've let your friends down, but worst of all, you've let yourself down'? Fear of such personal failure is part of what drives commitment to consistent strong performance in support of a cause. Spies recognise the strength of this principle and apply it on every occasion possible.

UNITY

As it happens, vocal enthusiasm from their handler for an agent's efforts will make them feel less alone. Sneaking around behind colleagues' backs, stealing information, can be a lonely business. It is understandable that an agent might feel socially isolated. Consequently, part of a spy's job is to create an alternative sense of belonging for the agent, a process that relates to the final principle of influence noted above: unity. This principle is summed up by Cialdini as 'People are inclined to say yes to someone they consider one of them.'[2] Thus, the spy must make the agent feel like they are part of a *club*.

1 Ibid., p. 294.
2 Ibid., p. 364.

A sense of unity – or club membership – can arise from being part of the same family or coming from the same locality or community. These forms of unity are unlikely to be much help to a spy operating overseas. But unity also arises from two or more people acting together. This is more promising. Studies have shown that people who sing together, pray together, dance together or walk together in lockstep are more likely to be cooperative with one another than people between whom these things are absent. Again, a spy is likely to have only limited opportunities to do any of these things with an agent. But they can develop a sense of unity in four other ways.

The first is mirroring. This is simply a case of adopting some of the postures and actions of the agent: crossing legs at the same time; taking a sip of tea at the same time; resting a hand on the table when the agent does so. Second is what Cialdini calls 'repeated reciprocal exchange': usually episodes of self-disclosure interleaved with similar episodes by the agent, with increasing depth of intimacy. This second technique requires the agent to take an active decision to join in but it can be very powerful in the hands of a skilled spy. Third is emphasising the shared adversity faced by the spy and the agent: people who face struggles together – such as soldiers on the battlefield – are more likely to assist one another later. This requires careful handling, as too much emphasis on risk may be off-putting for a nervous agent. Again, however, it is a powerful tool when wielded with skill.

The fourth ploy involves something altogether more natural within the spy–agent relationship. It is asking for advice. Not an opinion or a view, but specifically advice. This approach may feel counterintuitive, in that it seems to re-weight the balance of power in the agent's favour. But this is illusory. In fact, far from creating a sense of superiority on the part of the person asked over the person asking, requests for and the giving of advice create a sense of 'we-ness' between two parties. It makes both feel that they are part of the same team. And, if the spy can achieve this, they have pulled off the most important trick of all, because we all want our own teams to win.

We shall come back to this when we look at how to adapt a spy's thinking to enhance your influence in relationships with goals allies. But, first, I'd like to tell you a story about how subconscious use of some of the techniques outlined above altered my relationship with a much more powerful figure than me. My only job was to serve him beer.

*   *   *

Picture a pub in suburban Birmingham: the White Swan. A quiet Thursday afternoon in the late eighties, Culture Club's 'Karma Chameleon' playing on the jukebox. The lunchtime rush is over. There is a noisome smell of fat and the remains of steak and onion pies. The carpets are sticky with spilled beer and cigarette smoke has impregnated the stained upholstery of the window-seats.

There's a man leaning on the bar. Slick, prosperous, wearing a tailored Italian suit and Hermès tie. Middle-aged but toned from time on the squash court. Dyed black hair and a perma-tan. His red Alfa Romeo Spider waits in the car park, but he is in no hurry to leave. He is senior. There's nobody at his office to watch his timekeeping.

He's chatting to a tall, skinny, awkward young man, who keeps adjusting his cheap, black-rimmed glasses and re-tucking his regulation striped green shirt into ill-fitting black trousers. He brushes locks of mousy-ginger hair, parted in the middle, from his forehead. But the bangs immediately drop back into place. The only colour in his face is from a large spot on his chin.

No prizes for guessing which one was me.

I enjoyed working as a barman. In fact, it is probably the role – nestled among parliamentary researcher, stockbroker, diplomat, private security consultant, television personality, company director and now, writer – that I value most, for what it taught me about life. I believe it is something that every young – or not so young – person should experience once. It forced me to confront and deal with social differences, prejudice, dishonesty, conflict and coercion. It helped me improve my mental arithmetic, kept me fit (it is an active job) and introduced me to some fascinating, wonderful people, including my first serious girlfriend.

Most important of all, it taught me to re-think the balance of social power.

Derek was a lunchtime regular, usually with a group of colleagues, occasionally with clients. He was always the first in, arriving shortly after midday, to a fanfare of his own making. Nods, smiles and handshakes with other regulars that he recognised. The flapping of his long black woollen coat, as he shook it free of real or imagined raindrops, hung it on the hatstand and smoothed it carefully into place. Then, he would settle on a stool at one end of the bar and summon me over, with a twenty-pound note half-folded lengthwise, held between first and second fingers.

'A pint of Brew XI, please, Jules.' Always a pint of Brew XI, the hoppy keg ale brewed by Mitchells & Butlers, who owned the playing fields on which I had played truant as a kid. My own favourite, as it happened, so I was good at pulling a decent pint, with just the right measure of foaming head. If it was quiet, we would chat. He told me he was senior at the Birmingham offices of a global consulting firm: he might have been a partner, but he fudged this question. I told him I was a student on a gap year that hadn't so far worked out. He lived in Solihull, one of the more salubrious parts of the Midlands, near the river. I lived in Ladywood, one of the less salubrious, near the prison. He drove a sports car. I took the bus or walked. We laughed about the differences between us. Or, at least, *he* laughed about the differences between us.

I confess I felt inferior, doubting that I would ever reach Derek's state of financial and personal confidence. The imbalance between us – customer and waiter; master and servant – was painfully stark. But I quickly realised that I had control over something that Derek wanted.

The beer.

More slowly, it dawned on me that I had control over something else that Derek craved.

Attentiveness.

As the lunchtimes wore on, Derek's guests would arrive, in ones and twos, forming ever-expanding groups in 'his' corner of the bar. He would greet them throatily and beckon me over to take their orders, throwing banknotes on the counter as he turned to embrace, backslap and air-kiss his companions. It became obvious to me that he needed to play the Big Man: wealthy and generous; directing affairs; solicitous juniors at his beck and call. My fellow bar-staff didn't warm to his attitude, preferring to hover at the other end of the bar, tending to the orders of less ostentatious customers. A small voice in me whispered that it would be advantageous to give him what he wanted.

On seeing him come into the pub, I would start pulling a pint, so it was waiting for him by the time he finished his greetings and reached the bar. I complimented him on his dress sense and choice of car. Over time, I memorised what his friends, colleagues and clients liked and made sure their drinks were waiting for them, too. I smiled, was welcoming to all his guests, removed and replenished empty glasses promptly, kept the bar near them dry and clean and emptied their ashtrays regularly. I was responsive but discreet, unintrusive. In return, Derek left me generous tips, but it was never really about that. His sense of obligation grew with each well-served pint, with each smile. Soon, he started to linger after the others had left, to while away an hour or so, chatting to me in the pub's dead hour of the early afternoon.

The principle of reciprocation: check. He could see that I had gone out of my way to help him, regularly and reliably. Tips alone were not enough to repay this.

The principle of liking: check. Why hang around if he didn't like me? The smiles, the courteousness, the compliments – the gestures of liking towards him – had paid off.

He was curious. How had I ended up working a bar in my gap year? Shouldn't I be travelling the world, living it up on a beach in Bali or finding myself on a Buddhist retreat? I told him that I thought it possible to find oneself though menial work; it was just a case of not being frightened of what you might discover. I remember him looking at me for a long time, a slight frown creasing his forehead. 'You are a rare sort,' he said. I asked him what he meant. 'Well, here you are, a bright kid – one of the brightest, selected by Oxford University – pulling beers and dispensing wisdom. It's all a bit unexpected, that's all.'

The principle of authority: check. Oxford had accepted me. I must be the goods.

The principle of scarcity: check. If I was the goods, there were not many of me around, not in that part of town, not serving beers on a Thursday lunchtime.

One day, he came in with a friend I hadn't seen before. A serious man, in whose company Derek was also serious, and quieter. A local and successful businessman, like Derek. They were fellow Rotarians. Unusually, nobody else joined them and the three of us chatted as a group, when I wasn't serving other customers. His companion knew a handful of people I knew, through the local Conservative Association. We gossiped about them, laying the groundwork of commonality. We moved on to the economy. The two men listened carefully as I explained why I thought 'Big Bang' – the deregulation of the City – in 1986 would eventually lead to a financial crisis. I was passing off as original thought the gist of an article I had read for my Economics A level the previous year – a skill later to be honed through studying for my PPE degree. They nodded sagely and glanced at each other. It occurred to me suddenly that the situation had been orchestrated by Derek. Gathering up his cigarettes and lighter to leave, his friend said to me, 'You are wasted in here. Somebody should find you a proper job.'

The principle of social proof: check.

The next time I saw Derek, I was starting an evening shift. He wasn't staying for a drink, instead stopping by on his way home. He handed me an envelope.

'There's an application form in there,' he said. 'My firm runs an internship scheme. It's usually for students who have already started their courses. But I think you would be great for it, if you are willing to spend the summer in London.'

I nodded. 'Of course, thank you. I'll get my application in early.' I tucked the envelope behind the bottles of spirits that lined the back of the bar, for safekeeping.

Derek reached a hand across the bar to shake mine. 'I'll see you there, then. I've been transferred to the London office, so you won't be seeing me in here again.'

'That's a shame,' I said, 'I've enjoyed getting to know you.'

'Me too, Jules.' He pointed at the envelope behind me. 'You deserve a break. Just make sure you send in that application. And mention my name in your covering letter.'

It was only when writing my letter, the following day, that I realised I didn't know Derek's surname. I considered ringing his office, but it was after hours. I was also late for my shift and wanted to post my application on the way, as the deadline was looming. I thought about referring to him by his first name only but decided that would be odd. So, I settled on letting my application stand on its merits.

A word of advice, here. If someone gives you a referral, mention them by name when following up.

I heard nothing further about that application. Not even an acknowledgement of receipt. Perhaps it got lost in the post. More likely, as Derek had warned, the available internships were awarded to students who had already started their courses. Either way, I cursed myself for not having waited a day to check his name and include it in my application. Life was so much more complicated before the internet came along. So, I didn't get to spend the summer before university exploring London. But I did get to continue working at the White Swan, so it wasn't all bad.

It was to be over three years before I saw Derek again. By then, I had finished my degree and was busy messing up interviews, while making ends meet painting rooms for my father. I was spending a lot of time in the White Swan and other pubs around Harborne and, one evening, I spotted Derek in his usual corner, surrounded by acolytes, as on past occasions. He was up for the weekend, visiting old friends, and he greeted me as one. It felt strange to be on the same side of the counter as Derek, accepting a pint bought from a bartender who couldn't have looked less interested: I wanted to shake her.

'I was sorry not to see you in London,' Derek said. 'I guess you got a better offer.'

'I wish. Truth is, I didn't even get a reply to my application.' I took a swig of my pint, swallowing hard. 'My fault. I realised I didn't know your surname, so didn't mention you.'

Derek laughed heartily. 'You fool,' he said, tapping my head lightly. 'So much intelligence, so little common sense.'

'That's what my mum says.'

'She's right.' Derek waved for the bartender again, without success. 'Still, I guess you are fighting off the jobs now you have graduated.'

I explained that I wasn't, muttering something about recessions.

'Oh, yes, I remember you said Big Bang would end in tears. But fear not. There are graduate jobs aplenty at my place.' He handed me a business card. 'I'll have someone write to you. Just mention my name this time.'

Derek was true to his word. A week later, I received a letter from one of his colleagues in London, apologising for my internship application going unheeded and inviting me to apply for a full-time position. I remember one of the lines: 'Derek was very sorry that you were not able to join us in 1989. While he will play no role in the selection process for our Graduate Recruitment Programme, he is very keen that you should apply to join it this year.'

The principle of commitment and consistency: check.

I regretted not taking the job they later offered me, only because I would have enjoyed seeking out Derek and thanking him in person, as a colleague. I owed him that. Reciprocity can start a wonderful virtuous circle. And it would have checked off the principle of unity, too, as we would both have been on the same team. The full suite of Cialdini's seven principles.

Having denied myself that satisfying conclusion, I must be content with an amusing postscript. I happened to walk past the pub a few months before starting to write this book. It had been refurbished and new owners had replaced the nameboard that swung from a post out front. A shame. I really liked the old nameboard. On one side, it pictured a pristine pen with 'White Swan' written beneath it. On the other, the picture was of a grubby cygnet: underneath that, the words 'Dirty Duck'.

A pub with two identities. What a shame I don't believe in omens.

* * *

RECAP

- Recruitment is an achievement but it is also only a beginning. The spy now needs to exert influence to ensure her agent stays the course.
- Influence is different from persuasion. It involves earning long-term emotional buy-in, rather than a quick win.
- Dr Cialdini identifies seven principles of persuasion and influence: reciprocation, liking, social proof, authority, scarcity, commitment and consistency, and unity.
- Not all seven principles are relevant to the relationship between spy and agent, but most are, with unity being perhaps the most difficult to apply.
- Potential 'unitising' actions include physical mirroring, repeated reciprocal exchange, emphasising shared challenges, and the spy seeking advice from the agent.
- The overarching goal is to create conditions for the agent to feel that they are part of a team with the spy. The same applies to influencing goals allies.
- In the case of goals allies, the remaining six principles of influence can also be turned to advantage.

*   *   *

Some people are understandably uncomfortable with the concept of influence. They might regard it as a type of manipulation. Or consider influence techniques as somehow underhanded. While some of the stratagems outlined above can undoubtedly be used unethically, I don't share the view that they are inherently so. To illustrate why not, I invite you to think about influence from a different perspective, at least when it comes to building your relationship with a newly recruited goals ally.

I would like you to think about how you can *earn* their contin-ued support. In this respect, as illustrated with my story about Derek above, I think all seven of Cialdini's principles might be relevant, though they won't all be so in every case. It will be for you to decide which apply, given your specific circumstances.

So, how can you set about earning the attention of a goals ally, such that they are prepared to give up time and effort to help you achieve your goals? You can:

- provide them with, or promise them, something in return (reciprocation);
- attract their assistance by being a decent, thoughtful, positive and respectful person (liking);
- demonstrate your worth through endorsement by peers (social proof);
- demonstrate your worth through endorsement by experts (authority);
- be different from others that might deserve assistance (scarcity);
- help them by offering opportunities to continue efforts they have already committed to (commitment and consistency);
- invite them to be part of a team, with shared goals (unity).

Of course, this all amounts to the same thing as exercising influence. The only difference is that, in this instance, I 'framed' the principles in a different way, thereby – I hope – altering your perception of them for the better. There is nothing wrong with this approach and it is one that you can adopt yourself.

Cialdini terms it 'pre-suasion'. Introducing this idea, he takes us back to the concept of gardening, or cultivation (see Chapter Three (p. 68)). He writes that the 'highest achievers' he has observed in various fields of persuasion and influence 'set about their mission as skilled gardeners who know that even the finest seeds will not take root in stony soil or bear fullest fruit in poorly prepared ground. They spent much of their time toiling in the fields of influence thinking about and engaging in cultivation.' [1] One final quote from him to drive home the point: 'What we present first changes the way people experience what we present to them next.'[2]

Our task now, then, is to examine how you can use techniques of pre-suasion in strengthening the relationship with your goals ally, with reference to the seven established principles of influence (or, if you prefer, the principles of earning support). I aim here to make some practical, grounded suggestions, from which you can pick and choose, as appropriate.

TAKE NOTE

Or notes. Literally. Each time you find out something about your goals ally, make a note of it. Knowing when it is their birthday or wedding anniversary, the names of their children, what pets they have, details of their wider interests or insights into their reading tastes, can make all the difference as a relationship develops. But such details can be easily forgotten. So, write them down (in a way that respects the privacy of your goals ally and any legal obligations on you). This seems like an obvious idea, but I remember being surprised when I saw one of the Cazenove sales team jotting notes on the back of a business card handed to him by a new client over drinks. I asked him what he had written. 'Slimline tonic,' he said. 'The guy takes Slimline

1 Cialdini, *Pre-Suasion*, p.004.
2 Ibid, p.004.

tonic. Next time, I won't need to ask him. I'll just say, "Gin and Slimline for you?" and watch his smile grow.'

Your notes will serve two purposes. First, they will be prompts for you to buy small gifts at the right times. Nothing spectacular but tailored to be meaningful. Say, for instance, that you know your goals ally's birthday falls a week after your next scheduled get-together. And that she is an enthusiastic cook. Perhaps she has also mentioned that she is keen to visit Israel one day. A cookbook by Yotam Ottolenghi, or a gift voucher for one of his restaurants would be an apt – and probably surprising – present. A present that gives in two ways: in itself; and in demonstrating to your goals ally that you have paid attention to her interests. It is, indeed, the thought that counts.

Second, they will act as conversation-openers or excuses for thoughtful communications between meetings. 'I saw this and thought of you' is a powerful line in an email containing an attachment. So long as the attachment is relevant and not time-wasting, of course. Taking again the example of your goals ally and her desire to visit Israel, you might send her a link to one of the virtual tours of the country produced during the Covid-lockdown years. Similarly, if she is Jewish, you might want to send her a Rosh Hashanah card to mark the Jewish New Year. Other festival cards will be relevant to members of other communities.

These small actions, taken ahead of or at the outset of encounters with your goals ally, will incline them towards wanting to repay your kindness in some way (reciprocation) and towards finding you a more agreeable companion (liking).

SEEK ENDORSEMENTS

These can come in many forms, from likes on social media, through word of mouth and formal written references, to certificates of achievement. The important considerations are: first, that they should come from people in the same social or professional group as your goals ally, or from experts and authority figures; and second, that they should be seen or heard by your goals ally.

There is nothing at all wrong with asking a friend in common to put in a good word for you. Or with forwarding a positive review of writing, music-making or other creative endeavour; whatever is relevant to the help you are seeking from the goals ally. This is all social proof of your worthiness for their continued support. If you have recently won a prize – be it for photography, a sporting competition, a short story, or some computer programming; again, whatever is relevant – tell your goals ally at your next encounter. They will understand your excitement and absorb the fact that it confers authority on you. Communicating such endorsements immediately prior to or at an early stage of a meeting will help to frame later exchanges, positioning you as someone deserving of continued support.

DARE TO BE DIFFERENT

Your goals ally meets a lot of people and has a lot of demands on her time. Why should she give up any of that time for you? Differentiation helps to make your case. Perhaps you are the first member of your family to go to university. The first minority ethnic person to win the local schools' debating competition. One of only two disabled members of the local theatre group. Born and raised in the poorest postcode of the United Kingdom.

You will see appeals of this type at work in the political arena. Sadiq Khan, the mayor of London as I write, makes great play of the fact that his father was a bus driver.[1] The millionaire prime minister (at the time of writing), Rishi Sunak, has claimed that the 'best training' he ever had for running the country was 'working in a curry house'.[2] (Incidentally, I hold my hands up to purposely framing responses to that last point with use of the word 'millionaire' to describe Sunak.)

At one level, such anecdotes are designed to 'humanise' politicians, or to make them 'relatable'. But they are also used to differentiate the speaker, to suggest somehow that they are worthy of election because of their scarcity value in a political scene dominated by public-school and Oxbridge-educated white men. I don't decry such anecdotes, if they are truthful and not used in a purposely misleading way. There is a strong case for increasing diversity of representation in all areas of public and professional life in the UK. Accordingly, you need not be shy in promoting to goals allies those aspects of yourself that place you in a minority or disadvantaged group.

The chances are that you have already done so, in your recruitment pitch. But there is no harm in returning to the theme when framing ongoing requests for assistance. Think about the following sentence: 'As a disabled person who has completed the Three Peaks Challenge, I'd love to take a leading role in charities to support others like me, and I have an idea about how you could help me do that.' It is both honest

1 Facebook, Sadiq Khan. https://www.facebook.com/sadiqforlondon/videos/as-londoners-will-know-im-proud-that-my-dad-worked-as-a-bus-driver-its-a-tough-a/191948558715628/
2 Robbie Griffiths, 'Rishi Sunak says serving in a restaurant was his recipe for No 10 success', The Standard, 29 November 2022. https://www.standard.co.uk/news/londoners-diary/londoner-s-diary-rishi-sunak-curry-awards-phoebe-waller-bridge-dehenna-davison-andrew-lloyd-webber-b1043440.html

and pre-suasive, without being manipulative, self-pitying or self-aggrandising.

Some years ago, I was approached by an African friend with a request that I write a letter to support his (successful) application for UK residency. Immediately prior to his request, we had been discussing his track record as a high-profile anti-corruption campaigner: a rare beast in a country where such activists are routinely harassed. I would have written the reference, anyway, based on our many years of friendship. But I was moved to do so more quickly and in more glowing terms by this act of probably unintentional pre-suasion; a reminder of my friend's scarcity value. You will no doubt be able to develop equivalent formulas that are appropriate for your own circumstances.

PLANT FLAGS

This suggestion might require you to get your pen or pencil out again. It is a good idea to make a note each time your goals ally does something to help you. Then, plant flags by thanking them for their help, even for relatively small favours. You could do this verbally, immediately after the event (common courtesy would dictate that you do this anyway). Later, you might reiterate your gratitude by text message or by email. But it would be more impactful to mail them a thoughtfully selected card, with a handwritten message of thanks. Finally, you can refer to their previous acts of generosity and kindness when framing requests for further help.

Consider the comparative merits of this pair of requests: 'I know you are pressed for time, but could I ask you to nominate me for Fellowship of the Royal Society of Arts?'; or 'I really must thank you again for providing that testimonial for my non-profit start-up. It really helped get it off the ground. I think your

Fellowship of the Royal Society of Arts made your contribution stand out, so I'd like to get involved too. Would you consider nominating me?'

I don't need to spell out how one of those approaches frames the request in a negative way and the other in a positive, persuasive way. It also has the benefit of being polite, respectful, and demonstrating honest gratitude. I struggle to see anything manipulative in that.

ASK FOR ADVICE

I have always wanted to be a writer. I wrote my first novelette in long-hand, perched on my bed, aged fifteen. I have it still, though only one other person has ever read it (thank you, Natalie, for your kind comments, however much they were intended to shield me from the truth). Other attempts at novel-writing over the years have ended up in the recycle bin, either physically or digitally. Except two. The first of these has been rejected by numerous publishers. The second – I think much better – novel is still gathering virtual dust. Again, it has been seen by only one other person, himself a published novelist of great distinction. William Palmer is a friend of my father's, who suggested that I show my efforts to him.

When sharing a handful of chapters with William, I asked him not what he thought of them, but for feedback. For advice, in other words. He was most generous in response, providing not only warm words but going so far as to send me a suggested re-write of one scene, highlighting areas of potential improvement, and scribbling editorial notes on the remainder. It must have taken up quite a bit of his time and there was no reason for him to do this, other perhaps than his friendship with my father. I have not even met William in person. Nonetheless, my request for advice and guidance seemed to resonate with him and he wrote to me as he might to a fellow author, rather than an upstart of dubious talent. He treated me as belonging to the same team as him: *Team Writer*.

CASE STUDY

Two weeks after their lunch in Paris, Tom and Moussa met again, this time for a photoshoot that Tom had arranged with his friend Sabrine. Tom wanted to maximise his use of Moussa's time, so brought two pieces for each season to the shoot. He made temporary adjustments as they went along, where he had not had time to alter the clothes to fit Moussa. It worked out well and all three were happy with the results. Sabrine shared digital versions of the portfolio between them and, right away, Moussa uploaded photos of the summer designs to his social media accounts. He agreed that he would post the other photos as the pieces came into season. However, Moussa was concerned about a disagreement with his director and was obviously preoccupied. Tom realised that he would need to remind Moussa to post the remaining shots at the relevant times.

In the following months, unable to see Moussa as he was busy filming, Tom sent him a bottle of wine as thanks for his time – the same one that Moussa had chosen for their after-lunch drinks. He also made sure to remember Moussa's birthday, sending him a hand-made card featuring photos from the shoot. The two would also exchange links to articles about fashion designers that they both admired.

As the time approached that it would be appropriate for Moussa to put up shots of him wearing the autumn pieces, Tom compiled a series of screenshots from his own social media accounts. The screenshots were of responses from his followers that contained positive comments about Moussa. He emailed the selection to Moussa, with the following message: 'Hi, thanks so much again for posting the fab photos of you in my summer pieces. They caused quite a buzz, as you'll see from these comments. I hope we can do it again with the autumn jacket and the slacks. Now would be a great time to post those shots, if you have time. Please don't forget to tag me! Looking forward to a Crème de Châtaigne or two with you soon, now the chestnuts are falling.'

Moussa posted the shots that evening. He remembered to tag Tom. They were on the same team, after all.

Cialdini writes that 'providing advice puts a person in a merging state of mind, which stimulates a linking of one's own identity with another party's'.[1] The ideal state for relationships with goals allies is where identities are linked, or 'unitised'. It is serendipitous that one means of achieving this state is asking for advice, given that the advice sought is likely also to be an end in itself. This is because a valuable goals ally will be experienced and knowledgeable about your area of endeavour. In many cases, you will have much to learn from them. Thus, it pays to hone the skill of debriefing. We turn to this next, after I have introduced you to Eniola, whose very name was a desperate cry for unity.

* * *

The waiter's hand shook as he poured champagne. Eniola held up his glass, tight against the bottle's neck, to alleviate the trembling.

1 Cialdini, *Pre-Suasion*, p. 206.

'Thank you, sir.' The waiter returned the bottle to its ice and draped a napkin across his left arm. His eyes fell on a cigar-cutter, thrown carelessly onto the table, where its blade reflected the bucket. 'That is a beautiful thing,' he said. 'You have excellent taste.' Eniola picked up the cutter and turned it over once or twice, examining it thoughtfully. It was, so far as I could tell, made of a solid gold case, with a sterling silver blade, polished to a high shine. He snipped the end off a Cuban mini and I caught the warming, earthy-liquorice smell of the tobacco leaves.

'Will there be anything else, sir?' The waiter was lingering. Eniola regarded him for a moment, eyes narrowed, as though pondering whether to order still or sparkling water. Then, abruptly, he thrust the cigar-cutter towards him.

'Take it,' Eniola said. 'It's yours.'

It was not the first time that I had witnessed the rich generosity of a successful Nigerian but even I was surprised. I watched the waiter, as he weaved through the tables in the lobby area of the Abuja Intercontinental, back to the bar. He wore a broad smile, polishing his prize with his starched napkin.

'He's probably weighing up how much he thinks he can sell it for.' I regretted my words as soon as my eyes met Eniola's. He shrugged.

'It matters not what he does with it. It is his.'

'Sorry, that was ungenerous of me. Unlike you. That cutter must have been worth a lot.'

'It was,' Eniola said. 'But he paid me a compliment and that is more valuable.'

'You never fail to surprise me, Eniola,' I said.

It was true. Like many people, I went to Nigeria for the first time with some prejudiced ideas about its businesspeople. A persistent narrative about the prevalence of corruption and toxic masculinity within that world had guaranteed that. So, I had been lucky to meet Eniola on one of my first trips there, because he smashed all my preconceptions.

That had been several years before our pleasant, boozy evening at the Intercontinental. I had been dispatched to the country as a contractor, by a private security company that was assessing security arrangements in place for a range of commercial interests in the Niger Delta. Their client was the corporate group owned by Eniola. He had taken a hands-on interest in the project and we had become friends.

He had made millions of dollars from oil trading and related activities. When I met him, he was close to the then vice-president, Goodluck Jonathan, who would go on to become president in 2010. This connection doubtless helped Eniola's cause, but he was also hard working, conscientious, intelligent and talented. He had the spoils to show for it: homes in Lagos, Abuja, New York, London and Geneva; a fleet of expensive cars, most fitted with police sirens to get him through the heavy Lagos traffic; dressing rooms full of bespoke and designer suits; his own restaurant in Paris. He never wanted for anything. But he was a man of humility, quietly spoken, concerned for others and, as we have seen, exceptionally generous.

We were friends, but more than that. He once told me that he would do anything to help my business succeed. He introduced me to influential politicians (including Jonathan when he was president), dug up information for me and smoothed my path with officialdom. So long as I was friends with Eniola, I did not need to fear the ritual of being shaken down for bribes at Murtala Muhammed International Airport or at roadblocks. He put me up at his various homes, lent me chauffeur-driven vehicles and made office space available to me when I needed it.

He did all this because, one day during the security assessment, we shared a hair-raising, storm-buffeted flight from Port Harcourt to Bonny Island in his company helicopter. We dipped, bucked and shuddered through evil black clouds. A huge hail-stone smashed into the cockpit windshield, leaving a hairline crack. Even the pilot had jumped, and we all feared that we might ditch in the mangrove swamps of the Niger Delta, where armed pirates and oil smugglers patrolled the labyrinthine waters. That evening, shaken by the experience, he had downed half a bottle of Blue Label whisky and told me his deepest secret. I had reacted with – a little to his surprise – empathy and warm support.

Eniola wanted to be a woman.

This is a cultural taboo in Nigeria. While same-sex sexual activity is specifically criminalised there, the law is less clear-cut about transgenderism. But it is certainly not something that one would choose to advertise. Worse, for Eniola, he was born in the religiously conservative north of Nigeria where, according to the Human Dignity Trust, 'trans people may also face prosecution under state level Sharia laws'.[1] Consequently, Eniola had not come out as trans. His family had ostracised him nonetheless, sensing that, in his words, 'something was not right'. Young, fearful and isolated, he had fled to the south, to study engineering at the University of Lagos. While there, he converted to Christianity and adopted a new name. He told me that he had chosen Eniola because it is gender neutral.

This was a man in need of a family. In need of unity.

So, while not able to understand viscerally the torments he had suffered, I tried to empathise with him, and I offered him friendship and non-judgemental support. Mainly, I listened to him. I was, he told me, the first man that he had been able to speak to about his feelings, without feeling shunned. I

1 Human Dignity Trust, Nigeria. https://www.humandignitytrust.org /country-profile/nigeria/

introduced him to the works of Jan Morris, gifting him a copy of *Conundrum*, her book about transitioning from a man to woman. I was also able to persuade him to join online support groups, where he could explore his desire to transition with others better able to understand his feelings. I asked him whether he wanted me to think of him – and treat him – as a man or a woman. He was clear that I should regard him as a man, so long as it was always clear between us that he was a man who wanted to become a woman. I did my best to tread this line, always respectful of his wishes.

Our friendship, forged in the terrors of turbulent air travel, burgeoned on the ground. On Eniola's fortieth birthday, I bought him a bottle of single-malt whisky that had been bottled in the year of his birth. Soon after he gave away his cigar-cutter, I bought him another one. A cheaper version, gold-plated rather than solid gold. But engraved with his initials on one side and mine on the other. He cried when he unwrapped it. He gave me gifts too, mementoes from his home state and books by Nigerian authors he thought I should read. And he was unbending in his determination to support me professionally.

Most important, whatever each of us did for the other, it was always about *us*, a unit of mutual support.

Then, on 31 March 2015, Eniola's world fell apart.

That day, Goodluck Jonathan conceded defeat to his challenger, Muhammadu Buhari. And Buhari's men came for Eniola. It is not unheard of for businesspeople associated with one president in parts of Africa to be targeted by the succeeding regime. Usually, they are accused of corruption or other malfeasance, their assets are seized or frozen, and they are unable to continue conducting business in the country. But they are usually left unharassed in their personal lives. In Eniola's case, the persecution was particularly vicious. Already out of favour with a Muslim-led government for having abandoned Islam, he was outed as 'gay' by a former schoolmate. This made his life in Nigeria intolerable. So, he abandoned his properties and businesses and fled, for the second time in his life, this time to America. There, at least, he could make progress towards transitioning.

I saw him one last time before he was to commence that journey. We lunched at Boisdale, behind London's Victoria Station. Afterwards, we sat on the cigar terrace, and he cut a couple of Cubans for us. I was touched to note that he used the cigar-cutter I had given him some years earlier. As we smoked, we reminisced a little and then he told me about his plans to start a new life as a woman.

'But we'll stay in touch, won't we?' I asked.

Eniola shook his head, slowly.

'I would rather we didn't. A new life needs to be a new life and you are part of my old life.'

'I shall miss you,' I said.

'And I, you.' I thought I saw Eniola's eyes glisten with unshed tears. 'You have been a true friend, sometimes when I felt I had no others.'

'I will always be here, if you change your mind.'

He shook his head again, emphatically.

'I won't change my mind. I shall forge my own way without you. After all, I am used to it.' He leaned forward. 'I never told you the other reason I chose the name Eniola, did I?'

'You didn't. I thought one was enough.'

'It is an anagram,' he said. 'Do I need to unscramble it for you?'

It was my turn to shake my head, not trusting myself to speak. I got it.

Eniola, I thought. *I, alone.*

* * *

RECAP

- If the idea of using influence techniques makes you feel uncomfortable, try reframing it. Ask yourself how you can *earn* the support of goals allies.
- Framing is a technique of *pre-suasion*, which can be used when applying Cialdini's seven principles of influence to your relationships.
- Make notes of significant dates for your goals allies, and of their interests. Use these as prompts to present thoughtful gifts and send links to relevant online resources.
- Seek independent endorsements, prizes and other forms of recognition of your talents. Be sure to share these with your goals allies, ahead of or early in meetings.
- Don't be shy about letting your goals allies know what marks you out from other deserving causes, including belonging to marginalised or underprivileged groups.
- Seeking advice from your goals ally is valuable in its own right. It will also act as a 'unitising' force, inclining them to think of you as being on the same team.

CHAPTER EIGHT

The Revealing Power of Effective Debriefing

Agents can change the world. For better and for worse.

Dmitri Polyakov, code-name TOP HAT, was a high-ranking officer in the Soviet Union's military intelligence agency, the GRU. He was also a CIA source, reportedly providing enough intelligence to fill twenty-five file drawers.[1] According to former CIA director James Woolsey, TOP HAT's reporting 'kept the Cold War from becoming hot' and ultimately helped the west to prevail.[2] Polyakov started working with the CIA in 1961 and intelligence he provided was to make a difference as much as thirty years later. Information about anti-tank missiles acquired by Iraq from the Soviet Union helped the US military overcome their use during the first Gulf War of 1991.

So much for an agent changing the world for the better. In the run-up to the second Gulf War of 2003, another agent's reporting proved disastrous, bolstering the case for a ruinous and potentially illegal conflict. Rafid Ahmed Alwan al-Janabi was

---

1 Elaine Shannon, 'Death of the perfect spy', TIME, 24 June 2001. https://content.time.com/time/magazine/article/0,9171,164863,00.html
2 Erin Blakemore, 'The spy who kept the Cold War from boiling over', History, 15 July 2019. https://www.history.com/news/cold-war-soviet-spy-dmitri-polyakov

known by an apt codename, given the spin that he put on his reporting. He was known as CURVEBALL.

In fact, 'spin' is a generous word for a pack of lies. Al-Janabi was approached by the *Bundesnachrichtendienst* (BND), Germany's foreign intelligence agency, shortly after arriving in the country to claim asylum. He attracted attention from the BND because he claimed to have worked as a chemical engineer in Iraq, at a time when the US and the UK were building a case for invading Iraq to rid it of so-called weapons of mass destruction (WMD). CURVEBALL provided 'intelligence' cited by the US Secretary of State Colin Powell at the United Nations in February 2003. Powell said that 'one of the most worrisome things that emerges from the thick intelligence file we have on Iraq's biological weapons is the existence of mobile production facilities used to make biological agents [. . .] In a matter of months, they can produce a quantity of biological poison equal to the entire amount that Iraq claimed to have produced in the years prior to the [first] Gulf War.'[1] Deeply concerning, but also false, according to the *Guardian* newspaper.[2] These allegations were the product of CURVEBALL's imagination, drawn from intelligence debriefs of him. They were not the only element of the US's case for invading Iraq in 2003, but they were an undeniably important part of it.

An invasion that, according to Brown University, contributed directly or indirectly to between 280,000 and 315,000 deaths over the following twenty years. No WMD were found in Iraq following the invasion, despite extensive and expensive

1 https://www.theguardian.com/world/2003/feb/05/iraq.usa?INTCMP=SRCH
2 https://www.theguardian.com/world/2011/feb/15/curveball-iraqi-fantasist-cia-saddam

searches by over 1,600 UN and US inspectors.[1] It is fair to say that, aided and abetted by politicians who placed the findings of intelligence agencies front and centre in the case for war, CURVEBALL (and others) caused immense and lasting reputational damage to the west's diplomatic credibility.

The contrasting cases of TOP HAT and CURVEBALL illustrate two things: first, the centrality of effective debriefing skills in the relationship between a spy and an agent; and second, the need for spies to be adept at detecting deception. We shall look at these related matters in turn.

The term 'debrief' is military speak. It refers to a formal process of retrieving information from participants in a just-concluded operation or exercise. In the intelligence world, it is broadly synonymous with 'interview'. For present purposes, we shall treat a 'debrief' as part of the following cycle: first, the spy 'tasks' or 'briefs' the agent to retrieve intelligence relating to a particular matter; second, the agent sets about collecting the intelligence required; and third, the spy 'debriefs' the agent about what he has discovered.

With this cycle in mind, we can lay out some guidelines, or rules, to help the spy conduct an effective debrief: one that yields comprehensive, relevant, accurate and, perhaps, actionable intelligence.

The first rule applies at the briefing stage: *be objective in the briefing and don't incentivise the agent to supply biased intelligence.* Consider the following instruction to an agent: 'We need evidence of Saddam Hussein's WMD programme and how he is concealing it. I can pay you top dollar for anything you produce about these matters.' That's one approach. Another might be: 'We need to understand whether Saddam has an

1 Julian Borger, 'There were no weapons of mass destruction in Iraq', *Guardian*, 7 October 2004. https://www.theguardian.com/world/2004/oct/07/usa.iraq1

active programme to develop WMD and, if so, what it involves. The important thing is that we get an accurate picture, not to prove anything one way or the other.'

I have no idea whether any spies adopted phrases equivalent to the first of the two instructions above. But it is safe to assume that the political atmosphere at the time suggested to agents that a premium would be placed on reporting to corroborate the existence of a WMD programme. And that, accordingly, they might be paid handsomely for producing such 'intelligence'. In such febrile circumstances, it is all the more important that a spy handles their agent with impartiality.

The second rule applies during the collection phase, while the spy is waiting for the agent to complete their task and report back: *research the subject matter in detail.* Time spent learning what is already known about the subject of the agent's tasking enables the spy to project authority during the debrief and to ask more pertinent questions. It may also, incidentally, enhance the likelihood of the spy recognising attempts at deception.

The third rule applies immediately prior to the debrief: *create a comfortable and unthreatening space, in which the agent will have adequate time to relay their findings securely.* This speaks for itself, but we'll come back to how spies achieve it in Chapter Nine (p. 270).

The fourth and final rule applies during the debrief: *focus on the agent, asking searching questions, without guiding their responses.* There are a few components to this. Relax the agent first, inquiring about their welfare and attending to their comfort before beginning the formal interview. It is best to ask open questions; those that don't invite a straightforward 'yes' or 'no' response. Avoid loaded questions; those that contain assumptions. Ask the '5W and H' questions: who, what, why, where, when and how? Shorter questions are better than long, discursive enquiries.

Listen actively. This is also covered in Chapter Four (p. 103).

Establish how the agent knows what they claim to know. Challenge the agent – gently – if any of their material is internally contradictory or is inconsistent with what you already know about the subject. Maintain good eye contact, so that the agent knows *they* are your focus. Control movements so that the agent doesn't detect approval or disapproval of specific findings from your body language. Slow the agent down if they become over-excited. Take regular breaks during longer debriefs.

It is during a debrief that the spy's skills at detecting deception will come into play. A good spy will be on the alert for any evidence of deceit throughout the process.

Now, I'm afraid I have bad news for anyone who has come here in search of foolproof techniques used by spies to root out lies or misleading narratives. According to psychologist Professor Zoë Walkington, who has 'worked extensively as a consultant providing police training with regard to suspect interviewing',[1] most people's ability to detect deception is 'around chance level'. This is, according to Walkington, 'regardless of whether or not we're an ordinary person or someone who's had more specialist training, such as a police officer or a psychologist'.[2] Or a spy, indeed.

That is a general rule, though. And there are a few things a spy can do to tilt the balance in their favour, on a case-by-case basis.

First, they can assess an agent's motivations to lie. After all, assessing motivations is a core part of the job. If, for example, an agent is driven by hatred and resentment of their government, it is likely they will portray that government in as negative a light as possible. Perhaps even with the intention of persuading a foreign power to launch military action against it. Let's go

1 https://www.open.edu/openlearn/profiles/zw48
2 The Open University, Detecting Deception. https://learning.elucidat. com/course/5e15ef4ca5d25-5e15f0b95185a

back to the CURVEBALL case. Al-Janabi was an asylum seeker from Iraq and made no secret of his distaste for Saddam Hussein's regime. I have no doubt that these motivations were considered by his handlers. But maybe the political pressure to produce intelligence in support of the subsequent military invasion made it difficult for them also to view matters objectively. Who knows?

Second, over time, a spy can establish a baseline for their agent's behaviour during debriefs. Significant deviations from the baseline may be indicators of attempted deceptions. Deception specialist Paul Ekman points out that 'There is no sign of deceit itself – no gesture, no facial expression or muscle twitch – that in and of itself means that a person is lying.'[1] But, 'There are clues that the person is poorly prepared and clues of emotions that don't fit the person's line.' Such 'leakages', as Ekman calls them, are more likely to be detectable in an agent if their handler has made a prior effort to establish baselines when the agent is providing a narrative.

The two aspects that a liar will find most difficult to control are his face and voice, more than the words he speaks or the way in which he holds his body as he lies. For example, a former colleague of mine who liked to brag about real and imagined sexual conquests tended to blink more rapidly when he was being untruthful. I told him about this, and he sought to correct it. But he overcompensated, so I became more suspicious of him when he blinked *less* frequently. He was simply not able to exert natural-looking control over his facial expression when experiencing the heightened emotions associated with lying. It didn't help him that he also blushed at these times. And his voice would rise a few notes. He was very bad at lying. But I can't

1 Paul Ekman, *Telling Lies: Clues to Deceit in the Marketplace, Politics, and Marriage*, W. W. Norton & Company, 2009, p. 80.

draw any broad conclusions from this case. Rapid blinking, staring, blushing or a heightened voice pitch are not, in themselves, indicators of someone being deceitful. They only betrayed him to me because I had come to know his baseline.

It is possible to establish one rule of thumb, however. A mismatch between displayed emotions or body language and the subject matter under discussion is often telling. Some people may laugh when lying about something serious, for instance. Or they may try to make a joke about a serious matter, to distract from their lies, but their demeanour will not display humour. Again, not definitive, but a component of a body of evidence that might incline a spy to treat with caution their agent's comments.

Third, as noted above, being familiar with relevant subject matter also increases the likelihood of detecting deception. Especially if the agent is not aware of just how far the spy's knowledge extends. Conversely, if the agent believes that the spy knows a great deal about the subject, he may be diffident when presenting material that is genuinely new. There is a balance to be struck here. One approach might be a variation of the old rule 'Never ask a question to which you don't already know the answer.' Of course, this is not possible throughout a debrief, but a few questions of this nature scattered strategically might well trip up a careless liar. If challenged when gilding the lily about something minor, the agent will, most likely, try to avoid fabrications about more important matters.

Fourth, it may be worth revisiting a narrative out of chronological sequence. If an agent has invented a chronology, he is likely to have rehearsed it to himself sequentially. Consider the following (fictional) monologue: 'President Mugabe gave his usual closing speech at the end of the Politburo meeting. He said that he was determined to drive all the white farmers out of the country. Then he asked the Minister of Agriculture to lay out some options to achieve this. After the minister spoke, Mugabe slammed shut his notebook and shouted that his ideas were no good. Then he paced the room for a while, picking on attendees to give their ideas. Finally, he told everyone to leave, except me. He asked me to stay behind so he could tell me the following explosive piece of intelligence . . .' The spy is suspicious, so responds with, 'Sorry, I think I missed a bit. What did Mugabe do immediately before shouting at the minister?' If the agent has made it all up, he may have to replay the narrative mentally before answering. His subsequently delayed response would be a 'tell' for the spy.

A few additional quickfire thoughts for the deception-savvy spy. Lying tends to make people – sociopaths apart – uncomfortable, anxious and eager to get away: be wary of an agent who is in a hurry to leave. Be sceptical too of those who are in a rush to plead their truthfulness: the mythical second-hand car dealer Honest John calls himself that for a reason. And I am always suspicious of those who offer up unnecessary, overly specific details when telling a story: ask yourself why someone would say 'I left at 7.32,' rather than 'I left around 7.30.' I recognise this tactic for a very good reason: I have used it myself when attempting to cover my trails.

On which note, spies have a natural advantage when it comes to detecting deception; because it takes a thief to catch a thief. It is part of a spy's job to deceive at a high level themselves, so they may more readily recognise when others are trying to do the same thing.

A spy must often think about how to mislead people in positions of authority. I was a young boy when I first had to think about how to do that.

* * *

The first time I was interviewed by the police, I was thirteen. And I had very good reasons to deceive them.

It took them nearly a year after I collided with a car to seek my account of it. I was out of hospital by then, convalescing at home, hopping around on crutches. They came to interview me there. Two of them – a man and a woman. They were in plain clothes but were intimidating nonetheless, to a young boy. They sat together on the sofa in our living room. That was where the young policeman who came to tell us about my sister's death had sat a couple of years earlier. I was on a hard seat opposite them, flanked by my parents. Not sure if I was being treated as victim or criminal. Either way, I was trembling.

'Please tell us in your own words what happened that morning,' the policeman said, as his colleague flipped open a notebook. The room fell silent, except for a hiss of gas from the fire. Sophie, our quarter-Siamese black cat, curled up in front of it. I wished that I could lead her comfortable, uncomplicated life. I sat immobile, silent, for so long that the policeman prompted me; 'At least tell us what you can remember of it.'

The problem wasn't being unable to remember. It was *what* I remembered.

It had been a Monday morning and I was returning to school after a week's absence, ostensibly due to an episode of asthma. Dad had given me money for the bus fare but I decided to walk instead, planning to spend the money on sweets. I didn't usually eat lunch at school, preferring to avoid the canteen, where I was likely to be bullied. Instead, I would sneak out and buy chocolate at local shops. (My sweet tooth survives to this day. I am sucking on sherbet lemons as I write.)

The walk was about two miles and the long trudge held another attraction for me. It delayed the evil moment of my arrival at school. I was dragging myself there, satchel slung over my shoulder, eyes cast down to the pavement. About a third of the way into my walk, I came to a complex junction, where three roads met and there was no pedestrian crossing.

Two of the roads were key arteries and were busy at that time of the morning. So, I waited. And waited. Standing there, my dread at the prospect of returning to school grew. I was thinking in particular of one of my classmates, who sat next to me in lessons, whispering 'wheeeee-splat' at intervals. He relished taunting me about my sister jumping to her death from a fifth-floor window. When he wasn't doing that, he and his friends would shake me down for cash, knowing that I kept bus fare and dinner money back to buy sweets.

That morning, I could not face the idea of returning to the bullying, the taunting, the extortion and the indifferent teachers. Despairing at these thoughts, I looked up, saw a car coming towards me and, without further thought, stepped out in front of it.

I can't say for sure that I was suicidal. All I can say is that I was prepared to do anything it took to avoid going to school that day. But no way was I going to admit that in front of my parents. They had suffered enough with the loss of their daughter. I could not tell them I had deliberately walked in front of a moving vehicle. I could scarcely accept it myself.

The impact was painless but the car hit my skinny leg with a surprisingly loud bang. Then, I was cartwheeling through the air, to land, seated upright, on the other side of the road. Miraculously, there were no vehicles coming towards me on that side. Otherwise, I would certainly not be writing this. The difference between me living and dying at that point was measured in milliseconds.

Sitting there, I was suddenly overcome with a desire to be at school. I could tell all my classmates and teachers what had happened. I would be an object of interest, rather than ridicule and pity. I tried to stand up but was dismayed to find I couldn't. Then I noticed I was missing a shoe and I thought, *Dammit, I can't carry on walking to school without my shoe.* I twisted myself round to try and locate it. The car that had hit me had mounted the pavement and the driver, a woman, was standing next to it, head in hands. People were running towards me from all sides, others were holding up traffic at the junction. There was a lot of shouting: 'Is he okay?', 'Oh my God, someone call an ambulance', 'What happened?' Front doors slammed and, from all around, residents ran towards me, some half-dressed, others in dressing gowns. The slap of shoes on the pavement. Where was my shoe? If I could find it, I could carry on.

Never mind that my right thighbone was split clean in two, my leg bent at an unnatural right angle and folded neatly beneath me. There was no blood, so I was going to be okay.

A year later, sitting opposite two police officers, I didn't want to tell them any of that.

The policewoman leaned forward and stroked my upper arm. I realised that she had a kind face but I was still not sure she was on my side.

'Look,' she said. 'You were twelve when it happened. Nobody blames you. The child is never held to blame in these cases. But we need to know what happened so we can file a report and then we can decide if we should take the driver to court.'

I felt the colour drain from my face. It *was* my fault. I had stepped in front of that car deliberately. That poor woman, sobbing into her hands, her knees buckling under her. How must she have felt? What had I done to her? I couldn't let her go to court.

But I couldn't tell the truth, either.

So, miserable and nervous as I was, I sat there working out how best to lie. I remembered reading a saying in *Jennings and Darbishire*, a book that I loved: 'Oh what a tangled web we weave, when first we practise to deceive.' From that, I knew that I should keep my story simple and as close to the truth as possible. I should give the police officers only limited room within which to probe the veracity of what I was telling them. And I wanted to insert a detail that was checkable.

I took a deep breath and told them my story.

'I was walking to school. I got to the junction and it was busy, so I had to wait. I waited so long that I was worried about being late for school. I decided I would need to run for it. I saw the car coming but thought I could make it. But, as I stepped out, I looked down and realised my shoelace was undone. This slowed me down. When I looked up, it was too late. The car hit me and I landed on the other side of the road.' I paused. 'It was my fault, not hers.'

The policewoman leafed through her notepad. 'Oh yes,' she said, 'the driver told us that she found your shoe caught on her bumper. No wonder. It must have been loose with the lace undone.'

They got up to go, the policeman saying, 'It all seems very straightforward. We'll write to you when we have completed our report. But I don't think there will be any further action.'

I had got away with it. I had lied but I had lied well, I thought, and for good reason. I didn't feel what Ekman calls 'deception guilt' but neither did I feel 'duping delight'. I just felt relieved: for me, for my parents, for the driver.

My deception was contained. It was simple. There was no narrative distortion involved, just a tweak to the account of my state of mind when walking out into the road. And my story about the shoelace enabled the police to adduce something else to corroborate my account: something else that was independently true and verifiable. My shoe *had* come off.

There was another reason why I had wanted so badly to protect the driver. The day of the accident, as I was getting used to my leg being in traction and peeing into a bottle, a nurse came to me with a plastic bag. My shoe was in the bag. The nurse told me that the driver had brought it to the hospital herself, hoping to see me and say sorry. They said she was not allowed to see me, in case criminal proceedings were later brought against her. The poor woman. She had made the effort to return my shoe. She wanted to see that I was all right. She wanted to apologise, for something that was not her fault.

I owed her.

The principle of reciprocation is very powerful.

*   *   *

RECAP

- For spies working with agents to generate reliable and actionable intelligence, effective debriefing and detecting deception are two sides of the same coin.
- The spy 'tasks' an agent to retrieve intelligence; the agent collects the intelligence required; finally, the spy 'debriefs' the agent about what he has discovered.
- Preparation for debriefing starts with setting objective requirements, continues with mastering the subject and ends with arranging a safe space for an interview.
- Short, open, non-loaded, 5W and H questions are best. The spy needs to listen actively, establish sources of knowledge, challenge questionable claims and exude authority.
- Detecting deception is an art, not a science. To improve her chances, the spy assesses motivations for her agent to lie and establishes their baseline behaviours.
- The two aspects that a liar will find most difficult to control are his face and voice, more than the words he speaks or the way in which he holds his body as he lies.
- Asking questions about events out of their chronological sequence can wrongfoot and betray someone who has falsified a narrative.

- Spies have a natural advantage in detecting deception, as they practise it at a high level themselves and are familiar with its traits.

*   *   *

You may be asking yourself how relevant techniques of debriefing and deception detection are to your dealings with goals allies. The answer is, in the case of debriefing, highly relevant. In the case of deception detection, not so much, but there are lessons to be learned from them.

Let's start with the case for debriefing techniques. A good goals ally will not only be able to offer you practical assistance, they will also be a fount of valuable advice. They will have extensive life experience, career knowledge, people-handling know-how and first-hand exposure to a range of organisations with a bearing on your goals. In short, they will have wisdom. Why would you not want to learn from that?

So, you stand to learn a great deal from your mentor. But you should not assume either that they know what you need to learn from them, or that they know how best to tell you. In a healthy relationship with a goals ally, it is your responsibility to make life as easy as possible for them, at least when it comes to extending assistance to you, including advice. This doesn't mean that you should adopt a formal debriefing approach. That would be inappropriate in most cases. But there are a few ways in which you can benefit from thinking like a spy when it comes to learning from goals allies.

First: be clear about what it is that you *do* want to learn from them. You don't need to produce a formal requirements brief and send them to find out the answers to your questions – those are already in their head. But you should think carefully about how to phrase your requests. Rather than 'Please tell me about how you got into radio broadcasting', try 'What can you tell me about your early experiences in broadcasting that would be helpful to someone trying to break into that world?' Or, better still, 'What are your five top tips for the would-be radio presenter?' The more specific and the more relevant to your goals, the better.

Second: do your homework. Your goals ally's time is precious, as is yours. Don't waste it asking them about information that you can easily find online or by other means. Your aim should be to acquire what I call 'experience-based intelligence'. This is information that someone knows first-hand and which is not recoverable by any means other than talking to (or debriefing) them. For example, you don't need to ask a goals ally how to make an application for a Harvard scholarship. You can find that out with a few keystrokes. But a former scholar may have all sorts of advice to offer about how to enhance your chances of acceptance. So, ask them that. They will enjoy the second type of conversation much more than they would the first.

Third: create comfortable and conducive conditions for them to impart their knowledge. In part, this is about controlling the environment, a subject that we shall return to in Chapter Nine (p. 270). It is also about convenience. Find a time and place that works for your goals ally and make sure that you are not pressed for time at the encounter. If possible, keep your time commitment open-ended and establish early on how much time they have available to talk to you. As touched on before, it is worth checking in advance that the venue you choose will be open at the time you agree and that it won't close abruptly during your discussions.

To the extent that you can, reduce the likelihood of other interruptions. One obvious thing to do is put your mobile on silent or, better still, switch it off altogether. If you are meeting in an office and you can, reserve a conference room and switch

on the 'do not disturb' light. On this note, it is always worth
double-checking such arrangements. Some years ago, I hosted a
sensitive meeting for a private client in a hotel room in Luanda,
Angola, with a source who was particularly concerned that our
contact should be discreet. After welcoming him in, I hung the
'por favor, não perturbe' sign on the external door handle. Ten
minutes later, we were interrupted by a knock from the cham-
bermaid. I impatiently told her to go away, pointing at the sign.
It was only then that I noticed it was printed differently on each
side. I had mistakenly displayed the message *'por favor, arrume o
quarto'*: please make up the room. We all make mistakes.

Finally, when you and your goals ally are settled in, cappuc-
cinos at the ready, there are a few rules of thumb to remember
about the most effective way to manage the conversation. Most
important of all, *let them talk*. Obvious, yes, but easier said than
done, for many of us. We all want to throw in our tuppence-
worth during a conversation but try to curb the temptation. You
should be in receive rather than transmit mode. On which note,
if you need to refresh your memory on how to listen actively,
look back at Chapter Four (p. 103) before meeting a goals ally. Be
prepared to keep the conversation moving, by having in mind a
few supplementary questions. As is the case for spies, the best
questions are open and without in-built assumptions: 'What
were the key factors that landed you your first Ted Talk?' is better
than 'Which speakers' agent got you your first gig?' Short,
straightforward questions are preferable to long and convoluted
ones. All the while, be attentive to your goals ally's needs. Would
they like another drink? Something to eat? A comfort break?

It is okay to take occasional notes but ask their permission
first: 'Do you mind if I jot down a couple of notes as an *aide-
memoire*?' And keep them to a minimum.

It is also worth spending a little time thinking about body
language. I don't subscribe to the idea that a calculable

proportion of human communication is unspoken, but that is not important. It is obvious that certain postures, gestures and expressions are more conducive to open communication than others. You would be well advised to adopt them, to get the most out of a session with a goals ally in which you are seeking experience-based intelligence.

Working from the top down, the eyes are a good place to start. As Allan and Barbara Pease put it in *The Definitive Book of Body Language*, 'It is only when you see "eye to eye" with another person that a real basis for communication can be established.' They go on to claim that the meeting of gazes between two people for 60 to 70 per cent of a conversation is ideal for 'building rapport'.[1] But it should be noted that this does not apply in some cultures. And too much sustained eye contact can be unsettling in all cultures. If in doubt, a good rule is to take your cue from the goals ally, mirroring their own use of eye contact. It is also helpful to be aware of a distinction between the 'social gaze' – which roves around the triangular area of another's face between the eyes and the mouth – and the intimate gaze. The intimate gaze during one-to-one encounters roves around the triangular area between the eyes and the chest. Better not to confuse these two.

Moving down, concentrate on adopting an open posture. The primary means of achieving this is to keep your arms uncrossed. Not only does this signal to your companion that you are in a receptive mode, but studies also suggest that it *makes* you more receptive. In one such study, volunteers who kept their arms folded across their chests during a lecture recalled 38 per cent less of its content than others who adopted a relaxed, open posture, with their legs and arms uncrossed.[2] So, relax and open

1 Allan and Barbara Pease, *The Definitive Book of Body Language*, Orion, 2017, p. 175.
2 Ibid., p. 91.

yourself up to learning from your goals ally. Don't overdo it, though. A languid, slouching pose might suggest indifference or boredom. Instead, it does no harm to lean in towards the speaker, so long as you are careful not to invade their personal space.

You might also want to think about how to position your feet. It's never a good look to appear in a hurry to get away and your feet may subconsciously suggest that you do. Overall, it is best to keep both feet pointing generally towards your interlocutor. I fell foul of this myself, when meeting executives of an oil company based in Europe. They were looking for assistance to establish if their recently awarded exploration blocks in South Sudan were already being worked by competitors. I was reluctant to get involved but couldn't quite explain why, so I tried to engage with the oilmen, keeping good eye contact throughout, remaining attentive and smiling in all the right places. Afterwards, one of them called me to say I wouldn't be getting the job. He and his colleagues felt that the meeting had gone badly, because it was clear that I wanted to get away. Thinking back, I realised that I had sat on a sofa in one of the executive's plush offices, with both feet clearly angled towards the door. My body was doing the talking for me. I am delighted that its message was received loud and clear. Today, that oil company faces allegations of complicity in war crimes.

In a similar vein, you should avoid looking at your watch or glancing at your mobile while your goals ally is talking. Either is a sure-fire way to get them to shut up. Play it safe and put your phone away. However, don't be afraid to busy yourself with it if your companion takes a call during your encounter. This is a simple way of giving them space to get on with whatever important business they need to attend to. Better than drumming your fingers on the table and sighing.

Politeness – and good sense – dictates that, as the meeting draws to a close, you should thank your goals ally for their time and advice. An omission to do so will almost certainly be noted and will disincline the goals ally to be helpful in the future. They may even lie to you, making excuses as to why they cannot be of further assistance.

Which brings us onto the lessons to be learned from deception-detection techniques. It is unlikely that you will need to spot when a goals ally is misleading you. It can't be ruled out that they will exaggerate their own achievements and they may claim insights they don't really possess. But common sense will guide you to spot either of those relatively harmless deceptions. More important is that you learn to read your goals ally's body language – not to spot when they are lying but to work out if they are feeling unsettled at any stage. Not everyone is comfortable talking about their histories, especially if such discussions encroach on personal matters. You should be alive to this risk and be prepared to take a step back if you assess that you have strayed into uncomfortable territory.

As with detection of deception, this involves establishing a baseline. After a few meetings, you will soon get a sense of how your goals ally usually holds himself or herself when relaxed and positive. Be on the lookout for deviations from the baseline, particularly for evidence of a desire to leave or withdraw physically from you. As noted above, we tend to point our bodies towards an exit when we want to get away, so this is an obvious clue to watch for. Another one is their leaning back and away from you. You should also be sensitive to reduced eye contact. Just as you crossing your arms would send a defensive, closed signal, so it is with your goals ally – as long as that is not a natural position for them, as it is for some people. Be aware of where they place their coffee cup: holding it with their right hand with the cup on their left may be a subconscious formation of a single-arm barrier. Clenched hands might indicate anxiety or restraint. Use of their hand to support their head, on their chin or cheek, could suggest boredom. If they combine any of these negative signals with checking their watch or fiddling with their mobile, it may be time to draw your meeting to a close.

Much of this is, of course, common sense. But – as is often the case when learning to think like a spy – the difference is to be found in applying everyday techniques systematically and with intent. Perhaps the most significant lesson to learn is that the best results will be obtained when your focus is outward rather than inward. Situational awareness is all-important. So, our concluding chapter will focus more broadly on this subject (p. 270). After a story about an unusual situation that challenged both my worldview and my ability to detect deception.

* * *

If popular crime dramas are anything to go by, guilty interviewees often betray themselves by revealing information about crime scenes they couldn't know without being there. Apparently compelling. But I am not so sure, after my close encounter with Voodoo.

There are two myths about Voodoo (or, preferably, Vodou) that need busting before I explain. First, it is not a form of black magic. Rather, it is an ancient monotheistic religion that involves worship of a range of spirits and the belief that humans are essentially spirits in material form.[1] Second, its spiritual home is not in Haiti or any other Caribbean country. It is in Benin. And, within Benin, the capital of Vodou is the southern town of Ouidah, where I found myself in March 2009.

My colleague Sophie and I had completed an intelligence-gathering project in the commercial capital Cotonou and were visiting Ouidah out of curiosity. It is hardly a tourist spot. More

1 Britannica, Vodou. https://www.britannica.com/topic/Vodou

a humid hellhole; formerly a slave trading centre for over two hundred years. I was drenched in sweat as soon as we stepped out of the taxi that had ferried us there, so we headed to the nearest place that looked like it could provide shelter from the sun. The *Temple de Pythons* is exactly what it sounds like.

The people of Ouidah worship royal pythons as protectors of their former king. It is forbidden to harm the snakes, on pain of imprisonment. Many houses have 'python holes' at floor level, to allow them to come and go as they wish. Far from being considered a pest, a visiting python is welcomed as a bringer of good luck. For many visitors to the temple, where ball pythons from all over Benin live, it is the done thing to have one draped around their shoulders. I must have been faint from the sun because I agreed to this ritual. Sophie, sensible woman that she is, declined. As the surprisingly dry, cool creature writhed around my neck, I asked our guide what he would do if it went to bite me. His answer was, roughly, 'Nothing, because that is God's will.' I let him take the snake back with some relief.

Sophie and I sought out cold sodas, over which we agreed to walk *La Route de l'Esclave*. This is a four-kilometre dirt road, down which an estimated one million slaves[1] were marched to ships waiting to transport them across the Atlantic. Not the cheeriest of R&R activities but fascinating and thought-provoking. Sights along the route include the 'Tree of Oblivion', around which the slaves were walked seven times to forget their former, free lives, the 'Zomai House', where the captives waited to board the ships, and – somewhat unexpectedly – a western-style cemetery.

Sophie saw it first, was intrigued, and veered off the road to explore. I followed but, before I could enter the cemetery, my eye was caught by a pile of bones, feathers, blood and eggshells.

1 Memorias Situadas, Slave Route. https://www.cipdh.gob.ar/memorias-situadas/en/lugar-de-memoria/la-ruta-del-esclavo/

Puzzled and a little repulsed, I knelt to examine it. Sophie was waving me in, so I stood up and tried to step over the rotting pile. I say 'tried' because, as I walked towards the cemetery, I felt pressure on my chest, as if an invisible hand was pushing me back. I shook my head, told myself to stop being ridiculous and tried again. Again, pressure on my chest stopped me going forward. I wondered if I was having a heart attack but, as soon as I stepped backwards, the pressure was released. A little panicked, but trying not to show it, I called Sophie over.

'I know it sounds ridiculous,' I said, 'but I can't step over this pile of bones. Can you?'

Sophie laughed, hopped over the pile and then back again. 'It does sound ridiculous,' she said, heading back into the cemetery. 'Come on, I want to show you one of the inscriptions.' I took a deep breath, stepped forward and, once more, felt a gentle but unyielding hand push me away.

I decided against viewing the cemetery that day, braving Sophie's mockery instead.

I am a rational man, not given to superstition or belief in the supernatural. I put the experience down to heat stroke or dehydration: a trick of the mind. Nonetheless, it had unnerved me, as I admitted to another colleague on my first day back at the office. Fidelis, a devout Catholic, hails from Edo State in Nigeria and proved himself well versed in West African religious beliefs. As I told him about what had happened at the cemetery, he listened carefully, fingers steepled, his forehead furrowed and his kind eyes on mine.

When I had finished, he nodded slowly and asked, 'Was the pile of bones and feathers on a crossroads?'

I thought for a while, playing the scene over in my mind's eye.

'Yes,' I said, 'there was a footpath leading to the cemetery from the road and it was on the corner where they met. How did you know?'

Fidelis ignored my question. 'And Sophie could step over it?'

'Yes, no problem at all.'

The furrows on his forehead deepened. 'In that case,' he said, 'you must have had the python around your neck, and she didn't.'

I was stunned.

'That's mad,' I said. 'How can you possibly have known that? Did Sophie tell you about it?'

'No.' Fidelis gestured towards Sophie's unoccupied desk. 'She's not in yet.'

'She must have phoned you, then.'

Fidelis laughed. 'She doesn't have my number.' He handed me his phone. 'Here, have a look. You'll see we haven't spoken since you both left for Benin.'

I waved his phone away. It felt like too much to scroll through Fidelis's call log.

'No, I trust you. But how did you know, then? I haven't told anyone else.'

I watched Fidelis carefully as he spoke. I knew him well by then. We had sat together for over a year and had grown close personally, as well as professionally. I was his boss and there had been difficult, as well as joyful, discussions between us. I had a good baseline for his behaviour when telling the truth. In any case, he is one of the most honest, devout and respectful people I know. I believe that he would find it difficult to lie for any length of time without displaying significant levels of discomfort. Nonetheless, his words were difficult for a rational man to accept.

'You discovered a Vodou fetish,' he said. 'If someone has died tragically, some people believe that they have been inhabited by an evil spirit. They build a fetish at a crossroads near where their relative is buried. The spirit leaves the body of their loved one and makes a home in the fetish. But it can only stay there temporarily.'

'How does the spirit leave the fetish?'

Fidelis raised his eyes to mine. 'It enters the body of the first person to step over the fetish.'

Nonsense. Of course. But I felt a little sick, despite myself.

'Unless that person has protection from the python?' I asked.

Fidelis nodded. I continued watching him, sure that his face would betray him, that he would break out laughing, that he would call over our colleagues, to enjoy the joke he and Sophie had somehow cooked up at my expense. But nothing. If he was ragging me, he was a master of deception.

'But, what about Sophie? She stepped over the fetish. Is the evil spirit in her now?'

Fidelis shook his head adamantly. I could see he was distressed at the idea. 'No. I am sure it only works with people of the same sex.' He looked over to Sophie's desk, a shadow of apprehension crossing his face. At that moment, she walked into the office, and I could see the relief wash over him. I called her over.

'Great joke, Sophie,' I said. 'You both nearly got me. But I'm guessing you called Fidelis on his landline this morning, to plan it all.'

Sophie looked blank. 'What are you talking about?'

'Your joke on me about the python, protecting me at the cemetery.'

She laughed. 'Oh, yes, you were being a bit silly there,' she said. 'But what does that have to do with pythons?'

I looked from Sophie to Fidelis, checking for stolen glances, or a tell-tale upward curve of the lips. But, if they were both in on the joke, they were holding their own without any sign of effort.

'Okay, this has gone far enough,' I said, rattled now. 'Have you spoken to Fidelis since we got back from Benin, Sophie?'

'No, I haven't. I don't know what he has been telling you, but it has nothing to do with me.'

She went back to her desk.

'Fidelis,' I said. 'Now is the time to tell me if this is a wind-up. It's a good one, if so. Time to laugh about it with the others.'

He spread his hands. 'What can I say? I'm not messing with you. I'm just telling you what I know about Vodou. Some people in my state believe in it too.' That much is true. I had read about 'juju' practices in Edo State some time before. They are believed to play a role in people trafficking from that region: not the sort of thing that Fidelis would joke about.

The thought of juju gave me the cue for a final gambit. If I could inject a note of absurdity into the conversation, it might flush out the joke. 'Well, I guess that my mum's pet name for me was appropriate, then,' I said.

'What was that?

'Mum used to call me Juju, sometimes.'

This made Fidelis laugh, but his seriousness returned quickly. He looked me straight in the eye. 'I am telling you the truth, Juju,' he said. 'Think yourself lucky. You were protected by the python around your neck.'

I believed him, right then.

But rationality soon reasserts itself. Believing my friend implies accepting that there may be something in the superstitions and practices of Vodou, which I am reluctant to do. Disbelieving him means that I must override my instincts about his body language and my reading of his character. Perhaps that is the more sensible conclusion. After all, I noted earlier in this chapter that detecting deception is, for the most part, a game of chance.

So, come on, Fidelis, if you are reading this. It's been fourteen years. You got me good, and I'll laugh along with you.

Time to fess up, because my deception-detection skills have let me down on this one.

* * *

RECAP

- Debriefing techniques are relevant to interactions with a goals ally, who is likely to be a valuable source of experience-based intelligence unavailable elsewhere.
- It would not be appropriate to produce a formal requirements brief but be clear, concise and specific when asking what you would like to learn from a goals ally.
- Do your homework in advance, so you don't waste time on information available elsewhere. Create a conducive environment for the sharing of experiences.
- Give your goals ally space to speak, listen actively and have a prepared list of open, non-assumptive questions in mind. It's okay to take notes but polite to ask first.
- Be aware of your body language, adopting an open, receptive posture, focused on your goals ally. Maintain good eye contact without staring.
- You are unlikely to need deception-detection techniques but sensitivity to your goals ally's body language can provide clues to any discomfort they may feel.
- Establish baselines for their relaxed behaviour and watch out for deviations in body orientation, eye contact and use of arms and hands. Learn to be outward-focused.

CHAPTER NINE

The Protective Power of Controlling the Environment

We can't always rely on a python to protect us, so let's move on. From witchcraft to tradecraft.

Spies use the term 'tradecraft' for a suite of measures used to control the environment in which they communicate with their agents. As a reminder, Furnham and Taylor describe it as the means to 'ensure that potentially hostile people or technical devices do not observe their [handler and agent's] meetings'.[1] In this context, meetings can be taken to mean person-to-person contacts or the remote sharing of information.

There is one overriding reason why spies use tradecraft and that is *to protect the agent*. It doesn't take much thinking to work out why this is so important. It is pragmatic, in that to lose an agent would be to lose a valuable source of intelligence. It is symbolic, in that failure to protect one agent from discovery would make more difficult the job of convincing other targets to become agents. It is ethical, in that a spy owes a duty of care to an agent who is risking themselves at their behest. Hence, spies spend a lot of time learning about and practising tradecraft.

1 Furnham and Taylor, *The Psychology of Spies and Spying*, p. 114.

The techniques are used by intelligence agencies the world over and are proprietary to none.[1] They are also widely used in the private intelligence world.[2] They are taught by former government officials to commercial clients.[3] They are the subject of museum exhibitions and events.[4] And they have been written about extensively.[5] Nothing that follows reveals any secrets, confirms the use of specific techniques by any organisation, or is a threat to any country's national security.

Broadly speaking, tradecraft falls into three categories:

- Detection of followers;
- Use of secure premises; and
- Covert communications.

In the first group, there are two main techniques: anti-surveillance and counter-surveillance. In his book *Surveillance Tradecraft*, Peter Jenkins describes the former as 'actions or manoeuvres that a person carries out in order to confirm that he is under surveillance and by whom'. The latter are 'the methods or actions that a third party (person or team) carries out in order to identify the presence of a surveillance team'.[6] In both cases,

1 As covered by podcasts such as those produced by Spyscape (https://spyscape.com/article/spyscape-tradecraft-the-insiders-view-from-the-cia-kgb-mossad-and-more) and Washington DC's Spy Museum https://www.spymuseum.org/podcast/
2 Including by the company Diligence LLC: https://digroup-us.com/international-surveillance
3 See, for example, https://www.intelsecurity.co.uk/courses
4 See, for example, https://www.spymuseum.org/past-events/spy-fest-tradecraft-try-its/2023-01-27/
5 Including by Furnham and Taylor in *The Psychology of Spies and Spying*; Ferguson in *Spy*: Antonio and Jonna Mendez in *The Moscow Rules: The Secret CIA Tactics That Helped America Win the Cold War*, Public Affairs, 2020; and Peter Jenkins in *Surveillance Tradecraft: The Professional's Guide to Covert Surveillance Training*, Intel Publications, 2010, among many others.
6 Jenkins, *Surveillance Tradecraft*, p. 295.

the aim is to ensure (as far as possible) that hostile surveillance teams are not led to a meeting between a spy and their agent. The spy uses anti-surveillance to 'dry clean' herself, and counter-surveillance to do the same for the agent. In either case, should surveillance be detected, a planned meeting is aborted.

Anti-surveillance (AS) drills are designed so that it is not obvious to anyone watching – including surveillance teams – that they are being deployed. The target follows a pre-recced route, drawing followers into 'traps' in the hope of forcing them to reveal themselves through unusual behaviour. These might include moving rapidly between busy and quiet areas, so that followers need to speed up or slow down to maintain appropriate distance from their target. Or walking through a 'funnel', such as a narrow passageway for which there are no parallel routes and at the end of which there is a convenient stopping point for the spy to see who emerges from it behind them. Of course, the surveillance team also uses drills developed to enable them to evade detection, so interaction between followers and followed becomes a form of clandestine dance.

Counter-surveillance (CS) is a little easier than AS. Teams 'plot up' at various concealed vantage points along a pre-agreed route that the agent follows, to note whether the same person or people appear behind them on multiple occasions. Both AS and CS involve walking pre-set routes for which the walker has good cover. The routes involve numerous locations at which it is likely to be more than a coincidence if another person is spotted at more than one. In both cases, the golden rules are to look out for repeat sightings and unusual behaviour in others, without being spotted doing so. It is a skill.

Occasionally, surveillants make life easier for their target. On one occasion in Uganda, following a meeting at the president's office to discuss potential private security services for an upcoming diplomatic conference, I noticed a young woman shadowing me in the gardens of my hotel. I stopped and smiled at her. At first, she tried to pretend she hadn't noticed, then changed tack and approached me. 'Hi,' she said. 'I'm Elaine. I saw you earlier outside the president's office.' I put this fumble down to amateurishness, but surveillance teams do occasionally make their presence felt intentionally, for intimidation purposes. This was the case during my visit to Benin with Sophie, when a team searched my hotel room while we were downstairs taking dinner. I know they did, because they ripped the linings of my blazer and my suitcase, very obviously. It was the same blazer in which a scorpion nested a year or so later, in South Sudan. I avoided being stung by that scorpion: perhaps the python was still on my side.

Assuming the spy and the agent arrive safely and unaccompanied at their agreed meeting place, the next tradecraft task is to make sure the location is secure. If they meet in a public place, the spy will agree a cover reason for the two of them being there together. She will also manage seating arrangements so that their discussions will not be overheard. She will seat herself in such a way as to cover the entrance, so that she can appraise comings and goings for any threat. If in private, it is likely to be in premises controlled by her agency, which are routinely swept for concealed listening and video devices.

A few simple tactics can bamboozle would-be listeners, such as switching hotel rooms used for meetings at the last minute. This trick isn't guaranteed to work, though. I tried it once in Accra, Ghana, when meeting a nervous corporate whistleblower on behalf of a law firm. I told the receptionist that I needed to change rooms to get away from some construction noise, only to be told that the hotel was fully occupied. I rented a meeting room instead.

So long as the spy can control a location, in-person contact is the preferred form of communication with her agent. But this is not always possible, perhaps because the overall operating environment is too hostile (for example, in such places as Iran or North Korea). It may be that spy or agent needs to cancel an agreed meeting; in which case they will require a means of contact that is not in person. Or a risk assessment may conclude that it would be better to transfer packages of documentary intelligence remotely, to reduce the chances of the pair being caught in the act of an incriminating exchange. For contingencies such as these, there are both analogue and digital options to choose from.

On the analogue front, two tried and tested forms of communication are the lightning, or brush contact (BC), and the dead letter box (DLB). Neither is as exciting as it sounds. A brush contact simply involves a very brief encounter, in a prearranged area out of potential surveillants' sight, to hand over a small item – perhaps a roll of film or a short, written message. The handover can be made, for example, as one person passes another in the dogleg of a narrow passageway, following exchange of visual 'safe to proceed' signals. An amusing variant on the BC theme was used by Oleg Penkovsky's handler, Ruari Chisholm, with his wife's collaboration: as described in an article in London's *Evening Standard*, 'One exchange saw Penkovsky drop a box of "sweets," which in fact contained film copies of secret documents, into the pram of Chisholm's youngest child.'[1]

A dead letter box allows for exchange of bulkier items, as in the case of the FBI officer Robert Hanssen, who reported to the Russians undetected for many years. As described in an exhibition in New York's Spyscape, 'Hanssen exchanged money and secrets with his Russian handlers at Foxstone Park, near his home in Vienna, Virginia. He would secure a garbage bag full of intelligence to the

1 Katie Rosseinsky, 'The Courier: Greville Wynne,Oleg Penkovsky and the remarkable true story behind Benedict Cumberbatch's film', The Standard, 6 August 2021. https://www.standard.co.uk/culture/film/the -courier-true-story-greville-wynne-oleg-penkovsky-beneditch-cumber- batch-film-b949269.html

underside of a bridge in the park. Then, on his way home, he would stick a small piece of white tape onto one of the posts supporting the entrance sign (so his handlers knew he had made a drop).[1]

Of course, with the advent of technology, spies and agents now have access to secure digital communications systems. These systems typically involve sending highly encrypted messages over the web or by GSM (Global System for Mobile Communications). But they might also employ shorter-range means of information exchange, such as variants of Bluetooth technology or short-wave radio waves. On occasion, these short-range systems have given rise to almost comedic stories, such as that concerning a 'rock' in Moscow, discovered by the Russians to conceal a transceiver for communication with an agent. According to a report in the *Guardian*, a spokesman for Russia's Federal Security Service (FSB) claimed that 'the device, a twenty-first century version of the "dead letter drop", had a range of up to 20 metres and could send and receive coded signals to or from small palmtop computers, almost identical to those available on Britain's high streets'. The article went on to claim that 'it enabled British diplomats to communicate indirectly with their alleged Russian agents: it meant they never had to be in the same room as them'.[2]

In the private sector, intelligence practitioners (and the wider public) have access to commercially available systems of encrypted communication, such as Signal. Often, though, they opt to produce their own, to avoid potential 'back doors' built into off-the-shelf products for law enforcement (or, indeed, espionage) purposes. For most of us, commercial encryption packages are sufficient to

1 Reproduced from the *Spyscape Museum Booklet*, with the permission of John Hunt, Founder and CEO of Spyscape.
2 Nick Paton-Walsh, Richard Norton-Taylor and Ewen MacAskill, 'The Cold War is over, but rock in the park suggests the spying game still thrives', Guardian, 24 January 2006. https://www.theguardian.com/world/2006/jan/24/russia.politics

protect us against the threats that we all face – not from government intelligence agencies, but from criminals bent on committing fraud and identity theft. Big corporate organisations are more
likely to buy tailored packages, to protect them from (sometimes
state-sponsored) commercial espionage. It is all about adopting
mitigation measures appropriate to the threat.

Which brings us to another way at looking at what spies do.
They are, ultimately, players in the risk business. Risk in this
context is a function of vulnerability to threat. Spies are tasked
to collect intelligence about threats to national security. The
intelligence they produce is analysed to assess vulnerability to
those threats. Security services then implement mitigation
measures to reduce that vulnerability and, hence, the risk.

When handling an agent, a spy considers threats to their
security and assesses their vulnerability to those threats. She
then implements mitigation measures (tradecraft) to reduce the
agent's vulnerability to those threats.

Accordingly, to think like a spy when interacting with a goals
ally, you will need to get into the habit of thinking about what
threats exist to your relationship and the measures you can take
to mitigate those threats. That means thinking about controlling
the environment of your face-to-face meetings and your interim
means of communication. We'll look at how to do that next,
after a story about threat and risk management in the London of
the early nineties.

* * *

It is strange to think about it now, but to live in London in the early
1990s was to live in an environment of heightened deadly threat,
posed by the Provisional Irish Republican Army (PIRA). Everyone
was affected, so there was nothing particularly special about my
experience. Nonetheless, the PIRA began intensifying its campaign

of attacks in the capital in 1992, the year I moved there. And 1993 was particularly bad. At times, it seemed a bit personal.

I heard and felt my first IED explosion on 27 February that year. I was with my brother Tim in the aptly named World's End pub in Camden Town, embarking on an all-day drinking session. It was a Saturday, early afternoon, and the streets were filling up with tourists and locals heading to the market. A fair few had headed straight to the World's End from the tube station opposite. There was a pleasant, friendly hum of chatter in the air, punctuated by the clinks of glasses and the pops of crisp bags being opened. I think the Waterboys were playing on the jukebox: 'And a Bang on the Ear'.

The bomb was in a litter bin on the High Street, a few hundred yards from where my brother and I were tucking into our first pint of the day. We were in no doubt about what the noise was, even though neither of us had previously heard a live explosion. I remember being surprised at its abruptness: a *BLAM*, followed by a vacuum that sucked away all the noise of the world. A split second of silence, rather than the sound of falling masonry and reverberations that characterise blasts on television. My pint glass jumped a few millimetres and settled again, un-spilled. Then, the screaming and the shouting started. Followed by the wails of police and ambulance sirens.

Someone behind the bar was shouting to customers to stay inside the pub. Most ignored him, thronging to the doors. Two female students, on their first visit to London from Frankfurt, were rooted to their seats, faces drained of colour. We had exchanged a few words with them earlier, but they had made clear they weren't interested in our advances. Tim checked in with them, joking about the 'bloody awful' weather, as if it was a normal Saturday afternoon in London. In a way, it was. Once he had made sure the tourists were okay, we followed the others outside.

The police were already on the scene, as the IRA had issued an erroneous warning, convincing them to lead people towards the blast. By the time we got there, they had cordoned off the area and were not about to accept any help from two lads starting an all-day bender. We shrugged, and headed off down Camden Road, to pick up where we had left off, in the Old Eagle pub on Royal College Street. There, we watched the news unfold on TV.

Eighteen people were injured in that attack. Mercifully, nobody was killed.

Another Saturday, mid-morning, eight weeks later. Less hedonistic this time: I was near St Paul's Cathedral, walking to my office behind the Bank of England, planning to catch up on writing an end-of-month economic report. Another bang. Louder this time, sending shudders through the floor, reverberating like thunder and echoing for what felt like a minute. A massive truck bomb, detonated about a mile away, on Bishopsgate. It destroyed part of Liverpool Street Station and the nearby NatWest Tower, killed one person and injured forty-four others. I saw the funnel of smoke rising and turned back. Maybe I would spend the day in the pub, after all.

I was walking away from, rather than towards, my next near miss. Yet another Saturday, 2 October. I had been for dinner in Mayfair on the Friday evening and had caught the last Jubilee Line tube home from Green Park. I fell asleep and missed my stop at Swiss Cottage, getting out at Finchley Road instead, to walk to my flat on Belsize Park. I got in safely and didn't even hear the three bombs that exploded on Finchley Road sometime after midnight. It was only when I watched the news the following morning that I realised how close I had been to that incident.

The IRA mounted many other attacks in London that year: Oxford Street on 5 January; Harrods on 28 January; South Kensington tube station on 3 February; Crouch End, Archway and Highgate on 4 October; West Hampstead on 8 October;

Northfields Station on 20 December. In addition, there were countless false alarms, some following coded warnings, others caused by unattended baggage and the like. On 21 December, a series of coded warnings paralysed the underground system. It is not surprising that I found myself in the vicinity of a handful of incidents.

The net effect on me was, I am relieved to say, positive. I became, almost without realising it, highly threat aware. Most Londoners did, following a campaign on public transport to sensitise us all to the dangers of terrorism. Perhaps I was more sensitised than others because my behaviour altered significantly over that year. As well as being on the lookout for suspicious packages and avoiding crowded areas, I started taking personal protection measures to guard against attacks targeted at me. I varied my routes to and from work. Scanned streets for unusual behaviour, particularly after dark. Had new locks fitted at home. Avoided flashy accessories or carrying large amounts of cash. In short, I sharpened my situational awareness and taught myself to think routinely about personal threat and risk management.

This may sound a bit paranoid, but I don't see it that way. Paranoia cripples one's ability to function in the world. Threat awareness enhances one's ability to function safely, by 'switching on' at critical times, as I was to discover about a year later.

I was making my way home to Belsize Park, from a house party in Hampstead. Alone, despite my best efforts. It was a sultry summer's night, so I decided to walk, taking a route away from the main road. To the west of Haverstock Hill, there is a narrow passageway that cuts through one block, forming a short cut home. I approached on the opposite side of the road, crossing over just before drawing level with it. This gave me an opportunity to look back along the way I had come, as had become my habit by then. I saw a pair of youngish men a couple of hundred yards behind me. Something about their behaviour struck a discordant note with me. It seemed like they had suddenly slowed their pace as I looked back towards them. Without thinking, I 'switched on'.

Rather than head into the abandoned passageway, I turned sharp left and reversed direction, now on the other side of the road. I made sure to walk near the kerb, under the light of the lampposts, and took another look at the two men as I passed. I recognised one of them. He had been hanging around near the party as I left. Not a guest but not exactly a pest. Just someone smoking a spliff on a bench.

Repeat sightings and unusual behaviour. That was enough for me. I quickened my pace, heart pounding against my ribcage. The road we were on was lit but it was deserted, many of the residents having retired to bed long before. I had no confidence that anyone would respond to a knock on their door or a cry for help at that time of night: easier and safer to blame any noise on lively foxes, turn over and go back to sleep. As I passed them, I looked back and saw that the two men were crossing the road and reversing course themselves.

I ran.

First rule of self-defence: run away. Second rule: find somewhere safe. There was a twenty-four-hour garage on the corner with the main road, with a hatch at which the night staff dispensed cigarettes and snacks and took payments for petrol. I paid for a Mars Bar, and hovered, trying to steady my hand as I tore open the wrapper. From my new vantage point, I could see that my followers were waiting at a bus stop a short distance down Haverstock Hill. As far as I knew, there were no night buses running that route at the time.

I was reluctant to set off again on foot, so I asked the bored kiosk attendant if he would call me a cab. He was happy enough to do so, probably welcoming anything to break up the monotony.

'Where to?' he shouted through the hatch, phone clamped to his ear.

I realised that no driver would want to come out to carry me the half-mile or so home. So, I made up a destination further afield, planning to bung the driver a tenner for dropping me off sooner. The ploy worked, but I had ten minutes to wait before the car arrived. In all that time, the two men stood patiently at the bus stop, apparently waiting for a bus that was never going to come. More likely, waiting for me to leave the relative safety of the petrol station. I passed the time chatting to the kiosk attendant, trying to hide my mixture of nerves and relief, until my ride arrived.

We turned right out of the garage, and drove towards the bus stop, where the two men still stood. One of them, the spliff-smoker's companion, stared right at me in the passenger seat, as we drew level. In his left hand, he held an unlit cigarette. In his right, a flick-knife.

Without taking his unsmiling eyes off me, he gave me the merest glimpse of steel. My driver, unaware of his role as saviour, accelerated away.

'Thanks for picking me up,' I said. I like to imagine that I added, 'I would have been really cut up if you hadn't.' But the perfect line always occur to us after the moment has passed, doesn't it?

* * *

RECAP

- Tradecraft is used to prevent a spy's dealings with an agent from being observed by hostile parties. It involves controlling the environment of communication.

- The overriding point of tradecraft is to protect the agent, for pragmatic, symbolic and ethical reasons. A spy has an overriding duty of care to her agent.
- Tradecraft techniques – used by public and private agencies the world over – fall into three broad categories.
- First is detection of followers, including anti- and counter-surveillance: methods used to 'dry clean' spy and agent before a meeting.
- Second is use of secure premises: these might be carefully recced public settings or properties that are under an agency's direct control.
- Third is covert communications, including analogue techniques – like brush contacts and dead letter boxes – and digital transfer of encrypted data.
- Tradecraft requires a spy to adopt a threat and risk management mindset. The same mode of thinking can be adapted to enhance your interactions with goals allies.

* * *

In place of 'protect your agent', read 'respect your goals ally'.

Security is not about physical safety alone. Psychological safety matters too. And you owe it to your goals ally to look after theirs. At the same time, there are simple steps you can take to boost your own psychological wellbeing, as your relationship builds. The threats in both cases are the same: distraction, despondency and undue pressure or expectations. Any of these psychological 'followers' can destroy meaningful interactions.

As the spy does, it helps to break down your thinking about these threats into three parts:

- The approach to a meeting;
- Meeting venues; and
- Remote communication.

Obviously, you don't need to worry about hostile surveillance teams tailing you to a meeting with your goals ally. But you should take care not to take any personal demons into the meeting with you. Your responsibility is to focus on the needs of your ally, making it as easy as possible for them to give you assistance, advice or referrals. You won't be able to do this if you are distracted by the cares of the day. So, it is a good idea to 'dry clean' yourself psychologically, while making your way to an encounter.

For this reason, I always recommend walking to important meetings: it gives you time to 'switch on' to your emotional and mental state and compose yourself before a significant encounter. Medical experts tell us that walking 'has a positive influence on your hypothalamic-pituitary-adrenal (HPA) axis, which is your central nervous response system. This is good because the HPA axis is responsible for your stress response. When you exercise by walking, you calm your nerves, which can make you feel less stressed.'[1] A good walk can also enhance creativity, according to researchers at Stanford.[2] And it offers you the space to deal with anything that may threaten to distract you. It is a good idea to spend some time on your walk to a meeting focusing on worries or concerns that may get in the way of productive communication. Acknowledge them, describe them to yourself, promise yourself that you will come back to them at an appropriate time, and then park them.

1 WebMD, Mental Benefits of Walking. https://www.webmd.com/fitness-exercise/mental-benefits-of-walking
2 May Wong, 'Stanford study finds walking improves creativity', Stanford News, 24 April 2014. https://news.stanford.edu/2014/04/24/walking-vs-sitting-042414/

Spies tend to arrive early at meetings with targets and agents. You should aim to do so when meeting a goals ally. This way, you will be able to select the optimal seating arrangements: we'll come back to this. An early arrival will also allow you to find somewhere quiet (perhaps a restroom) to groom yourself. Wash your hands and face, comb your hair, reapply makeup and adjust your clothing. The ritual may give your self-confidence a last fillip. On which note, there is another trick worth trying. Adopt the 'winner's pose' for a minute or so: arms stretched out above you in a V shape, chin lifted, mouth open. Like a victorious athlete crossing the finish line well ahead of the pack. If this feels like too much, try the 'power pose' instead: standing with hands on hips, shoulders spread, legs apart, head up and facing forward.

Some social psychologists believe that body language has an emotional effect on the adopter as well as on observers. One such is Dr Amy Cuddy of Harvard Business School, who says that 'our bodies change our minds . . . and our minds change our behaviour . . . and our behaviour changes our outcomes.'[1] She is an enthusiastic proponent of power posing in challenging situations, claiming that such use of body language not only helps you 'fake it 'til you make it' but can be used to 'fake it 'til you *become* it'. I should add that other academics have questioned the validity of Cuddy's claims.[2] To these spoilsports, I say, what the hell? For a minute out of your day, it's worth a try.

So, you can use your route to a meeting with a goals ally as a way of giving the followers of distraction and despondency the slip. But you have no control over how a goals ally behaves

1 TED.com. https://www.ted.com/talks/amy_cuddy_your_body_language_may_shape_who_you_are?language=en
2 Nicolas Cesare, 'Do power poses really improve your confidence?', Newsweek, 29 September 2023. https://www.newsweek.com/do-power-poses-work-boost-confidence-1829907

before meeting you. They may be plagued by distracting thoughts and a negative mindset. There is not very much you can do about these threats, but you are not entirely powerless against them. That is, if you have some control over selection of the meeting venue.

This brings us back to Cialdini and his concept of pre-suasion. He claims that 'background cues in one's physical environment can guide how one thinks there'.[1] As an example, he cites the case of a project manager who was surprised to discover that her team designed the most effective corporate incentive programmes when working in a centrally located, glass-walled office, from which they were able to observe employees at work and moving around. Cialdini posits that this is because 'she and her team needed ongoing visual exposure to employees who would be covered by the programs'.[2] Another example is imagery used to motivate call-centre employees, such as posters depicting sprinters breaking through a finishing tape.

I am not suggesting that you put up posters where you meet a goals ally. You don't need to, because you can select venues that may achieve the same end, which is to pre-suade the goals ally to focus on your area of endeavour. As Cialdini says, 'It is possible for influencers to achieve their goals by shifting *others* [Cialdini's emphasis] to environments with supportive cues.' For example, if you are talking about how to achieve sporting success, try meeting in a sports bar or a gym's café. If your ambitions are artistic, galleries often have public meeting places that you can use; the same applies to photography exhibitions. If you are trying to make it as an author, how about meeting your writing mentor at a bookshop coffee bar? Musicians should head for public bars at music venues, actors for those at

1 Cialdini, *Pre-Suasion*, p. 119.
2 Ibid., p. 118.

theatres. If you are a budding entrepreneur, find out if you can use the premises of your local Chamber of Commerce or Institute of Directors. Third sector and development work? Find a Fairtrade coffee shop or explore your local Royal British Legion club.

With a little imagination, you should be able to find a venue that fits your specific pre-suasion requirements in most towns and cities. This will help to focus your goals ally, clearing their heads of the distraction threat.

Once at your selected venue, think carefully about seating arrangements. As Allan and Barbara Pease say in *The Definitive Book of Body Language*, 'Where you sit in relation to other people is an effective way of obtaining cooperation from them.'[1] You seek collaboration with a goals ally, so a collaborative set-up is appropriate.

Assuming a rectangular or square table, Pease and Pease set out four options. The 'corner position' is for 'people who are engaged in friendly, casual conversation': it involves sitting at a right angle of the table, with chairs facing towards one another. The 'co-operative position' is for when 'two people are thinking alike or both working on a task together': here, the seats are on the same side of the table, again orientated towards each other. The 'competitive/defensive position' is often used in business settings and involves protagonists facing one another from opposite sides of the table: however, it is also used in social settings, especially restaurants, allowing good eye contact and respect for one another's personal space. Finally, the 'independent position', in which two people sit diagonally opposite one another, 'is taken by people when they don't want to interact with each other'.

Self-evidently, you can rule out the independent position, but you will need to think about individual circumstances when

1 Ibid., p. 332.

deciding which of the three remaining options is appropriate. I would tentatively suggest avoiding the co-operative position unless you and your goals ally are working on a task together, such as reviewing your CV or examining some of your photographs or artwork. The corner position is an attractive option, as it provides enough of a barrier to protect your goals ally's personal space. But there will be some people who find that position unsettling and overly familiar. You will soon get a sense if you are dealing with such a person, in which case the somewhat misleadingly named 'competitive/defensive position' might be the better choice. If a restaurant or coffee table is relatively small, this position provides for an appropriate level of intimacy while demonstrating respect for the other person's boundaries.

One other consideration is that, while spies prefer to sit facing *into* a venue – preferably with a good view of the entrance – you would be better advised to allow a goals ally to sit with their back to a solid wall. They are more likely to relax in this position than they would with an open space behind them. This is one reason why hosts often show their guests respect by inviting them to sit looking outwards.

'Respect' is the key word here. Remember, your overriding responsibility is to respect your goals ally and to make every effort to give them a sense of psychological safety. Intrusive, overbearing or pressuring behaviour is to be avoided at all costs. This applies when deciding how to sit in relation to your goals ally during face-to-face meetings. It applies equally to remote communications with them between meetings.

This may seem counterintuitive, but casual comms can be destructive to relationships, especially those in written form. It pays to be cautious when using email, SMS, iMessage, WhatsApp, Signal or similar platforms. This is partly because, stripped of accompanying non-verbal signals, written messages

can be especially susceptible to misinterpretation. The shorter
the message, the greater this risk. Furthermore, use of emojis or
other short-cuts might exacerbate the problem. As a rule of
thumb, it is a good idea to restrict short messages to unemo-
tional and uncontentious matters, such as agreeing times and
places for meetings. That said, there is a case for sending occasional links to articles or other content of mutual interest online:
just try to ensure that the underlying material is uncontroversial. If in doubt, don't press send.

Another problem is that indiscriminate or heavy use of
messaging systems can feel pressuring: remember that undue
pressure is a significant threat to relationships with goals
allies. Again, a rule of thumb is useful here: restrict yourself to
reciprocal messaging. That is, try not to send more than one
message (maybe two, if you realise something in the first needs
clarifying) before receiving a response. Allow your goals ally
to set the pace and establish the best times of day for exchange
of messages. Use their preferred form of communication if
they have one. If not, it may be worth considering whether the
communications system you select fits the nature of your
interactions.

For example, artists and musicians are unlikely to be drawn
to the end-to-end encrypted platform Signal. Security consultants and diplomats, conversely, may view Instagram and X
with suspicion. With the plethora of systems now available, it is
worth giving careful thought to whether the principles of persuasion may apply when it comes to controlling the digital, as
well as the physical, environment.

In fact, it is worth thinking carefully about how people
communicate in general. To do this is to think like a spy. Because,
ultimately, spying is about understanding and managing
communication between two people. We'll explore this theme
further in Final Thoughts (p. 297). First, though, let's look at

how a colleague of mine got on during a day of particularly challenging tradecraft tasks, back on the streets of London.

*   *   *

Jo was convinced she had been under surveillance for most of the day. I was certain she hadn't been, for reasons that will become clear. But I could understand why she might have been confused. It had been an exhausting nine hours for her.

It had started at 8am, with an operational briefing in private rooms on St Martin's Lane, provided for our use by a friendly contact. I outlined the purpose of the day's operation: to disrupt the smuggling of antiquities stolen in Iraq, Syria and elsewhere, for sale on the black market in London. We had an agent that we thought might be willing to provide intelligence: names of the criminals involved; smuggling routes; details of stolen items and their whereabouts; numbers of offshore bank accounts used to launder the proceeds. But the agent involved – codenamed JACKDAW – was extremely nervous about being revealed to his former collaborators as an informant. Furthermore, we did not fully trust JACKDAW. After all, this was a man with a violent, criminal past. It was vital to handle him with enhanced levels of tradecraft: the famed 'Moscow Rules'.

JACKDAW had refused to agree a meeting time and venue in advance. The most he would do was arrange a brush contact, with details of where his handler (Jo) could meet to debrief him later that day. To complicate matters, he insisted on using a form of encryption using T. S. Eliot's *The Love Song of J. Alfred Prufrock* as the key. The level of paranoia he was displaying concerned me, so I had decided that Jo should practise anti-surveillance (AS) throughout. The previous day, I had recced an AS route from the briefing room to the brush contact point near Temple. After her briefing, Jo memorised the route map and details of

the lightning contact, before making her way to it alone, as
JACKDAW had stipulated.

She set off, through Covent Garden and Somerset House,
onto the Embankment and towards Victoria Embankment
Gardens. There, she exchanged 'safe to proceed' signals with a
man she didn't know and made her way to steps leading up
from a narrow passageway into Temple, the legal heart of
London. The unknown man followed on and passed her as she
climbed the stairs, slipping a small USB stick into her hand as he
did so. Not a single word was exchanged between them. At the
top of the stairs, he turned left, and Jo carried on ahead, to find
a coffee shop where she could open the device on a burner
laptop that I had given her at the briefing.

It took her a while to decipher the apparently random set of
numbers in front of her, counting down the lines of Eliot's poem,
then across to a specific word and then again to locate the corre-
sponding letter in that word. But she got there, finally, only to
realise that she had no time to lose. JACKDAW wanted to meet
her just twenty minutes after she had decrypted his message,
across town at St Ermin's near St James's Park. Jo knew the
hotel. It had been used as a base by British intelligence opera-
tives during the Second World War. JACKDAW obviously
enjoyed the game of espionage.

She figured the quickest way to St Ermin's would be by tube
and ran to Temple Station, just in time to jump on a District Line
train heading west. She was a couple of minutes late. By the
time she located JACKDAW on a discreet balcony, he was
getting up to leave. 'I don't like being kept waiting,' he told her.

*Maybe don't mess around with brush contacts and encrypted
messages, then,* Jo thought, suppressing the urge to say it to his
face. JACKDAW was the agent. The man in danger, she
reminded herself. Her responsibilities were towards him.

He wasn't done with the awkwardness, though. JACKDAW

told Jo that he knew only a part of the information that we needed. He was working as an intermediary for another figure, one who was still involved with the smuggling gang. This person – JACKDAW called him John Bryant – had fallen out with the gang's leader and was prepared to share intelligence on him for money. Jo could meet Bryant later that day, for the first time. It was up to her to persuade him that she could be trusted with information that would betray his former colleagues. She had a little time to grab lunch and then was expected at the Millennium Hotel on Grosvenor Square: this was where the former Russian intelligence officer Alexander Litvinenko had been poisoned with Polonium-210 a few years earlier. Bryant would be waiting for her there.

More scurrying across London and more lonely anti-surveillance drills, before meeting a man that she would have to persuade to trust her with his life.

Bryant made no secret of his sexism. Why should he trust a woman? Didn't the Services recruit men any longer? It was 'political correctness gone mad' to have a young woman like Jo dealing with someone like him. What were her superiors thinking?

But she handled it. Jo had come across boors like Bryant before, all too often. She kept her calm, letting the storm of Bryant's prejudice blow itself out. She took time to build a rapport with him, to demonstrate her concern for his wellbeing. She gave him the reassurances he needed to hear. She demonstrated professional unflappability. Pushed the right influence buttons. It took time and it took patience, but Bryant finally relented. He had left a package of information in a dead letter box, he told her. It contained everything we needed to know. The names of people involved, details of stolen antiquities, their current locations, times of their intended shipment to private collectors, the reasons why they were so desirable, the means of their extraction from war zones. The who, what, why, where, when, and how of the entire smuggling operation. It was gold dust.

But there was one last thing. Bryant wanted half a million pounds in exchange for the dead letter box's location. It was a deal breaker if she couldn't get him the money. She had to think fast. The sum was way beyond the budget we had authorised. She considered promising the payment later but was reluctant to make a promise she knew she would be unable to keep. Bryant refused a lower offer, slamming his teacup down with anger at what he called an 'insult'. Jo raised her offer again. Another contemptuous refusal. She moved again, this time to the full amount she had been told she could offer. Bryant laughed and told her: 'Look, I like you. You're a young girl and you are out of your depth. Last chance here. I'll tell you where the dead letter box is if you agree to pay me four-fifty.' Four hundred and fifty thousand pounds, still a multiple of the sum Jo had to play with.

So, she said no. And Bryant stormed out.

Jo had no choice. Anti-surveillant must become surveillant. She watched him leave by the front door, noting that he turned left onto Grosvenor Square. Moving faster now, she slipped off her blue jacket and folded it into her backpack. She gathered her long blonde hair into a bun and put on a baseball cap, emblazoned with the words 'I love New York'. The cap would go if she thought Bryant spotted her at any point. As it was, she was confident he would not recognise her after just thirty minutes in her company and following her quick changes. Once out of the door, she saw Bryant on the other side of the square, past the old US Embassy and heading towards Upper Brook Street. She quickened her pace, and paralleled him on Upper Grosvenor Street, while radioing in for back-up.

She ran to the junction with Park Street, knowing there was nowhere for Bryant to turn off before then, and waited. Sure enough, a short while later, she spotted him two blocks up, obvious from his green bomber jacket. He was heading straight for the park. So, she ran ahead of him again and hurtled through the foot tunnel under Park Lane. Tourists jumped to the side of the tunnel as she panted her way through it. Emerging into the daylight, she shielded her eyes and looked towards Marble Arch. It took a while, but she spotted Bryant again, held up at a pedestrian crossing, in the central reservation by the Animals in War Memorial. Once over the road, he went into the park and headed south-west, so that they would meet if she carried on straight.

She hung back, under cover of the trees that lined the pathway running alongside Park Lane. He emerged into the open and she gave him plenty of space as he crossed the open parkland. It wasn't hard to keep eyes on him and he didn't seem especially surveillance aware. Compared with JACKDAW, this man was an amateur.

Meantime, I scrambled back-up. By the time she had trailed Bryant to Exhibition Road, just south of the Royal Albert Hall, she was joined by two plain-clothes police officers. Together, the three formed a surveillance net around Bryant, and kept him under rotating observation until he reached the London Oratory on Brompton Road. He turned left into Cottage Place and made his way to a car park near the Oratory Gardens. The team closed in. Bryant stopped and turned through 360 degrees, scanning for any followers. All he saw were three young friends, two men and a woman, walking into the Brompton Café and Bookshop. He ducked behind a tree, observed by the group of friends from the café doorway. Jo recognised it as a tree once used by the KGB for dead letter drops. Perhaps he wasn't such an amateur, after all.

As Bryant reached into a knot in the tree, to pull out a package, the three friends – Jo and the two policemen – ran over to him.

'Excuse me, sir. Police. Would you mind explaining to me what you are doing here?'

Jo's cheeks were pink with excitement as she told me the story of her day, during her debrief. I topped up her glass of wine and waved to the waiter for another bottle.

'And did you detect surveillance at any point?' I asked.

Jo nodded. 'Oh yes. There were three of them.'

'Could you describe them?'

'A guy in Adidas trainers, blue sweatshirt and black tracksuit bottoms. Mousy hair. About six feet tall. He trailed me through Covent Garden. Then there was a black-haired woman who got on the tube with me at Temple. She ran to catch it, just behind me, and moved into the same carriage as me. She had plaited hair and was wearing a white blouse with a red knee-length leather skirt. And I couldn't be sure, but I thought that I saw a skinny bloke in jeans and a collarless shirt in the Costa where I stopped to decrypt JACKDAW's message, then later in Hyde Park.'

'Impressively detailed descriptions,' I said, leafing through my operational notes. 'But I can confirm that you were not under surveillance today.'

Jo's brow furrowed. 'Are you sure? I could have sworn that the black-haired woman was following me, at least.'

'I am one hundred per cent sure,' I said. 'But don't worry. You are not the first to report false positives and you won't be the last.'

How could I be so sure?

Because it was all a simulation. Live Action Role Play. Jo was taking part in a two-day corporate team-building event, revolving around a fictional espionage operation. It involved both teamwork and competitive solo work, as she had done that day. I had written the scenarios and the role-player briefs and taken operational control. The whole event was peopled with actors.

I ran several of these events, through a private company I formed for the purpose. Clients included businesspeople, corporate employees, students and the children of high-net-worth families. Observing their performances, I was struck by two things.

First, I was amazed at how readily participants 'switched on' and became situationally aware, as Jo had. Sure, there were plenty of false sightings of surveillance teams. But invariably, the players gave me detailed descriptions of the appearance and behaviour of random people they briefly encountered during the events. False positives are to be expected from first-time practitioners of anti-surveillance and – at least from a security point of view – are preferable to false negatives. The important point is that, when prompted to do so, everyone concerned proved that they could be keen observers of the environment around them.

The other thing that surprised me was how effective participants were in their meetings with role-player agents. Without exception, they bought into the scenarios and approached meetings with determination to get hold of the intelligence they needed. It seemed to me that, when I primed participants with a storyline of injustice or wrongdoing, an atavistic instinct kicked in. It would bring to the surface their latent determination to ensure that right prevailed. And it brought out skills of influence, charm and communication, even in the absence of formal training. The actors who role-played the agents were uniformly impressed by how well they had been handled, whether by a grizzled businessman or a student, young or old, male or female. Time after time.

This second observation was eye-opening for me. I thought carefully about what I could learn from it. Eventually, I concluded that it confirmed what I had always suspected. A suspicion which led me to write this book: that everyone has it within them to Think Like a Spy.

Including you.

* * *

RECAP

- A spy's number one priority is protecting her agent's physical security. Yours is watching out for your goals ally's psychological wellbeing.
- You owe them undistracted attention when seeking their help. So, walk to meetings and emotionally 'dry clean' yourself en route.
- Arrive early at the venue and take some time to groom and compose yourself. You might find striking a 'power pose' for a minute induces a positive frame of mind.
- One form of pre-suasion is selecting a meeting venue themed around your area of endeavour. This may help to focus the goals ally on your needs.
- Where you sit in relation to your goals ally will affect your communication with them. Aim for a cooperative arrangement without invading their personal space.
- Exercise caution when using SMS or social media to communicate between meetings. Keep such comms short, objective and to an appropriate minimum.
- As with meeting venues, there are numerous messaging options to choose from, enabling you to select one most appropriate to dealings with your goals ally.
- These are important considerations, because spying is all about understanding and managing communication between two people.

Final Thoughts about Thinking Like a Spy

A few months before starting to write this book, I was in New York, catching up with family and friends. One evening, I met a former CIA man, Jared, and a mutual mate, Clive, for drinks. It was one of Manhattan's sweaty summer evenings and we were meandering, without much of a plan other than to get hold of some cold beers. As we approached Times Square, Clive went ahead to buy some vaping liquid. Chatting between us, Jared and I soon lost sight of Clive, but strolled on nonetheless, assuming we would find him soon enough.

We were halfway along West 45th, outside the Museum of Broadway, when Clive jogged up to us, beads of sweat on his forehead and visibly irritated.

'I was on the other side of the Square. Didn't you see me waving?'

'Sorry, Clive,' I said. 'We didn't see you through the crowds.'

Clive tutted and drew heavily on his vape stick. He glared at Jared. 'I thought you were meant to be good at that sort of thing.'

This pushed one of Jared's buttons. 'Don't be ridiculous,' he snapped. 'That's like pitching a ball behind a catcher's back and jeering at him for not scooping it up.'

It's not a perfect analogy and Jared may have been protesting a little too much. But there is something in his objection.

Thinking like a spy is not a default state for anybody. It is not a constant mode of being.

Whether conducting anti-surveillance, eliciting information from a target or debriefing a tricky agent, a spy will approach each task deliberately, with intent. She will marshal mental resources that lie latent in all of us and point them towards the task at hand, at the right time. In a phrase that I have used a few times before, she will 'switch on'.

So, what *does* it mean to switch on and Think Like a Spy?

Aside from injecting intention and purpose into dealings with others, it means practising:

- self-awareness, the better to understand the impact of your words and actions on those around you;
- others-awareness, the better to appreciate the needs and desires of your interlocutors; and
- situational awareness, the better to assess and mitigate threats in your immediate environs.

A big part of it is tapping into being a people-person. Spying – as we have used the term in this book – is about engaging with the real world, rather than being absorbed in screens. It remains, at its best, an analogue pastime, because the most important secrets are often kept in people's heads rather than in cyberspace. Accordingly, thinking like a spy requires you to think collaboratively, to engage in effective teamwork. Good spying is about working effectively *with* people, ethically and responsibly. This requires polished communication skills.

Have a look at the following sentences:

- 'Good game the other day.'
- 'We have been awarded a project by the office of the president here.'

- 'Because you were all cowards.'
- 'I am asking you to save a man's life. Surely that is the important thing.'
- 'The satisfaction of knowing that you have helped an old friend when he needs you.'

Do you recognise them? They are all phrases lifted from stories told throughout this book, covering challenges that I faced in Zimbabwe, the DRC, South Sudan, Somalia and elsewhere. All very different comments, but they have one thing in common. They were all *pivotal*. They influenced my listeners and changed the course of events, for the better. Together, they illustrate the power of effective, targeted communication.

Spies need to use powerful communication skills around the intelligence cycle: when approaching, cultivating, recruiting and running agents, and when reporting their findings. Which brings us full circle, to my final point: thinking like a spy means thinking in cycles.

One day, if you have communicated well with your goals allies around your personal cycle of achievement, you will get the news you have been longing for. It might be the offer of a new job, a promotion, award of a coveted prize or scholarship, a welcome letter from an elite club, or an invitation to submit your treatment for a proposed TV series. Whatever it is, it will be an end in its own right. But it will also be a beginning. You will have achieved one goal in your life's journey. Of course, you must pause and celebrate achieving that goal.

But then it will be time to start over. Time to think again about your long-term goals. Time to review your new position and reset your short-term goals. Time to identify and target new allies for the next stage of your life.

Time to get back on your cycle.

Acknowledgements

It is fitting in a book about alliances to acknowledge a few key allies, for their support in producing it.

First, I invite the extraordinary characters of my various stories to take a bow. Without them, I would have nothing to say. But there are others behind the scenes, equally valuable, to whom I send my thanks and loving gratitude:

Dad and Mum, for surrounding us all with books, ideas, debate, and love. And for nurturing my fascination with words;

Dan Llywelyn Hall, for encouraging me to work on this idea in the first place. The sun was shining that day, as we sat outside the Cain Valley Hotel;

Dave Daniel, for sticking by me, in the face of less clement metaphorical weather. Third time lucky, eh?;

Nick Walters, Tom Asker, Maddie Mogford and the teams at DLA and Hachette, for believing in me and this idea. And for your enthusiasm, professionalism and ongoing support;

The fascinating folk at humanstory.io, for teaching me how to tell a story. Yours is so much more fascinating than mine;

Jacob Cockcroft and Don Levett, for gallivanting around London, helping to run games that got me thinking hard about what it means to think like a spy;

Lt Col Tim Spicer, Brigadier James Ellery and Dominic Armstrong, for putting me in some unusual situations. And getting me out of others. A handful ended up on these pages;

John Hunt, for inviting me to play a small part in the Spyscape adventure and allowing me to use some of the content from that absorbing venue;

Zane Ferula, for much wisdom that got me through challenging times, some of which made it into this book;

Robert Burton, for invaluable guidance on physical and mental wellbeing, that helped to keep me and this work in good shape; and

Michael Kearsey, for being a stalwart business partner and a steadfast personal ally. Thank you for keeping the wheels turning while mine were mired in writing.

Special thanks also to the wonderful women, children and men of Africa. Many of my stories are, in fact, *your* stories and I am eternally grateful.

Not least, of course, my undying love and thanks to Laura: for being you; for the Florida road trip when we nailed this idea; for tolerating a distracted me since then.

And for agreeing to become my wife. Some alliances are for life.

END

Index

Abdullahi Yusuf Ahmed, 205
Abuja, Nigeria, 237
Academic's Handbook, The, 20
access, 175–6, 188
Accra, Ghana, 273
advice, 220, 235–7
agents, xxv–xxvi
alcohol, 41, 72, 171, 176
Ali Mohammed Ghedi, 203
altruism, 159, 161, 163, 174, 187
Ames, Aldrich, 176
Amsterdam, Netherlands, 118
Angelou, Maya, 52
Angola, 259
anti-surveillance, 271–2, 279–81,
    289–90, 294
appearance, 36–7, 217–18
approval, 218
aristocracy, 14
Aristotle, 161
Arizona State University, 215
assets, xxv
Atak, Ajak Gai, 128, 131–6
attraction, 70–83
attractiveness, 217–18
authority, 215, 216, 224, 228, 232

Baidoa, Somalia, 202, 203, 209
Balamou, Samira, 95–100
Barwell, Peter, 182–8
Beck, Aaron, 55
Belstead, John Ganzoni, 2nd Baron,
    12

Benin, 263–8, 273
Berlin Wall, fall of (1989), xvi, 148
Big Bang (1986), 224–5, 227
Big Five personality traits, 106, 107,
    121, 123, 132, 137
Birmingham, West Midlands, xviii,
    xxi, 10, 61, 76, 87, 182–3, 187–8,
    221–7
Bishopsgate bombing (1993), 278
Bloxham School, Oxfordshire, 184,
    187–8
Blunt, Anthony, 144
body language
    confidence and, 284, 296
    deception and, 249–50
    rapport and, 52, 72–3, 260–61, 269
branding, 47–54, 67, 83, 90
Branson, Richard, 48
Bregman, Rutger, 84
Brew XI, 222
bribery, 58, 92–9, 154–7, 207
Brown University, 245
brush contact (BC), 274, 289
Budapest, Hungary, 152, 153
Buddhism, 162–3
Buffett, Warren, 142
Buhari, Muhammadu, 241
Bulgaria, 30–31
Bundesnachrichtendienst (BND), 245
Burgess, Guy, 144
Burnett, John, 202
Burns, Robert, 69
business project life cycle, 4

Cairncross, John, 144
Camara, Moussa Dadis, 92
Cambridge Five, 74, 144
Camden Town bombing (1993),
    277–8
Carnegie, Dale, 73
carry credentials, 37
Cazenove & Co., 14–16, 47–8, 81, 82,
    230–31
Central Intelligence Agency (CIA),
    142, 176
Channel Four, xxii
character sketches, 123
charity, 23, 123, 162–3
child soldiers, 131–6
Chisholm, Ruari, 274
chronological narratives, 250–51
Churchill, Winston, 9, 13, 16, 78, 79
Cialdini, Robert
    Influence, 215–16, 219, 227, 228,
        237
    Pre-suasion, 201, 229–30, 233–4,
        243, 285
City of London, xxii, 14, 47–8,
    224–5, 227
club membership, see unity
coercion, 140, 145–6, 157, 158
Cognitive Behavioural Therapy
    (CBT), 43, 54–6, 67
Cold War (1947–91), xv, 74–5
    Ames' disclosures, 176
    Cambridge Five, 74, 144
    Cuban missile crisis (1962), xv
    Hanssen's disclosures, xv, 142,
        274–5
    Penkovsky's disclosures, xiv–xv,
        274
    Polyakov's disclosures, 244
collaboration, 18, 24, 29, 121, 125,
    137, 179
Colonel Attack, 128, 131–6
commitment, 218–19, 227, 228
commonality, 107–8, 120
communications, 271, 274–6, 282,
    289, 291, 296
Conakry, Guinea, 92–100
Condé, Alpha, 92–3, 94, 98
Confucius, 192

Conservative Party, 9, 11–14, 183,
    224–5
consistency, 218–19, 227, 228
Constant Gardener, The (le Carré), 68
contingencies, 177, 181, 188, 194,
    197, 210
Conundrum (Morris), 241
Council House, Birmingham, 183
counter-surveillance, 271, 272–3
cover, 30–67, 138
    defensive, 32, 33, 39, 45, 56, 66
    natural, 33, 45
    offensive, 32–3, 37, 39, 45, 56, 66
    official, 33, 45
    personality, 40–44, 45, 49–56, 67,
        83
    practicalities, 34–6, 45
    presentation, 34, 36–7, 45, 47
    proposition, 34, 37–40, 45, 46–7, 69
    targeting and, 33, 37–8
covert communications, 271, 274–6,
    282, 296
Cuban missile crisis (1962), xv
Cuddy, Amy, 284
cultivation, 68–100
    acquaintance, 68, 70, 83
    approach, 68, 69, 70, 83–92
    friendship, 68, 70–83
    trust, 68, 75, 83
culture, 6–7
CURVEBALL, 143, 244–7, 248–9
cycles, 3–4, 299

Dalai Lama, 160
Dalí, Salvador, 211
dark-side traits, 8
De Neve, Jan-Emmanuel, 142
dead letter boxes (DLBs), 274, 275,
    291–2
debriefing, 244–69
    body language and, 259–61, 269
    deception and, 248–56, 262–3, 269
    definition, 246
    listening, 247–8, 256, 259, 269
    objectivity, 246
    questions, 247, 256, 257–8, 269
    research, 247, 250, 256, 258
    space and, 247, 256, 258

deception, 46, 248–57, 262–3, 269
  body language, 249–50
  chronology and, 250–51
  duping delight, 255
  guilt, 255
  motivations, 248
  research and, 250
DeFalco, Nicole, 214
Defense Counterintelligence and
    Security Agency (DCSA), 113,
    124
defensive cover, 32, 33, 39, 45, 56,
    66
Definitive Book of Body Language, The
    (Pease), 260, 286
Democratic Republic of Congo
    (DRC), 56–66
desire to please, 146, 147, 157, 159,
    162, 174, 180
DGSE, xxv
Diallo, Cellou Dalein, 92
diamond mining, 92–100
differentiation, 232–4
digital communications systems,
    275
Dinka people, 131
disguises, 36
dog whisperers, 53
dry cleaning, 272, 282, 283, 296
duping delight, 255

East Germany (1949–90), xvi–xvii
Eddie the Eagle, 71–2
Edgbaston, Birmingham, xxi
Edo State, Nigeria, 265, 268
Edwards, Michael, 71–2
ego
  elicitation and, 107, 109–10, 120
  motivation, 140, 144–5, 157, 159,
    162–3, 174
  pitch and, 187
Einstein, Arik, 92
Ekman, Paul, 249, 255
elicitation, 103–37
  commonality, 107–8, 120
  ego, appeal to, 107, 109–10, 120
  listening, 103, 112–14, 121
  motivation and, 107, 127, 161

  personality traits and, 106, 107,
    121, 123–4, 132
  provocation, 107, 110, 120, 133–6
  questions, use of, 111–12, 121
  reciprocity, 107, 108–9, 120
  roadmap, 122–5
Eliot, Thomas Stearns, 141, 289
emotional contagion, 71
emotional openness, 71
empathy-altruism hypothesis, 161
endorsements, 229, 232, 243
Ethiopia, 132, 203
Eudaimonia, 166
European Parliament, 9, 11–12
Examinations Board, 41, 44
experience-based intelligence, 258,
    260
Extractive Industries Transparency
    Initiative (EITI), 93
extrication, 177, 181, 188, 189, 194,
    197–8
eye contact, 64, 248, 260–61, 262,
    269, 286

false representation, 46
familiarity, 70–71
Farsi, xxi
Fassie, Brenda, 167–8
Federal Bureau of Investigation
    (FBI), xv, 104, 105, 142, 176
Felix, Christopher, 32–3
Fenton, Joe, xv
Ferguson, Harry, 68, 70, 75, 146,
    178–9
fight or flight mode, 55
Fish, Michael, 78
flattery, 51, 73, 109, 206, 218
Flynn, Francis, 84
followers, detection of, 271–3,
    279–81, 282, 289–90
football, 28
forward-facing characteristics, 40,
    45, 83
Fraud Act (2006), 46
friendship, 68, 70–83
  emotional openness, 71, 83
  gifts and, 74, 75, 83
  interest and, 73–82, 83

mere exposure effect, 70–71
reciprocity of liking, 72
similarity-attraction effect, 73
spontaneous trait transference, 71
trust and, 75
FSB, 275
Furnham, Adrian, 6, 8, 33, 142, 146, 180, 215, 270

gap years, 9–11, 42, 221–7
gardening, 68, 229
General Data Protection Regulation (GDPR), 123, 137
Ghana, 273
Glaser, Judith, 113
goal setting, 29, 48–9
    elicitation, 122, 137
    SMART model, 18, 122, 137
goals allies
    debriefing, 257–63, 269
    influence, 221–37, 243
    recruitment, 121–2, 137, 147, 157–66, 174, 181–210
    targeting, 16–24, 29, 46–7, 49–54, 56, 83, 100
    tradecraft, 276, 282–8
Goma, DRC, 60
GRADE, 147, 159–63, 174, 187, 194, 200
    Altruism, 159, 161, 163, 174, 187
    Desire to Please, 159, 162, 174, 187
    Ego, 159, 162–3, 174, 187
    Gratitude, 159–60, 174, 187
    Responsibility, 159, 160–61, 174, 187
gratitude, 159–60, 174, 187
Grosvenor, Paul, 58, 66
GRU, xv, 244
Guinea, 92–100
Gulf War
    First (1990–91), 244
    Second (2003), 143, 213, 244–6

Hansard, 13
Hanssen, Robert, xv, 142, 274–5
Harare, Zimbabwe, 7, 25–8, 62
Harith, Muhammad, 143
Harry Potter (Rowling), 54

Haverstock Hill, London, 279–81
hedonism, 161
Hierarchy of Needs, 140–41
Hilton Hotels, 59
Homeland Security 105
House of Commons, 12–14
HPA axis, 283
Human Dignity Trust, 240
human intelligence (HUMINT), 75
humour, 71
Hungary, 148–57

ideology, 140, 144, 157, 158, 180
Image Intelligence (IMINT), xxv–xxvi
influence, 213–43
    advice, 220, 235–7
    authority, 215, 216, 224, 228, 232, 243
    commitment/consistency, 218–19, 227, 228
    differentiation, 232–4
    liking, 217–18, 224, 228, 229, 231
    note taking, 230–31
    planting flags, 234–5
    reciprocation, 217, 220, 224, 227, 228, 229, 231
    scarcity, 215, 216, 224, 228
    social proof, 215, 216, 225, 228, 232, 243
    unity, 219–21, 227, 228, 235, 237–42, 243
Influence (Cialdini), 215–16, 219, 227, 228, 243
intellect, 7–8
intelligence cycle, 3–4
interviews, 76–82
IQ tests, xx
Iran, 274
Iran, xx
Iraq, 143, 213, 244–7
Ireland, 183
Irish Republican Army (IRA), 276–9
Islamic Courts Union (ICU), 202–3, 206
Islamism, 202
Israel, 93, 94

JACKDAW, 289–91
al-Janabi, Rafid Ahmed Alwan, 143, 244–7, 248–9
Japan, 114–20
Jenkins, Peter, 271
Jennings and Darbishire, 254
Jonathan, Goodluck, 239, 241
JP Morgan, 14
Juba, South Sudan, 129, 130, 134
juju, 268

Kabat-Zinn, Jon, 193
Kabila, Joseph, 56–7
Kabila, Laurent, 57
Kant, Immanuel, 160
Kaplan, Gilbert, 141
Karen Blixen Coffee House, Nairobi, 202, 203, 206
Karinthy, Frigyes, 20
karma, 162–3
Kennedy, John Fitzgerald, xv
Kenya, 202, 203
KGB, xv, 74–5, 139, 142–3, 293
Khan, Sadiq, 233
khat, 203, 204
Kiir, Salva, 128
Kinshasa, DRC, 56–66

Labour Party, 9, 11–12, 14, 183
Ladywood, Warwickshire, 222
Lampl, Peter, 23
Law Society, 20
le Carré, John, 68
Liar's Poker (Lewis), 15
libraries, 20
liking, 217–18, 224, 228, 229, 231
LinkedIn, 20
listening
    debriefing, 247–8, 256, 259, 269
    elicitation, 103, 112–14, 121
Litvinenko, Alexander, xvi
Love Song of J. Alfred Prufrock, The (Eliot), 289
Luanda, Angola, 259
Luhrmann, Mark 'Baz', 201

Maastricht Treaty (1992), 183
Macintyre, Ben, 74

Maclean, Donald, 144
Maher, Bill, 73
Mahler, Gustav, 141
Major, John, 183
Manchester United FC, 28
Maslow, Abraham, 140–41
meditation, 192–3
mentoring, 23, 29, 89, 127, 160, 182–8
mere exposure effect, 70–71
MICED, 139–46, 147, 157–8
    Coercion, 140, 145–6, 157, 158
    Desire to Please, 146, 147, 157
    Ego, 140, 144–5, 157
    Ideology, 140, 144, 157, 158
    Money, 140–43, 157, 158
Microsoft, 20
Milgram, Stanley, 20
mindfulness, 192–3
mining, 57–66, 92–100
mirroring, 52, 72–3
Mitchells & Butlers, 222
Mnangagwa, Emmerson, 57
Mogadishu, Somalia, 202, 204–9
money, 140–43, 157, 158, 180
Morris, Jan, 241
Moscow Rules, 289
Mossad, xxv, 92, 93, 96
motivation, 107, 127, 138–74
    altruism, 159, 161, 163, 174
    coercion, 140, 145–6, 157, 158
    deception and, 248–9, 256
    desire to please, 146, 147, 157, 159, 162, 174, 180
    ego, 140, 144–5, 157, 159, 162–3, 174
    elicitation and, 107, 127, 161
    gratitude, 159–60, 174
    ideology, 140, 144, 157, 158, 180
    money, 140–43, 157, 158, 180
    pitch and, 177, 180, 187
    responsibility, 159, 160–61, 174
Mtoto, Patrice, 60–65
Mugabe, Robert, 24–5, 57
Myers–Briggs model, 123–4, 137, 191

N'djili Airport, Kinshasa, 58–9
Nairobi, Kenya, 202, 203, 206, 208, 209

NASA, 105
National Security Service (NSS),
    128
natural cover, 33, 45
Netherlands, 118, 119–20
niceness, 43
Nichomachean Ethics (Aristotle), 161
Nigeria, 237–43, 265, 268
noblesse oblige, 15, 160, 187
Nolan, John, 104
North Korea, 274
Northern Ireland, xv, 276–9

Obama, Barack, 1
offensive cover, 32–3, 37, 39, 45, 56,
    66
official cover, 33, 45
Open Society Foundations, 93
Open Source Intelligence (OSINT),
    xxv–xxvi, 4, 17
organograms, 5–6
Ouidah, Benin, 263–8
Oxford University, xxii, 76, 78, 155,
    224

Palais du Peuple, Kinshasa, 60–66
Palmer, William, 235
pangas, 26
Pease, Allan and Barbara, 260, 286
Penkovsky, Oleg, xiv–xv, 274
personal achievements cycle, 29
    cover, 37, 40, 45–56, 67, 90
    cultivation, 76–100
    goal setting, 29, 48–9, 83
    influence, 221–37
    motivation and, 147, 158
    targeting, 16–24, 29, 46–7, 48–54,
        56
    tradecraft, 276, 282–8
personal brand, 47–54, 67, 83, 90
personality traits
    Big Five, 106, 107, 121, 123, 132,
        137
    cover and, 40–44, 45, 49–56, 83
    elicitation and, 106, 107, 121,
        123–4, 132
    Myers–Briggs model, 123–4, 137,
        191

pitch and, 178, 191
    profiling, 6–9, 17, 19–24
persuasion, 213–15, 228
philanthropy, *see* charity
Philby, Kim, 144
pitch, 175–210
    access and, 175–6, 188
    clarity of intent, 178–9, 188
    contingencies, 177, 181, 188, 194,
        197, 210
    extrication/retreat, 177, 181, 188,
        189, 194, 197–8, 210
    headspace and, 190–93
    language and, 178–80, 188, 194,
        195–6
    mood, 177–8, 188, 194, 195, 210
    motivation and, 177, 180, 187, 194
    personality traits and, 178
    positioning, 175–6, 193
    security and, 180, 189
    setting, 177, 178, 194–5, 210
    suitability and, 176, 193–4, 210
Polyakov, Dmitri, 244
Powell, Colin, 245
power pose, 284, 296
praise, 218
pre-suasion, 201, 229–30, 233–4, 243,
    285
pretexting, 46
privacy, 123, 137
private intelligence consultancies,
    xxiii
Project Trust, The, 9
proposition, 34, 37–40, 45, 46–7, 69
prosocial behaviour, 159, 160, 174
Provisional Irish Republican Army
    (IRA), xv
provocation, 107, 110, 120, 133–6
psychological hedonism, 161
Psychology of Spies, The (Furnham
    and Taylor), 6, 8, 33, 142, 146,
    180, 215, 270
pythons, 264–8

questions
    debriefing, 247, 256, 257–8, 269
    elicitation, 111–12, 121

Reader's Digest, xx
reciprocity, 24, 183, 256
    cultivation and, 74–5, 86
    elicitation and, 107, 108–9, 120
    influence and, 217, 220, 224, 227, 228, 229, 231
    motivation and, 162, 174
    pitch and, 179
reciprocity of liking, 72
recruitment
    definition of, 189
    elicitation, 103–37
    motivation, 107, 127, 138–74
    pitch, 175–210
religion, 158, 160
requirement setting, 3, 4, 12–13, 16–17
respect, 287
responsibility, 159, 160–61, 174, 187
Richardson brothers, 11
Robert the Bruce, King of Scots, 69
role models, 52–3, 67
Rolodex, 185
Ronaldo, Cristiano, 28
Rooney, Wayne, 28
Roppongi, Tokyo, 114–20
Rotary International, 224
Rumbek, South Sudan, 128–36, 273
Russian Federation, xv–xvi, 30–31, 142–3, 176, 275
Rwanda, 26, 57, 60, 61

scarcity, 215, 216, 224, 228
Schindler's List (1993 film), 144–5, 156
School of Oriental and African Studies, London, xxi
sciatica, 129, 130
secure premises, use of, 271, 273–4, 282
security, 180
self-verification theory, 73–4
Senegal, 7
senses, 90–92
al-Shabaab, 206
Shariah law, 202, 240

Shcherbakov, Alexandr, 142–3
Short Course in the Secret War, A (Felix), 32–3
Signal, 275, 287, 288
Signals Intelligence (SIGINT), xxv–xxvi
similarity-attraction effect, 73
six degrees of separation, 20
Skripal, Sergei, xvi
Skyscape, New York, xiv–xv, 274
slavery, 264
SMART model, 18, 122, 137
Smith, Michael, 146
smuggling, 289–95
social media, 19–20, 22, 29, 48, 85, 86, 87, 88, 162, 287–8
social proof, 215, 216, 225, 228
Solihull, West Midlands, 222
Somalia, 201–9
Sophocles, 160
Soros, George, 93
sources, xxv
South Africa, 56, 57, 58, 167
South Sudan, 128–36, 140, 273
Southern People's Liberation Army (SPLA), 128–36
Soviet Union (1922–91), xiv–xv, 74–5, 139, 142–3, 148
    Ames' disclosures, 176
    Cambridge Five, 74
    Cuban missile crisis (1962), xv
    dissolution (1988–91), 148
    Hanssen's disclosures, xv, 142, 274–5
    Penkovsky's disclosures, xiv–xv, 274
    Polyakov's disclosures, 244
spontaneous trait transference, 71
spy, definition of, xxv
Spy (Ferguson), 68, 70, 75, 146, 178–9
stalking, 23
Stanford University, 85, 88, 283
Stasi, xvii
Stoics, 166
Succession, 140
Sudan, 128–36
suitability, 176

Summerfield Park, Birmingham, 182
Sunak, Rishi, 233
surveillance, 271–3, 279–81, 289–90, 292–5
Surveillance Tradecraft (Jenkins), 271
Sutton Trust, 23
'switching on', 164, 283, 298
Szirak Castle Hotel, Hungary, 148, 152–3

table positions, 286
targeting, 4–29
  cover and, 33, 37–8, 46–7, 49–54, 56, 90
  goals allies, 16–24, 29, 46–7, 49–54, 56, 83
  identification, 4–6, 19
  personality profiling, 6–9, 17, 19–24
  pitch and, 175–6, 193
  willingness and, 19, 21–4
Taylor, John, 6, 8, 33, 142, 146, 180, 215, 270
thanking, 234, 261–2
Thatcher, Margaret, 9, 12, 40
Theory of Human Motivation, A' (Maslow), 141
Tokyo, Japan, 114–20
TOP HAT, 244
Touré, Ahmed Sékou, 95, 97
tradecraft, 180–81, 189, 270–96
  communications, 271, 274–6, 282, 289, 291, 296
  followers, detection of, 271–3, 279–81, 282, 289–90, 292–5
  secure premises, use of, 271, 273–4, 282, 296
transactional exchanges, 24, 87, 183
transgender people, 240–43
Troubles (c. 1968–98), xv, 276–9
trust, 38, 68, 75, 83
Tsvangirai, Morgan, 24–5

Uganda, 272–3

United Kingdom
  Cambridge Five, 74, 144
  Iraq invasion (2003), 143, 213, 245
  Northern Ireland Troubles (c. 1968–98), xv, 276–9
  Thatcher government (1979–90), 9, 12, 40, 224–5
United States
  Ames' disclosures (1985–94), 176
  Cuban missile crisis (1962), xv
  Gulf War (1990–91), 244
  Hanssen's disclosures (1979–2001), xv, 142, 274–5
  Iraq invasion (2003), 143, 213, 244–6, 248–9
  Penkovsky's disclosures (1961–2), xiv–xv, 274
  Polyakov's disclosures (1961–86), 244
unity, 219–21, 227, 228, 235, 237–42, 243
upbringing, 7

Val d'Isère, France, 15
values, 190–92
Vodou, 263–8
vulnerability, 71–2

Walkington, Zoë, 248
wallet litter, 37
Waste Land, The (Eliot), 141
Where Soldiers Fear to Tread (Burnett), 202
Whitby, Michael, Baron, 11
White Swan, Birmingham, 221–7
willingness, 19, 21–4, 139
winner's pose, 284
de Witte, Melissa, 84
Woolsey, James, 244
World's End pub, Camden Town, 277
Writers' and Artists' Yearbook, 20

Zanu-PF, 24–8
Ziglar, Hilary 'Zig', 101
Zimbabwe, 7, 24–8, 57, 62